PEARSON CUSTOM
COMPUTER SCIENCE

College of Southern Maryland
ITS 1110
2014 edition

PEARSON

Please visit our website at *www.pearsonlearningsolutions.com*.

Attention Bookstores: For permission to return any unsold stock, contact us at *pe-uscustomreturns@pearson.com*.

Pearson Learning Solutions, 501 Boylston Street, Suite 900, Boston, MA 02116
A Pearson Education Company
www.pearsoned.com

Printed in the United States of America.

ISBN 10: 1-269-30010-5
ISBN 13: 978-1-269-30010-0

Table of Contents

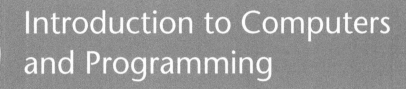

Introduction to Computers and Programming

TOPICS

1   Introduction

Think about some of the different ways that people use computers. In school, students use computers for tasks such as writing papers, searching for articles, sending email, and participating in online classes. At work, people use computers to analyze data, make presentations, conduct business transactions, communicate with customers and coworkers, control machines in manufacturing facilities, and many other things. At home, people use computers for tasks such as paying bills, shopping online, communicating with friends and family, and playing computer games. And don't forget that cell phones, iPods®, BlackBerries®, car navigation systems, and many other devices are computers too. The uses of computers are almost limitless in our everyday lives.

Computers can do such a wide variety of things because they can be programmed. This means that computers are not designed to do just one job, but to do any job that their programs tell them to do. A *program* is a set of instructions that a computer follows to perform a task. For example, Figure 1 shows screens from two commonly used programs: Microsoft Word and PowerPoint.

Figure 1 Commonly used programs

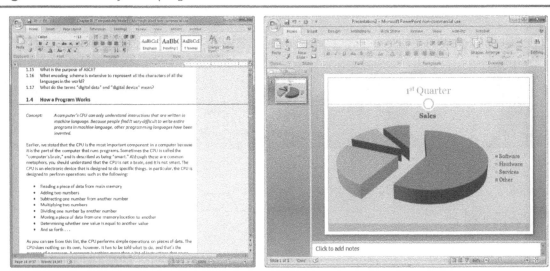

Programs are commonly referred to as *software*. Software is essential to a computer because without software, a computer can do nothing. All of the software that we use to make our computers useful is created by individuals known as programmers or software developers. A *programmer,* or *software developer,* is a person with the training and skills necessary to design, create, and test computer programs. Computer programming is an exciting and rewarding career. Today, you will find programmers working in business, medicine, government, law enforcement, agriculture, academics, entertainment, and almost every other field.

Before you begin exploring the fundamental concepts of computer programming concepts, you need to understand a few basic things about computers and how they work. This chapter will build a solid foundation of knowledge that you will continually rely on as you study computer science. First, we will discuss the physical components that computers are commonly made of. Next, we will look at how computers store data and execute programs. Finally, we will discuss the major types of software that computers use.

Hardware

CONCEPT: The physical devices that a computer is made of are referred to as the computer's hardware. Most computer systems are made of similar hardware devices.

The term *hardware* refers to all of the physical devices, or *components,* that a computer is made of. A computer is not one single device, but a system of devices that all work together. Like the different instruments in a symphony orchestra, each device in a computer plays its own part.

If you have ever shopped for a computer, you've probably seen sales literature listing components such as microprocessors, memory, disk drives, video displays, graphics cards, and so on. Unless you already know a lot about computers, or at least have a friend who does, understanding what these different components do can be confusing. As shown in Figure 2, a typical computer system consists of the following major components:

- The central processing unit (CPU)
- Main memory
- Secondary storage devices
- Input devices
- Output devices

Figure 2 Typical components of a computer system (photo credits listed clockwise from top: Poprugin AlekseyShutterstock, OZaiachinShutterstock, Abramov ValeryShutterstock, Poprugin AlekseyShutterstock, jocicShutterstock, LusoimagesShutterstock, Gregory GerberShutterstock, Smile StudioShutterstock, Norman ChanShutterstock., andrewsht - Fotolia, Feng YuShutterstock, SupertrooperShutterstock, alexvavShutterstock, AquilaShutterstock, Anders Sj manShutterstock)

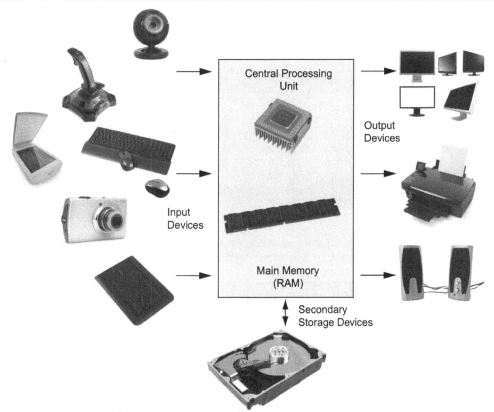

Let's take a closer look at each of these components.

The CPU

When a computer is performing the tasks that a program tells it to do, we say that the computer is *running* or *executing* the program. The *central processing unit*, or *CPU*, is the part of a computer that actually runs programs. The CPU is the most important component in a computer because without it, the computer could not run software.

In the earliest computers, CPUs were huge devices made of electrical and mechanical components such as vacuum tubes and switches. Figure 3 shows such a device. The two women in the photo are working with the historic ENIAC computer. The *ENIAC*, considered by many to be the world's first programmable electronic computer, was built in 1945 to calculate artillery ballistic tables for the U.S. Army. This machine, which was primarily one big CPU, was 8 feet tall, 100 feet long, and weighed 30 tons.

Today, CPUs are small chips known as *microprocessors*. Figure 4 shows a photo of a lab technician holding a modern-day microprocessor. In addition to being much smaller than the old electro-mechanical CPUs in early computers, microprocessors are also much more powerful.

Figure 3 The ENIAC computer (photo courtesy of U.S. Army Historic Computer Images)

Figure 4 A lab technician holds a modern microprocessor (photo courtesy of Intel Corporation)

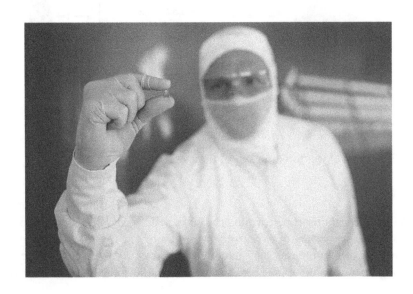

Main Memory

You can think of *main memory* as the computer's work area. This is where the computer stores a program while the program is running, as well as the data that the program is working with. For example, suppose you are using a word processing program to write an essay for one of your classes. While you do this, both the word processing program and the essay are stored in main memory.

Main memory is commonly known as *random-access memory,* or *RAM*. It is called this because the CPU is able to quickly access data stored at any random location in RAM. RAM is usually a *volatile* type of memory that is used only for temporary storage while a program is running. When the computer is turned off, the contents of RAM are erased. Inside your computer, RAM is stored in chips, similar to the ones shown in Figure 5.

Figure 5 Memory chips (photo © Garsya/Shutterstock)

Secondary Storage Devices

Secondary storage is a type of memory that can hold data for long periods of time, even when there is no power to the computer. Programs are normally stored in secondary memory and loaded into main memory as needed. Important data, such as word processing documents, payroll data, and inventory records, is saved to secondary storage as well.

The most common type of secondary storage device is the disk drive. A *disk drive* stores data by magnetically encoding it onto a circular disk. Most computers have a disk drive mounted inside their case. External disk drives, which connect to one of the computer's communication ports, are also available. External disk drives can be used to create backup copies of important data or to move data to another computer.

In addition to external disk drives, many types of devices have been created for copying data, and for moving it to other computers. For many years floppy disk drives were popular. A *floppy disk drive* records data onto a small floppy disk, which can be removed from the drive. Floppy disks have many disadvantages, however. They hold only a small amount of data, are slow to access data, and are sometimes unreliable. The use of floppy disk drives has declined dramatically in recent years, in favor of superior devices such as USB drives. *USB drives* are small devices that plug into the computer's USB (universal serial bus) port, and appear to the system as a disk drive. These drives do not actually contain a disk, however. They store data in a special type of memory known as *flash memory*. USB drives, which are also known as *memory sticks* and *flash drives,* are inexpensive, reliable, and small enough to be carried in your pocket.

Optical devices such as the *CD* (compact disc) and the *DVD* (digital versatile disc) are also popular for data storage. Data is not recorded magnetically on an optical disc, but is encoded as a series of pits on the disc surface. CD and DVD drives use a laser to detect the pits and thus read the encoded data. Optical discs hold large amounts of data, and because recordable CD and DVD drives are now commonplace, they are good mediums for creating backup copies of data.

Input Devices

Input is any data the computer collects from people and from other devices. The component that collects the data and sends it to the computer is called an *input device*. Common input devices are the keyboard, mouse, scanner, microphone, and digital camera. Disk drives and optical drives can also be considered input devices because programs and data are retrieved from them and loaded into the computer's memory.

Output Devices

Output is any data the computer produces for people or for other devices. It might be a sales report, a list of names, or a graphic image. The data is sent to an *output device,* which formats and presents it. Common output devices are video displays and printers. Disk drives and CD recorders can also be considered output devices because the system sends data to them in order to be saved.

Checkpoint

1 What is a program?

2 What is hardware?

3 List the five major components of a computer system.

4 What part of the computer actually runs programs?

5 What part of the computer serves as a work area to store a program and its data while the program is running?

6 What part of the computer holds data for long periods of time, even when there is no power to the computer?

7 What part of the computer collects data from people and from other devices?

8 What part of the computer formats and presents data for people or other devices?

3 How Computers Store Data

CONCEPT: All data that is stored in a computer is converted to sequences of 0s and 1s.

A computer's memory is divided into tiny storage locations known as *bytes*. One byte is only enough memory to store a letter of the alphabet or a small number. In order to do anything meaningful, a computer has to have lots of bytes. Most computers today have millions, or even billions, of bytes of memory.

Each byte is divided into eight smaller storage locations known as bits. The term *bit* stands for *binary digit*. Computer scientists usually think of bits as tiny switches that can be either on or off. Bits aren't actual "switches," however, at least not in the conventional sense. In most computer systems, bits are tiny electrical components that can hold either a positive or a negative charge. Computer scientists think of a positive charge as a switch in the *on* position, and a negative charge as a switch in the *off* position. Figure 6 shows the way that a computer scientist might think of a byte of memory: as a collection of switches that are each flipped to either the on or off position.

Figure 6 Think of a byte as eight switches

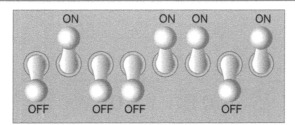

When a piece of data is stored in a byte, the computer sets the eight bits to an on/off pattern that represents the data. For example, the pattern shown on the left in Figure 7 shows how the number 77 would be stored in a byte, and the pattern on the right shows how the letter A would be stored in a byte. In a moment you will see how these patterns are determined.

Figure 7 Bit patterns for the number 77 and the letter A

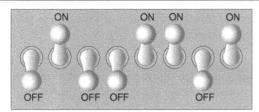 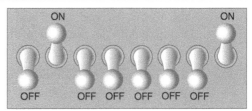

The number 77 stored in a byte.   The letter A stored in a byte.

Storing Numbers

A bit can be used in a very limited way to represent numbers. Depending on whether the bit is turned on or off, it can represent one of two different values. In computer systems, a bit that is turned off represents the number 0 and a bit that is turned on represents the number 1. This corresponds perfectly to the *binary numbering system*. In the binary numbering system (or *binary*, as it is usually called) all numeric values are written as sequences of 0s and 1s. Here is an example of a number that is written in binary:

```
10011101
```

The position of each digit in a binary number has a value assigned to it. Starting with the rightmost digit and moving left, the position values are 2^0, 2^1, 2^2, 2^3, and so forth, as shown in Figure 8. Figure 9 shows the same diagram with the position values calculated. Starting with the rightmost digit and moving left, the position values are 1, 2, 4, 8, and so forth.

Figure 8 The values of binary digits as powers of 2

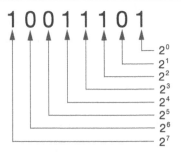

Figure 9 The values of binary digits

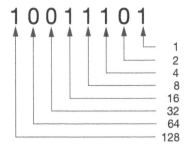

To determine the value of a binary number you simply add up the position values of all the 1s. For example, in the binary number 10011101, the position values of the 1s are 1, 4, 8, 16, and 128. This is shown in Figure 10. The sum of all of these position values is 157. So, the value of the binary number 10011101 is 157.

Figure 11 shows how you can picture the number 157 stored in a byte of memory. Each 1 is represented by a bit in the on position, and each 0 is represented by a bit in the off position.

Figure 10 Determining the value of 10011101

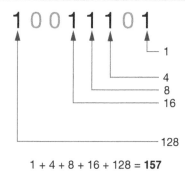

$$1 + 4 + 8 + 16 + 128 = \textbf{157}$$

Figure 11 The bit pattern for 157

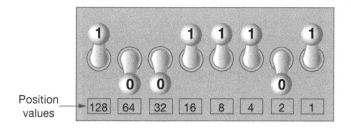

$$128 + 16 + 8 + 4 + 1 = \textbf{157}$$

When all of the bits in a byte are set to 0 (turned off), then the value of the byte is 0. When all of the bits in a byte are set to 1 (turned on), then the byte holds the largest value that can be stored in it. The largest value that can be stored in a byte is $1 + 2 + 4 + 8 + 16 + 32 + 64 + 128 = 255$. This limit exists because there are only eight bits in a byte.

What if you need to store a number larger than 255? The answer is simple: use more than one byte. For example, suppose we put two bytes together. That gives us 16 bits. The position values of those 16 bits would be 2^0, 2^1, 2^2, 2^3, and so forth, up through 2^{15}. As shown in Figure 12, the maximum value that can be stored in two bytes is 65,535. If you need to store a number larger than this, then more bytes are necessary.

Figure 12 Two bytes used for a large number

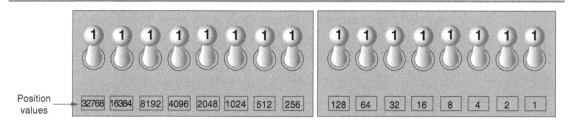

$$32768 + 16384 + 8192 + 4096 + 2048 + 1024 + 512 + 256 + 128 + 64 + 32 + 16 + 8 + 4 + 2 + 1 = \textbf{65535}$$

TIP: In case you're feeling overwhelmed by all this, relax! You will not have to actually convert numbers to binary while programming. Knowing that this process is taking place inside the computer will help you as you learn, and in the long term this knowledge will make you a better programmer.

Storing Characters

Any piece of data that is stored in a computer's memory must be stored as a binary number. That includes characters, such as letters and punctuation marks. When a character is stored in memory, it is first converted to a numeric code. The numeric code is then stored in memory as a binary number.

Over the years, different coding schemes have been developed to represent characters in computer memory. Historically, the most important of these coding schemes is *ASCII,* which stands for the *American Standard Code for Information Interchange.* ASCII is a set of 128 numeric codes that represent the English letters, various punctuation marks, and other characters. For example, the ASCII code for the uppercase letter A is 65. When you type an uppercase A on your computer keyboard, the number 65 is stored in memory (as a binary number, of course). This is shown in Figure 13.

Figure 13 The letter A is stored in memory as the number 65

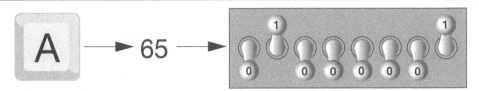

TIP: The acronym ASCII is pronounced "askee."

In case you are curious, the ASCII code for uppercase B is 66, for uppercase C is 67, and so forth. Appendix A shows all of the ASCII codes and the characters they represent.

The ASCII character set was developed in the early 1960s, and was eventually adopted by most all computer manufacturers. ASCII is limited, however, because it defines codes for only 128 characters. To remedy this, the Unicode character set was developed in the early 1990s. *Unicode* is an extensive encoding scheme that is compatible with ASCII, and can also represent the characters of many of the world's languages. Today, Unicode is quickly becoming the standard character set used in the computer industry.

Advanced Number Storage

Earlier you read about numbers and how they are stored in memory. While reading that section, perhaps it occurred to you that the binary numbering system can be used to represent only integer numbers, beginning with 0. Negative numbers and real numbers (such as 3.14159) cannot be represented using the simple binary numbering technique we discussed.

Computers are able to store negative numbers and real numbers in memory, but to do so they use encoding schemes along with the binary numbering system. Negative numbers are encoded using a technique known as *two's complement,* and real numbers are encoded in *floating-point notation.* You don't need to know how these encoding schemes work, only that they are used to convert negative numbers and real numbers to binary format.

Other Types of Data

Computers are often referred to as digital devices. The term *digital* can be used to describe anything that uses binary numbers. *Digital data* is data that is stored in binary, and a *digital device* is any device that works with binary data. In this section we have discussed how numbers and characters are stored in binary, but computers also work with many other types of digital data.

For example, consider the pictures that you take with your digital camera. These images are composed of tiny dots of color known as *pixels.* (The term pixel stands for *picture element.*) As shown in Figure 14, each pixel in an image is converted to a numeric code that represents the pixel's color. The numeric code is stored in memory as a binary number.

Figure 14 A digital image is stored in binary format (photo on the right courtesy of Tony Gaddis/ Pearson Education)

100101011101000010101101

The music that you play on your CD player, iPod, or MP3 player is also digital. A digital song is broken into small pieces known as *samples.* Each sample is converted to a binary number, which can be stored in memory. The more samples that a song is divided into, the more it sounds like the original music when it is played back. A CD-quality song is divided into more than 44,000 samples per second!

Checkpoint

9 What amount of memory is enough to store a letter of the alphabet or a small number?

10 What do you call a tiny "switch" that can be set to either on or off?

11 In what numbering system are all numeric values written as sequences of 0s and 1s?

12 What is the purpose of ASCII?

13 What encoding scheme is extensive to represent all the characters of all the languages in the world?

14 What do the terms "digital data" and "digital device" mean?

How a Program Works

CONCEPT: A computer's CPU can only understand instructions that are written in machine language. Because people find it very difficult to write entire programs in machine language, other programming languages have been invented.

Earlier, we stated that the CPU is the most important component in a computer because it is the part of the computer that runs programs. Sometimes the CPU is called the "computer's brain," and is described as being "smart." Although these are common metaphors, you should understand that the CPU is not a brain, and it is not smart. The CPU is an electronic device that is designed to do specific things. In particular, the CPU is designed to perform operations such as the following:

- Reading a piece of data from main memory
- Adding two numbers
- Subtracting one number from another number
- Multiplying two numbers
- Dividing one number by another number
- Moving a piece of data from one memory location to another
- Determining whether one value is equal to another value
- And so forth . . .

As you can see from this list, the CPU performs simple operations on pieces of data. The CPU does nothing on its own, however. It has to be told what to do, and that's the purpose of a program. A program is nothing more than a list of instructions that cause the CPU to perform operations.

Each instruction in a program is a command that tells the CPU to perform a specific operation. Here's an example of an instruction that might appear in a program:

```
10110000
```

To you and me, this is only a series of 0s and 1s. To a CPU, however, this is an instruction to perform an operation[1]. It is written in 0s and 1s because CPUs only understand instructions that are written in *machine language*, and machine language instructions are always written in binary.

A machine language instruction exists for each operation that a CPU is capable of performing. For example, there is an instruction for adding numbers; there is an instruction for subtracting one number from another; and so forth. The entire set of instructions that a CPU can execute is known as the CPU's *instruction set*.

---

[1] The example shown is an actual instruction for an Intel microprocessor. It tells the microprocessor to move a value into the CPU.

NOTE: There are several microprocessor companies today that manufacture CPUs. Some of the more well-known microprocessor companies are Intel, AMD, and Motorola. If you look carefully at your computer, you might find a tag showing a logo for its microprocessor.

Each brand of microprocessor has its own unique instruction set, which is typically understood only by microprocessors of the same brand. For example, Intel microprocessors understand the same instructions, but they do not understand instructions for Motorola microprocessors.

The machine language instruction that was previously shown is an example of only one instruction. It takes a lot more than one instruction, however, for the computer to do anything meaningful. Because the operations that a CPU knows how to perform are so basic in nature, a meaningful task can be accomplished only if the CPU performs many operations. For example, if you want your computer to calculate the amount of interest that you will earn from your savings account this year, the CPU will have to perform a large number of instructions, carried out in the proper sequence. It is not unusual for a program to contain thousands, or even a million or more machine language instructions.

Programs are usually stored on a secondary storage device such as a disk drive. When you install a program on your computer, the program is typically copied to your computer's disk drive from a CD-ROM, or perhaps downloaded from a Web site.

Although a program can be stored on a secondary storage device such as a disk drive, it has to be copied into main memory, or RAM, each time the CPU executes it. For example, suppose you have a word processing program on your computer's disk. To execute the program you use the mouse to double-click the program's icon. This causes the program to be copied from the disk into main memory. Then, the computer's CPU executes the copy of the program that is in main memory. This process is illustrated in Figure 15.

Figure 15 A program is copied into main memory and then executed (photo credits from left to right: chevanonShutterstock, Anders Sj manShutterstock, marpanShutterstock)

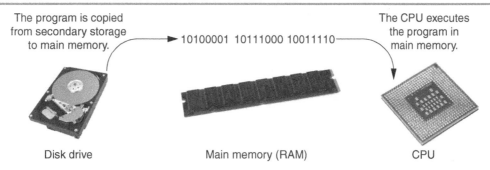

The program is copied from secondary storage to main memory.

10100001 10111000 10011110

The CPU executes the program in main memory.

Disk drive   Main memory (RAM)   CPU

When a CPU executes the instructions in a program, it is engaged in a process that is known as the *fetch-decode-execute cycle*. This cycle, which consists of three steps, is repeated for each instruction in the program. The steps are:

1. **Fetch** A program is a long sequence of machine language instructions. The first step of the cycle is to fetch, or read, the next instruction from memory into the CPU.
2. **Decode** A machine language instruction is a binary number that represents a command that tells the CPU to perform an operation. In this step the CPU decodes the instruction that was just fetched from memory, to determine which operation it should perform.
3. **Execute** The last step in the cycle is to execute, or perform, the operation.

Figure 16 illustrates these steps.

Figure 16 The fetch-decode-execute cycle (photo credits from left to right: Peter GuessShutterstock, marpanShutterstock)

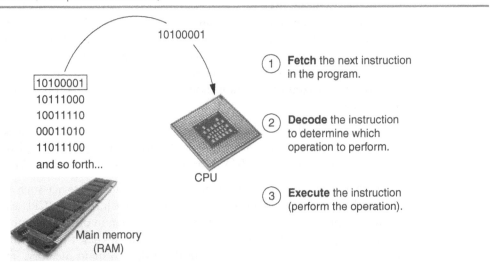

From Machine Language to Assembly Language

Computers can only execute programs that are written in machine language. As previously mentioned, a program can have thousands, or even a million or more binary instructions, and writing such a program would be very tedious and time consuming. Programming in machine language would also be very difficult because putting a 0 or a 1 in the wrong place will cause an error.

Although a computer's CPU only understands machine language, it is impractical for people to write programs in machine language. For this reason, *assembly language* was created in the early days of computing[2] as an alternative to machine language. Instead of using binary numbers for instructions, assembly language uses short words that are known as *mnemonics*. For example, in assembly language, the mnemonic add typically means to add numbers, mul typically means to multiply numbers, and mov typically means to move a value to a location in memory. When a programmer uses assembly language to write a program, he or she can write short mnemonics instead of binary numbers.

---

[2] The first assembly language was most likely developed in the 1940s at Cambridge University for use with a historical computer known as the EDSAC.

NOTE: There are many different versions of assembly language. It was mentioned earlier that each brand of CPU has its own machine language instruction set. Each brand of CPU typically has its own assembly language as well.

Assembly language programs cannot be executed by the CPU, however. The CPU only understands machine language, so a special program known as an *assembler* is used to translate an assembly language program to a machine language program. This process is shown in Figure 17. The machine language program that is created by the assembler can then be executed by the CPU.

Figure 17 An assembler translates an assembly language program to a machine language program

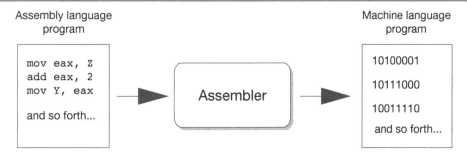

High-Level Languages

Although assembly language makes it unnecessary to write binary machine language instructions, it is not without difficulties. Assembly language is primarily a direct substitute for machine language, and like machine language, it requires that you know a lot about the CPU. Assembly language also requires that you write a large number of instructions for even the simplest program. Because assembly language is so close in nature to machine language, it is referred to as a *low-level language*.

In the 1950s, a new generation of programming languages known as *high-level languages* began to appear. A high-level language allows you to create powerful and complex programs without knowing how the CPU works, and without writing large numbers of low-level instructions. In addition, most high-level languages use words that are easy to understand. For example, if a programmer were using COBOL (which was one of the early high-level languages created in the 1950s), he or she would write the following instruction to display the message "Hello world" on the computer screen:

```
Display "Hello world"
```

Doing the same thing in assembly language would require several instructions, and an intimate knowledge of how the CPU interacts with the computer's video circuitry. As you can see from this example, high-level languages allow programmers to concentrate on the tasks they want to perform with their programs rather than the details of how the CPU will execute those programs.

Since the 1950s, thousands of high-level languages have been created. Table 1 lists several of the more well-known languages. If you are working toward a degree in computer science or a related field, you are likely to study one or more of these languages.

Table 1 Programming languages

Language	Description
Ada	Ada was created in the 1970s, primarily for applications used by the U.S. Department of Defense. The language is named in honor of Countess Ada Lovelace, an influential and historical figure in the field of computing.
BASIC	Beginners All-purpose Symbolic Instruction Code is a general-purpose language that was originally designed in the early 1960s to be simple enough for beginners to learn. Today, there are many different versions of BASIC.
FORTRAN	**FOR**mula **TRAN**slator was the first high-level programming language. It was designed in the 1950s for performing complex mathematical calculations.
COBOL	**C**ommon **B**usiness-**O**riented **L**anguage was created in the 1950s, and was designed for business applications.
Pascal	Pascal was created in 1970, and was originally designed for teaching programming. The language was named in honor of the mathematician, physicist, and philosopher Blaise Pascal.
C and C++	C and C++ (pronounced "c plus plus") are powerful, general-purpose languages developed at Bell Laboratories. The C language was created in 1972 and the C++ language was created in 1983.
C#	Pronounced "c sharp." This language was created by Microsoft around the year 2000 for developing applications based on the Microsoft .NET platform.
Java	Java was created by Sun Microsystems in the early 1990s. It can be used to develop programs that run on a single computer or over the Internet from a Web server.
JavaScript™	JavaScript, created in the 1990s, can be used in Web pages. Despite its name, JavaScript is not related to Java.
Python	Python is a general-purpose language created in the early 1990s. It has become popular in business and academic applications.
Ruby	Ruby is a general-purpose language that was created in the 1990s. It is increasingly becoming a popular language for programs that run on Web servers.
Visual Basic	Visual Basic (commonly known as VB) is a Microsoft programming language and software development environment that allows programmers to create Windows®-based applications quickly. VB was originally created in the early 1990s.

Each high-level language has its own set of words that the programmer must learn in order to use the language. The words that make up a high-level programming language are known as *key words* or *reserved words*. Each key word has a specific meaning, and cannot be used for any other purpose. You previously saw an example of a COBOL statement that uses the key word `display` to print a message on the screen. In the Python language the word `print` serves the same purpose.

In addition to key words, programming languages have *operators* that perform various operations on data. For example, all programming languages have math operators that perform arithmetic. In Java, as well as most other languages, the + sign is an operator that adds two numbers. The following adds 12 and 75:

```
12 + 75
```

In addition to key words and operators, each language also has it own *syntax,* which is a set of rules that must be strictly followed when writing a program. The syntax rules dictate how key words, operators, and various punctuation characters must be used in a program. When you are learning a programming language, you must learn the syntax rules for that particular language.

The individual instructions that you use to write a program in a high-level programming language are called *statements*. A programming statement can consist of key words, operators, punctuation, and other allowable programming elements, arranged in the proper sequence to perform an operation.

NOTE: Human languages also have syntax rules. Do you remember when you took your first English class, and you learned all those rules about infinitives, indirect objects, clauses, and so forth? You were learning the syntax of the English language.

Although people commonly violate the syntax rules of their native language when speaking and writing, other people usually understand what they mean. Unfortunately, computers do not have this ability. If even a single syntax error appears in a program, the program cannot be executed.

Compilers and Interpreters

VideoNote

Compiling and Executing a Program

Because the CPU understands only machine language instructions, programs that are written in a high-level language must be translated into machine language. Once a program has been written in a high-level language, the programmer will use a compiler or an interpreter to make the translation.

A *compiler* is a program that translates a high-level language program into a separate machine language program. The machine language program can then be executed any time it is needed. This is shown in Figure 18. As shown in the figure, compiling and executing are two different processes.

Figure 18 Compiling a high-level program and executing it (photo Credit: marpanShutterstock)

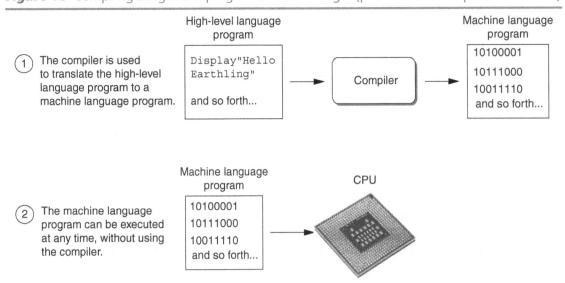

① The compiler is used to translate the high-level language program to a machine language program.

② The machine language program can be executed at any time, without using the compiler.

An *interpreter* is a program that both translates and executes the instructions in a high-level language program. As the interpreter reads each individual instruction in the program, it converts it to a machine language instruction and then immediately executes it. This process repeats for every instruction in the program. This process is illustrated in Figure 19. Because interpreters combine translation and execution, they typically do not create separate machine language programs.

Figure 19 Executing a high-level program with an interpreter (photo Credit: marpanShutterstock)

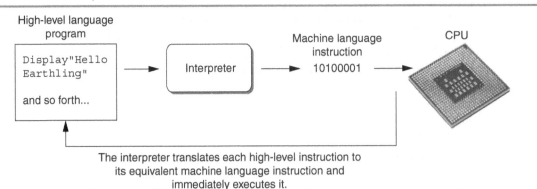

The interpreter translates each high-level instruction to its equivalent machine language instruction and immediately executes it.

This process is repeated for each high-level instruction.

NOTE: Programs that are compiled generally execute faster than programs that are interpreted because a compiled program is already translated entirely to machine language when it is executed. A program that is interpreted must be translated at the time it is executed.

The statements that a programmer writes in a high-level language are called *source code*, or simply *code*. Typically, the programmer types a program's code into a text editor and then saves the code in a file on the computer's disk. Next, the programmer uses a compiler to translate the code into a machine language program, or an interpreter to translate and execute the code. If the code contains a syntax error, however, it cannot be translated. A *syntax error* is a mistake such as a misspelled key word, a missing punctuation character, or the incorrect use of an operator. When this happens the compiler or interpreter displays an error message indicating that the program contains a syntax error. The programmer corrects the error and then attempts once again to translate the program.

Integrated Development Environments

Although you can use a simple text editor such as Notepad (which is part of the Windows operating system) to write a program, most programmers use specialized software packages called *integrated development environments* or *IDEs*. Most IDEs combine the following programs into one software package:

- A text editor that has specialized features for writing statements in a high-level programming language
- A compiler or interpreter
- Useful tools for testing programs and locating errors

Figure 20 shows a screen from Microsoft Visual Studio, a popular IDE for developing programs in the C++, Visual Basic, and C# languages. Eclipse™, NetBeans, Dev-C++, and jGRASP™ are a few other popular IDEs.

Figure 20 An integrated development environment

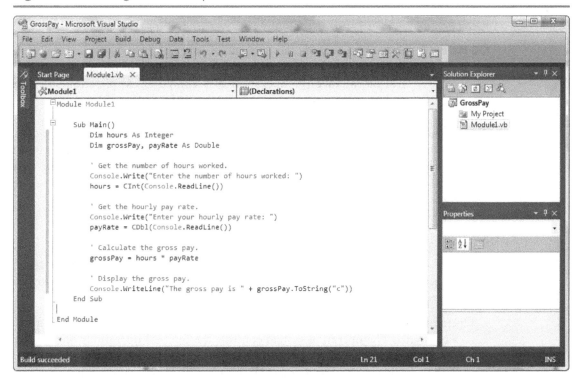

 **Checkpoint**

15 A CPU understands instructions that are written only in what language?

16 A program has to be copied into what type of memory each time the CPU executes it?

17 When a CPU executes the instructions in a program, it is engaged in what process?

18 What is assembly language?

19 What type of programming language allows you to create powerful and complex programs without knowing how the CPU works?

20 Each language has a set of rules that must be strictly followed when writing a program. What is this set of rules called?

21 What do you call a program that translates a high-level language program into a separate machine language program?

22 What do you call a program that both translates and executes the instructions in a high-level language program?

23 What type of mistake is usually caused by a misspelled key word, a missing punctuation character, or the incorrect use of an operator?

 # 5 Types of Software

CONCEPT: Programs generally fall into one of two categories: system software or application software. System software is the set of programs that control or enhance the operation of a computer. Application software makes a computer useful for everyday tasks.

If a computer is to function, software is not optional. Everything that a computer does, from the time you turn the power switch on until you shut the system down, is under the control of software. There are two general categories of software: system software and application software. Most computer programs clearly fit into one of these two categories. Let's take a closer look at each.

System Software

The programs that control and manage the basic operations of a computer are generally referred to as *system software*. System software typically includes the following types of programs:

Operating Systems. An *operating system* is the most fundamental set of programs on a computer. The operating system controls the internal operations of the computer's hardware, manages all of the devices connected to the computer, allows data to be saved to and retrieved from storage devices, and allows other programs to run on the computer. Figure 21 shows screens from four popular operating systems: Windows, iOS, Mac OS®, and Linux®.

Utility Programs. A *utility program* performs a specialized task that enhances the computer's operation or safeguards data. Examples of utility programs are virus scanners, file compression programs, and data backup programs.

Software Development Tools. *Software development tools* are the programs that programmers use to create, modify, and test software. Assemblers, compilers, and interpreters are examples of programs that fall into this category.

Figure 21 Screens from the Windows, iOS, Mac OS, and Linux operating systems

Windows

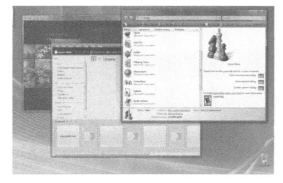

iOS

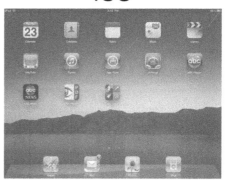

Mac OS

Linux

Application Software

Programs that make a computer useful for everyday tasks are known as *application software*. These are the programs that people normally spend most of their time running on their computers. Figure 1, at the beginning of this chapter, shows screens from two commonly used applications—Microsoft Word, a word processing program, and Microsoft PowerPoint, a presentation program. Some other examples of application software are spreadsheet programs, email programs, Web browsers, and game programs.

✓ Checkpoint

24 What fundamental set of programs controls the internal operations of the computer's hardware?

25 What do you call a program that performs a specialized task, such as a virus scanner, a file compression program, or a data backup program?

26 Word processing programs, spreadsheet programs, email programs, Web browsers, and game programs belong to what category of software?

Review Questions

Multiple Choice

1. A(n) _____ is a set of instructions that a computer follows to perform a task.
   a. compiler
   b. program
   c. interpreter
   d. programming language

2. The physical devices that a computer is made of are referred to as _____.
   a. hardware
   b. software
   c. the operating system
   d. tools

3. The part of a computer that runs programs is called _____.
   a. RAM
   b. secondary storage
   c. main memory
   d. the CPU

4. Today, CPUs are small chips known as _____.
   a. ENIACs
   b. microprocessors
   c. memory chips
   d. operating systems

5. The computer stores a program while the program is running, as well as the data that the program is working with, in _____.
   a. secondary storage
   b. the CPU
   c. main memory
   d. the microprocessor

6. This is a volatile type of memory that is used only for temporary storage while a program is running.
   a. RAM
   b. secondary storage
   c. the disk drive
   d. the USB drive

7. A type of memory that can hold data for long periods of time—even when there is no power to the computer—is called _____.
   a. RAM
   b. main memory
   c. secondary storage
   d. CPU storage

8. A component that collects data from people or other devices and sends it to the computer is called _____.
   a. an output device
   b. an input device
   c. a secondary storage device
   d. main memory

9. A video display is a(n) _____.
   a. output device
   b. input device
   c. secondary storage device
   d. main memory

10. A _____ is enough memory to store a letter of the alphabet or a small number.
    a. byte
    b. bit
    c. switch
    d. transistor

11. A byte is made up of eight _____.
    a. CPUs
    b. instructions
    c. variables
    d. bits

12. In a(n) _____ numbering system, all numeric values are written as sequences of 0s and 1s.
    a. hexadecimal
    b. binary
    c. octal
    d. decimal

13. A bit that is turned off represents the following value: _____.

    a. 1
    b. –1
    c. 0
    d. "no"

14. A set of 128 numeric codes that represent the English letters, various punctuation marks, and other characters is _____.

    a. binary numbering
    b. ASCII
    c. Unicode
    d. ENIAC

15. An extensive encoding scheme that can represent the characters of many of the languages in the world is _____.

    a. binary numbering
    b. ASCII
    c. Unicode
    d. ENIAC

16. Negative numbers are encoded using the _____ technique.

    a. two's complement
    b. floating-point
    c. ASCII
    d. Unicode

17. Real numbers are encoded using the _____ technique.

    a. two's complement
    b. floating-point
    c. ASCII
    d. Unicode

18. The tiny dots of color that digital images are composed of are called _____.

    a. bits
    b. bytes
    c. color packets
    d. pixels

19. If you were to look at a machine language program, you would see _____.

    a. Java code
    b. a stream of binary numbers
    c. English words
    d. circuits

20. In the _____ part of the fetch-decode-execute cycle, the CPU determines which operation it should perform.

    a. fetch
    b. decode
    c. execute
    d. immediately after the instruction is executed

21. Computers can only execute programs that are written in _____.
    a. Java
    b. assembly language
    c. machine language
    d. C++

22. The _____ translates an assembly language program to a machine language program.
    a. assembler
    b. compiler
    c. translator
    d. interpreter

23. The words that make up a high-level programming language are called _____.
    a. binary instructions
    b. mnemonics
    c. commands
    d. key words

24. The rules that must be followed when writing a program are called _____.
    a. syntax
    b. punctuation
    c. key words
    d. operators

25. A(n) _____ program translates a high-level language program into a separate machine language program.
    a. assembler
    b. compiler
    c. translator
    d. utility

True or False

1. Today, CPUs are huge devices made of electrical and mechanical components such as vacuum tubes and switches.

2. Main memory is also known as RAM.

3. Any piece of data that is stored in a computer's memory must be stored as a binary number.

4. Images, like the ones you make with your digital camera, cannot be stored as binary numbers.

5. Machine language is the only language that a CPU understands.

6. Assembly language is considered a high-level language.

7. An interpreter is a program that both translates and executes the instructions in a high-level language program.

8. A syntax error does not prevent a program from being compiled and executed.

9. Windows Vista, Linux, UNIX®, and Mac OS X are all examples of application software.

10. Word processing programs, spreadsheet programs, email programs, Web browsers, and games are all examples of utility programs.

Short Answer

1. Why is the CPU the most important component in a computer?

2. What number does a bit that is turned on represent? What number does a bit that is turned off represent?

3. What would you call a device that works with binary data?

4. What are the words that make up a high-level programming language called?

5. What are the short words that are used in assembly language called?

6. What is the difference between a compiler and an interpreter?

7. What type of software controls the internal operations of the computer's hardware?

Exercises

1. Use what you've learned about the binary numbering system in this chapter to convert the following decimal numbers to binary:

   11
   65
   100
   255

VideoNote

Converting Binary to Decimal

2. Use what you've learned about the binary numbering system in this chapter to convert the following binary numbers to decimal:

   1101
   1000
   101011

3. Look at an ASCII character set and determine the codes for each letter of your first name.

4. Use the Web to research the history of the BASIC, C++, Java, and Python programming languages, and answer the following questions:
   - Who was the creator of each of these languages?
   - When was each of these languages created?
   - Was there a specific motivation behind the creation of these languages? If so, what was it?

Answers to Checkpoint Questions

1   A program is a set of instructions that a computer follows to perform a task.

2   Hardware is all of the physical devices, or components, that a computer is made of.

3   The central processing unit (CPU), main memory, secondary storage devices, input devices, and output devices.

4   The CPU

5   Main memory

6   Secondary storage

7   Input device

8   Output device

9   One byte

10   A bit

11   The binary numbering system.

12   It is an encoding scheme that uses a set of 128 numeric codes to represent the English letters, various punctuation marks, and other characters. These numeric codes are used to store characters in a computer's memory. (ASCII stands for the American Standard Code for Information Interchange.)

13   Unicode

14   Digital data is data that is stored in binary, and a digital device is any device that works with binary data.

15   Machine language

16   Main memory, or RAM

17   The fetch-decode-execute cycle.

18   It is an alternative to machine language. Instead of using binary numbers for instructions, assembly language uses short words that are known as mnemonics.

19   A high-level language

20   Syntax

21   A compiler

22   An interpreter

23   A syntax error

24   The operating system

25   A utility program

26   Application software

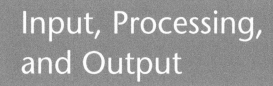

Input, Processing, and Output

TOPICS

1. Designing a Program
2. Output, Input, and Variables
3. Variable Assignment and Calculations
4. Variable Declarations and Data Types
5. Named Constants
6. Hand Tracing a Program
7. Documenting a Program
8. Designing Your First Program

1 Designing a Program

CONCEPT: Programs must be carefully designed before they are written. During the design process, programmers use tools such as pseudocode and flowcharts to create models of programs.

Programmers typically use high-level languages to write programs. However, all professional programmers will tell you that a program should be carefully designed before the code is actually written. When programmers begin a new project, they never jump right in and start writing code as the first step. They begin by creating a design of the program.

After designing the program, the programmer begins writing code in a high-level language. Recall that each language has its own rules, known as syntax, that must be followed when writing a program. A language's syntax rules dictate things such as how key words, operators, and punctuation characters can be used. A syntax error occurs if the programmer violates any of these rules.

If the program contains a syntax error, or even a simple mistake such as a misspelled key word, the compiler or interpreter will display an error message indicating what the error is. Virtually all code contains syntax errors when it is first written, so the programmer will typically spend some time correcting these. Once all of the syntax errors and simple typing mistakes have been corrected, the program can be compiled and translated into a machine language program (or executed by an interpreter, depending on the language being used).

From Chapter 2 of *Starting Out with Programming Logic and Design,* Third Edition. Tony Gaddis.

Once the code is in an executable form, it is then tested to determine whether any logic errors exist. A *logic error* is a mistake that does not prevent the program from running, but causes it to produce incorrect results. (Mathematical mistakes are common causes of logic errors.)

If there are logic errors, the programmer *debugs* the code. This means that the programmer finds and corrects the code that is causing the error. Sometimes during this process, the programmer discovers that the original design must be changed. This entire process, which is known as the *program development cycle,* is repeated until no errors can be found in the program. Figure 1 shows the steps in the process.

Figure 1 The program development cycle

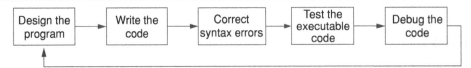

This text focuses entirely on the first step of the program development cycle: designing the program. The process of designing a program is arguably the most important part of the cycle. You can think of a program's design as its foundation. If you build a house on a poorly constructed foundation, eventually you will find yourself doing a lot of work to fix the house! A program's design should be viewed no differently. If your program is designed poorly, eventually you will find yourself doing a lot of work to fix the program.

Designing a Program

The process of designing a program can be summarized in the following two steps:

1. Understand the task that the program is to perform.
2. Determine the steps that must be taken to perform the task.

Let's take a closer look at each of these steps.

Understand the Task That the Program Is to Perform

It is essential that you understand what a program is supposed to do before you can determine the steps that the program will perform. Typically, a professional programmer gains this understanding by working directly with the customer. We use the term *customer* to describe the person, group, or organization that is asking you to write a program. This could be a customer in the traditional sense of the word, meaning someone who is paying you to write a program. It could also be your boss, or the manager of a department within your company. Regardless of who it is, the customer will be relying on your program to perform an important task.

To get a sense of what a program is supposed to do, the programmer usually interviews the customer. During the interview, the customer will describe the task that the program should perform, and the programmer will ask questions to uncover as many details as possible about the task. A follow-up interview is usually needed because customers rarely mention everything they want during the initial meeting, and programmers often think of additional questions.

The programmer studies the information that was gathered from the customer during the interviews and creates a list of different software requirements. A *software requirement* is simply a single function that the program must perform in order to satisfy the customer. Once the customer agrees that the list of requirements is complete, the programmer can move to the next phase.

> **TIP:** If you choose to become a professional software developer, your customer will be anyone who asks you to write programs as part of your job. As long as you are a student, however, your customer is your instructor! In every programming class that you will take, it's practically guaranteed that your instructor will assign programming problems for you to complete. For your academic success, make sure that you understand your instructor's requirements for those assignments and write your programs accordingly.

Determine the Steps That Must Be Taken to Perform the Task

Once you understand the task that the program will perform, you begin by breaking down the task into a series of steps. This is similar to the way you would break down a task into a series of steps that another person can follow. For example, suppose your little sister asks you how to boil water. Assuming she is old enough to be trusted around the stove, you might break down that task into a series of steps as follows:

1. Pour the desired amount of water into a pot.
2. Put the pot on a stove burner.
3. Turn the burner to high.
4. Watch the water until you see large bubbles rapidly rising. When this happens, the water is boiling.

This is an example of an *algorithm,* which is a set of well-defined logical steps that must be taken to perform a task. Notice that the steps in this algorithm are sequentially ordered. Step 1 should be performed before Step 2, and so on. If your little sister follows these steps exactly as they appear, and in the correct order, she should be able to boil water successfully.

A programmer breaks down the task that a program must perform in a similar way. An algorithm is created, which lists all of the logical steps that must be taken. For example, suppose you have been asked to write a program to calculate and display the gross pay for an hourly paid employee. Here are the steps that you would take:

1. Get the number of hours worked.
2. Get the hourly pay rate.
3. Multiply the number of hours worked by the hourly pay rate.
4. Display the result of the calculation that was performed in Step 3.

Of course, this algorithm isn't ready to be executed on the computer. The steps in this list have to be translated into code. Programmers commonly use two tools to help them accomplish this: pseudocode and flowcharts. Let's look at each of these in more detail.

Pseudocode

Each programming language has strict rules, known as syntax, that the programmer must follow when writing a program. If the programmer writes code that violates these rules, a syntax error will result and the program cannot be compiled or executed. When this happens, the programmer has to locate the error and correct it.

Because small mistakes like misspelled words and forgotten punctuation characters can cause syntax errors, programmers have to be mindful of such small details when writing code. For this reason, programmers find it helpful to write their programs in pseudocode (pronounced "sue doe code") before they write it in the actual code of a programming language.

The word *pseudo* means fake, so *pseudocode* is fake code. It is an informal language that has no syntax rules, and is not meant to be compiled or executed. Instead, programmers use pseudocode to create models, or "mock-ups" of programs. Because programmers don't have to worry about syntax errors while writing pseudocode, they can focus all of their attention on the program's design. Once a satisfactory design has been created with pseudocode, the pseudocode can be translated directly to actual code.

Here is an example of how you might write pseudocode for the pay calculating program that we discussed earlier:

```
Display "Enter the number of hours the employee worked."
Input hours
Display "Enter the employee's hourly pay rate."
Input payRate
Set grossPay = hours * payRate
Display "The employee's gross pay is $", grossPay
```

Each statement in the pseudocode represents an operation that can be performed in any high-level language. For example, all languages provide a way to display messages on the screen, read input that is typed on the keyboard, and perform mathematical calculations. For now, don't worry about the details of this particular pseudocode program. As you progress through this chapter you will learn more about each of the statements that you see here.

NOTE: As you read the examples in this text, keep in mind that pseudocode is not an actual programming language. It is a generic way to write the statements of an algorithm, without worrying about syntax rules. If you mistakenly write pseudocode into an editor for an actual programming language, such as Python or Visual Basic, errors will result.

Flowcharts

Flowcharting is another tool that programmers use to design programs. A *flowchart* is a diagram that graphically depicts the steps that take place in a program. Figure 2 shows how you might create a flowchart for the pay calculating program.

Notice that there are three types of symbols in the flowchart: ovals, parallelograms, and rectangles. The ovals, which appear at the top and bottom of the flowchart, are called *terminal symbols*. The *Start* terminal symbol marks the program's starting point and the *End* terminal symbol marks the program's ending point.

Between the terminal symbols are parallelograms, which are used for both *input symbols* and *output symbols,* and rectangles, which are called *processing symbols.* Each of these symbols represents a step in the program. The symbols are connected by arrows that represent the "flow" of the program. To step through the symbols in the proper order, you begin at the *Start* terminal and follow the arrows until you reach the *End* terminal. Throughout this chapter we will look at each of these symbols in greater detail.

There are a number of different ways that you can draw flowcharts, and your instructor will most likely tell you the way that he or she prefers you to draw them in class. Perhaps the simplest and least expensive way is to simply sketch the flowchart by hand with pencil and paper. If you need to make your hand-drawn flowcharts look more professional, you can visit your local office supply store (or possibly your campus bookstore) and purchase a flowchart template, which is a small plastic sheet that has the flowchart symbols cut into it. You can use the template to trace the symbols onto a piece of paper.

The disadvantage to drawing flowcharts by hand is that mistakes have to be manually erased, and in many cases, require that the entire page be redrawn. A more efficient and professional way to create flowcharts is to use software. There are several specialized software packages available that allow you to create flowcharts.

Figure 2 Flowchart for the pay calculating program

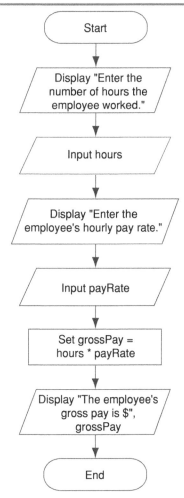

NOTE: Flowcharting symbols and techniques can vary from one book to another, or from one software package to another. If you are using specialized software to draw flowcharts, you might notice slight differences between some of the symbols that it uses, compared to some of the symbols used in this text.

 Checkpoint

1 Who is a programmer's customer?

2 What is a software requirement?

3 What is an algorithm?

4 What is pseudocode?

5 What is a flowchart?

6 What are each of the following symbols in a flowchart?

- Oval
- Parallelogram
- Rectangle

2 Output, Input, and Variables

CONCEPT: Output is data that is generated and displayed by the program. Input is data that the program receives. When a program receives data, it stores it in variables, which are named storage locations in memory.

Computer programs typically perform the following three-step process:

1. Input is received.
2. Some process is performed on the input.
3. Output is produced.

Input is any data that the program receives while it is running. One common form of input is data that is typed on the keyboard. Once input is received, some process, such as a mathematical calculation, is usually performed on it. The results of the process are then sent out of the program as output.

Figure 3 illustrates these three steps in the pay calculating program that we discussed earlier. The number of hours worked and the hourly pay rate are provided as input.

Figure 3 The input, processing, and output of the pay calculating program

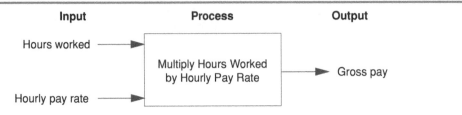

The program processes this data by multiplying the hours worked by the hourly pay rate. The results of the calculation are then displayed on the screen as output.

In this section, you will look at some simple programs that perform two of these steps: output and input. In the next section, we will discuss how to process data.

Displaying Screen Output

Perhaps the most fundamental thing that you can do in a program is to display a message on the computer screen. As previously mentioned, all high-level languages provide a way to display screen output. In this text, we use the word `Display` to write pseudocode statements for displaying output on the screen. Here is an example:

```
Display "Hello world"
```

The purpose of this statement is to display the message *Hello world* on the screen. Notice that after the word `Display`, we have written `Hello world` inside quotation marks. The quotation marks are not to be displayed. They simply mark the beginning and the end of the text that we wish to display.

Suppose your instructor tells you to write a pseudocode program that displays your name and address on the computer screen. The pseudocode shown in Program 1 is an example of such a program.

Program 1

```
Display "Kate Austen"
Display "1234 Walnut Street"
Display "Asheville, NC 28899"
```

It is important for you to understand that the statements in this program execute in the order that they appear, from the top of the program to the bottom. This is shown in Figure 4. If you translated this pseudocode into an actual program and ran it, the first statement would execute, followed by the second statement, and followed by the third statement. If you try to visualize the way this program's output would appear on the screen, you should imagine something like that shown in Figure 5. Each `Display` statement produces a line of output.

NOTE: Although this text uses the word `Display` for an instruction that displays screen output, some programmers use other words for this purpose. For example, some programmers use the word `Print`, and others use the word `Write`. Pseudocode has no rules that dictate the words that you may or may not use.

Figure 4 The statements execute in order

```
 1   Display "Kate Austen"
 2   Display "1234 Walnut Street"
 3   Display "Asheville, NC 28899"
```

Figure 5 Output of Program 1

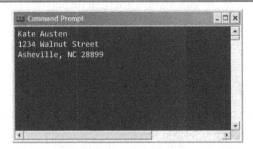

Figure 6 shows the way you would draw a flowchart for this program. Notice that between the *Start* and *End* terminal symbols there are three parallelograms. A parallelogram can be either an output symbol or an input symbol. In this program, all three parallelograms are output symbols. There is one for each of the Display statements.

Figure 6 Flowchart for Program 1

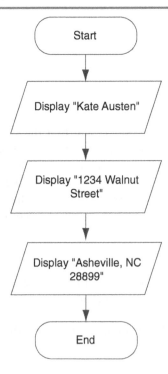

Sequence Structures

It was mentioned earlier that the statements in Program 1 execute in the order that they appear, from the top of the program to the bottom. A set of statements that execute in the order that they appear is called a *sequence structure*. In fact, all of the programs that you will see in this chapter are sequence structures.

A *structure,* also called a *control structure,* is a logical design that controls the order in which a set of statements execute. In the 1960s, a group of mathematicians proved that only three program structures are needed to write any type of program. The simplest of these structures is the sequence structure. Later, you will learn about the other two structures—decision structures and repetition structures.

Strings and String Literals

Programs almost always work with data of some type. For example, Program 1 uses the following three pieces of data:

```
"Kate Austen"
"1234 Walnut Street"
"Asheville, NC 28899"
```

These pieces of data are sequences of characters. In programming terms, a sequence of characters that is used as data is called a *string*. When a string appears in the actual code of a program (or in pseudocode, as it does in Program 1) it is called a *string literal*. In program code, or pseudocode, a string literal is usually enclosed in quotation marks. As mentioned earlier, the quotation marks simply mark where the string begins and ends.

We will always enclose string literals in double quote marks ("). Most programming languages use this same convention, but a few use single quote marks (').

Variables and Input

VideoNote

Variables and Input

Quite often a program needs to store data in the computer's memory so it can perform operations on that data. For example, consider the typical online shopping experience: You browse a Web site and add the items that you want to purchase to the shopping cart. As you add items to the shopping cart, data about those items is stored in memory. Then, when you click the checkout button, a program running on the Web site's computer calculates the total of all the items you have in your shopping cart, applicable sales taxes, shipping costs, and the total of all these charges. When the program performs these calculations, it stores the results in the computer's memory.

Programs use variables to store data in memory. A *variable* is a storage location in memory that is represented by a name. For example, a program that calculates the sales tax on a purchase might use a variable named `tax` to hold that value in memory. And a program that calculates the distance from Earth to a distant star might use a variable named `distance` to hold that value in memory.

In this section, we will discuss a basic input operation: reading data that has been typed on the keyboard. When a program reads data from the keyboard, usually it stores that data in a variable so it can be used later by the program. In pseudocode we will read data from the keyboard with the `Input` statement. As an example, look at the following statement, which appeared earlier in the pay calculating program:

```
Input hours
```

The word Input is an instruction to read a piece of data from the keyboard. The word hours is the name of the variable in which that the data will be stored. When this statement executes, two things happen:

- The program pauses and waits for the user to type something on the keyboard, and then press the [Enter] key.
- When the [Enter] key is pressed, the data that was typed is stored in the hours variable.

Program 2 is a simple pseudocode program that demonstrates the Input statement. Before we examine the program, we should mention a couple of things. First, you will notice that each line in the program is numbered. The line numbers are not part of the pseudocode. We will refer to the line numbers later to point out specific parts of the program. Second, the program's output is shown immediately following the pseudocode. From now on, all pseudocode programs will be shown this way.

Program 2

```
1 Display "What is your age?"
2 Input age
3 Display "Here is the value that you entered:"
4 Display age
```

Program Output (with Input Shown in Bold)

```
What is your age?
24 [Enter]
Here is the value that you entered:
24
```

The statement in line 1 displays the string "What is your age?" Then, the statement in line 2 waits for the user to type a value on the keyboard and press [Enter]. The value that is typed will be stored in the age variable. In the example execution of the program, the user has entered 24. The statement in line 3 displays the string "Here is the value that you entered:" and the statement in line 4 displays the value that is stored in the age variable.

Notice that in line 4 there are no quotation marks around age. If quotation marks were placed around age, it would have indicated that we want to display the word *age* instead of the contents of the age variable. In other words, the following statement is an instruction to display the contents of the age variable:

```
Display age
```

This statement, however, is an instruction to display the word *age*:

```
Display "age"
```

> **NOTE:** In this section, we have mentioned the user. The *user* is simply any hypothetical person that is using a program and providing input for it. The user is sometimes called the *end user*.

Figure 7 Flowchart for Program 2

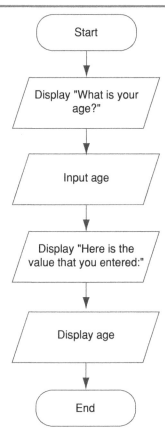

Figure 7 shows a flowchart for Program 2. Notice that the Input operation is also represented by a parallelogram.

Variable Names

All high-level programming languages allow you to make up your own names for the variables that you use in a program. You don't have complete freedom in naming variables, however. Every language has its own set of rules that you must abide by when creating variable names.

Although the rules for naming variables differ slightly from one language to another, there are some common restrictions:

- Variable names must be one word. They cannot contain spaces.
- In most languages, punctuation characters cannot be used in variable names. It is usually a good idea to use only alphabetic letters and numbers in variable names.
- In most languages, the first character of a variable name cannot be a number.

In addition to following the programming language rules, you should always choose names for your variables that give an indication of what they are used for. For example, a variable that holds the temperature might be named temperature, and a variable that holds a car's speed might be named speed. You may be tempted to give variables names like x and b2, but names like these give no clue as to what the variable's purpose is.

Because a variable's name should reflect the variable's purpose, programmers often find themselves creating names that are made of multiple words. For example, consider the following variable names:

```
grosspay
payrate
hotdogssoldtoday
```

Unfortunately, these names are not easily read by the human eye because the words aren't separated. Because we can't have spaces in variable names, we need to find another way to separate the words in a multiword variable name, and make it more readable to the human eye.

One way to do this is to use the underscore character to represent a space. For example, the following variable names are easier to read than those previously shown:

```
gross_pay
pay_rate
hot_dogs_sold_today
```

Another way to address this problem is to use the *camelCase* naming convention. camelCase names are written in the following manner:

- You begin writing the variable name with lowercase letters.
- The first character of the second and subsequent words is written in uppercase.

For example, the following variable names are written in camelCase:

```
grossPay
payRate
hotDogsSoldToday
```

Because the camelCase convention is very popular with programmers, we will use it from this point forward. In fact, you have already seen several programs in this chapter that use camelCase variable names. The pay calculating program shown at the beginning of the chapter uses the variable name payRate. Later in this chapter, Program 9 uses the variable names originalPrice and salePrice, and Program 11 uses the variable names futureValue and presentValue.

NOTE: This style of naming is called camelCase because the uppercase characters that appear in a name are sometimes reminiscent of a camel's humps.

Displaying Multiple Items with One Display Statement

If you refer to Program 2 you will see that we used the following two Display statements in lines 3 and 4:

```
Display "Here is the value that you entered:"
Display age
```

We used two Display statements because we needed to display two pieces of data. Line 3 displays the string literal "Here is the value that you entered:" and line 4 displays the contents of the age variable.

Most programming languages provide a way to display multiple pieces of data with one statement. Because this is a common feature of programming languages, frequently we will write `Display` statements in our pseudocode that display multiple items. We will simply separate the items with a comma, as shown in line 3 of Program 3.

Program 3

```
1 Display "What is your age?"
2 Input age
3 Display "Here is the value that you entered: ", age
```

Program Output (with Input Shown in Bold)

```
What is your age?
24 [Enter]
Here is the value that you entered: 24
```

Take a closer look at line 3 of Program 3:

```
Display "Here is the value that you entered: ", age
```

Notice the space.

Notice that the string literal `"Here is the value that you entered: "` ends with a space. That is because in the program output, we want a space to appear after the colon, as shown here:

```
Here is the value that you entered: 24
```

Notice the space.

In most cases, when you are displaying multiple items on the screen, you want to separate those items with spaces between them. Most programming languages do not automatically print spaces between multiple items that are displayed on the screen. For example, look at the following pseudocode statement:

```
Display "January", "February", "March"
```

In most programming languages, such as statement would produce the following output:

```
JanuaryFebruaryMarch
```

To separate the strings with spaces in the output, the `Display` statement should be written as:

```
Display "January ", "February ", "March"
```

String Input

Programs 2 and 3 read numbers from the keyboard, which were stored in variables by `Input` statements. Programs can also read string input. For example, the pseudocode in Program 4 uses two `Input` statements: one to read a string and one to read a number.

Program 4

```
1 Display "Enter your name."
2 Input name
3 Display "Enter your age."
4 Input age
5 Display "Hello ", name
6 Display "You are ", age, " years old."
```

Program Output (with Input Shown in Bold)

```
Enter your name.
Andrea [Enter]
Enter your age.
24 [Enter]
Hello Andrea
You are 24 years old.
```

The Input statement in line 2 reads input from the keyboard and stores it in the name variable. In the example execution of the program, the user entered Andrea. The Input statement in line 4 reads input from the keyboard and stores it in the age variable. In the example execution of the program, the user entered 24.

Prompting the User

Getting keyboard input from the user is normally a two-step process:

1. Display a prompt on the screen.
2. Read a value from the keyboard.

A *prompt* is a message that tells (or asks) the user to enter a specific value. For example, the pseudocode in Program 3 gets the user to enter his or her age with the following statements:

```
Display "What is your age?"
Input age
```

In most programming languages, the statement that reads keyboard input does not display instructions on the screen. It simply causes the program to pause and wait for the user to type something on the keyboard. For this reason, whenever you write a statement that reads keyboard input, you should also write a statement just before it that tells the user what to enter. Otherwise, the user will not know what he or she is expected to do. For example, suppose we remove line 1 from Program 3, as follows:

```
Input age
Display "Here is the value that you entered: ", age
```

If this were an actual program, can you see what would happen when it is executed? The screen would appear blank because the Input statement would cause the program to wait for something to be typed on the keyboard. The user would probably think the computer was malfunctioning.

The term *user-friendly* is commonly used in the software business to describe programs that are easy to use. Programs that do not display adequate or correct instructions are frustrating to use, and are not considered user-friendly. One of the simplest things that you can do to increase a program's user-friendliness is to make sure that it displays clear, understandable prompts prior to each statement that reads keyboard input.

> **TIP:** Sometimes we computer science instructors jokingly tell our students to write programs as if "Uncle Joe" or "Aunt Sally" were the user. Of course, these are not real people, but imaginary users who are prone to making mistakes if not told exactly what to do. When you are designing a program, you should imagine that someone who knows nothing about the program's inner workings will be using it.

 Checkpoint

7 What are the three operations that programs typically perform?

8 What is a sequence structure?

9 What is a string? What is a string literal?

10 A string literal is usually enclosed inside a set of what characters?

11 What is a variable?

12 Summarize three common rules for naming variables.

13 What variable naming convention do we follow in this text?

14 Look at the following pseudocode statement:

```
Input temperature
```

What happens when this statement executes?

15 Who is the user?

16 What is a prompt?

17 What two steps usually take place when a program prompts the user for input?

18 What does the term *user-friendly* mean?

 ## Variable Assignment and Calculations

CONCEPT: You can store a value in a variable with an assignment statement. The value can be the result of a calculation, which is created with math operators.

Variable Assignment

In the previous section, you saw how the `Input` statement gets a value typed on the keyboard and stores it in a variable. You can also write statements that store specific values in variables. The following is an example, in pseudocode:

```
Set price = 20
```

This is called an assignment statement. An *assignment statement* sets a variable to a specified value. In this case, the variable `price` is set to the value 20. When we write an assignment statement in pseudocode, we will write the word `Set`, followed by the name of the variable, followed by an equal sign (=), followed by the value we want to store in the variable. The pseudocode in Program 5 shows another example.

Program 5

```
1 Set dollars = 2.75
2 Display "I have ", dollars, " in my account."
```

Program Output

```
I have 2.75 in my account.
```

In line 1, the value 2.75 is stored in the `dollars` variable. Line 2 displays the message "I have 2.75 in my account." Just to make sure you understand how the `Display` statement in line 2 is working, let's walk through it. The word `Display` is followed by three pieces of data, so that means it will display three things. The first thing it displays is the string literal `"I have "`. Next, it displays the contents of the `dollars` variable, which is 2.75. Last, it displays the string literal `" in my account."`

Variables are called "variable" because they can hold different values while a program is running. Once you set a variable to a value, that value will remain in the variable until you store a different value in the variable. For example, look at the pseudocode in Program 6.

Program 6

```
1 Set dollars = 2.75
2 Display "I have ", dollars, " in my account."
3 Set dollars = 99.95
4 Display "But now I have ", dollars, " in my account!"
```

Program Output

```
I have 2.75 in my account.
But now I have 99.95 in my account!
```

Line 1 sets the `dollars` variable to 2.75, so when the statement in line 2 executes, it displays "I have 2.75 in my account." Then, the statement in line 3 sets the `dollars` variable to 99.95. As a result, the value 99.95 replaces the value 2.75 that was previously stored in the variable. When line 4 executes, it displays "But now I have 99.95 in my account!" This program illustrates two important characteristics of variables:

- A variable holds only one value at a time.
- When you store a value in a variable, that value replaces the previous value that was in the variable.

NOTE: When writing an assignment statement, all programming languages require that you write the name of the variable that is receiving the value on the left side of the = operator. For example, the following statement is incorrect:

```
Set 99.95 = dollars        ◀── This is an error!
```

A statement such as this would be considered a syntax error.

NOTE: In this text, we have chosen to start variable assignment statements with the word `Set` because it makes it clear that we are setting a variable to a value. In most programming languages, however, assignment statements do not start with the word `Set`. In most languages, an assignment statement looks similar to the following:

```
dollars = 99.95
```

If your instructor allows it, it is permissible to write assignment statements without the word `Set` in your pseudocode. Just be sure to write the name of the variable that is receiving the value on the left side of the equal sign.

In flowcharts, an assignment statement appears in a processing symbol, which is a rectangle. Figure 8 shows a flowchart for Program 6.

Figure 8 Flowchart for Program 6

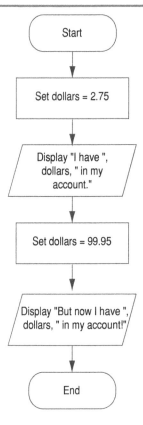

VideoNote

Performing
Calculations

Performing Calculations

Most real-world algorithms require calculations to be performed. A programmer's tools for performing calculations are *math operators*. Programming languages commonly provide the operators shown in Table 1.

Table 1 Common math operators

Symbol	Operator	Description
+	Addition	Adds two numbers
–	Subtraction	Subtracts one number from another
*	Multiplication	Multiplies one number by another
/	Division	Divides one number by another and gives the quotient
MOD	Modulus	Divides one number by another and gives the remainder
^	Exponent	Raises a number to a power

Programmers use the operators shown in Table 1 to create math expressions. A *math expression* performs a calculation and gives a value. The following is an example of a simple math expression:

```
12 + 2
```

The values on the right and left of the + operator are called *operands*. These are values that the + operator adds together. The value that is given by this expression is 14.

Variables may also be used in a math expression. For example, suppose we have two variables named hours and payRate. The following math expression uses the * operator to multiply the value in the hours variable by the value in the payRate variable:

```
hours * payRate
```

When we use a math expression to calculate a value, normally we want to save that value in memory so we can use it again in the program. We do this with an assignment statement. Program 7 shows an example.

Program 7

```
1 Set price = 100
2 Set discount = 20
3 Set sale = price - discount
4 Display "The total cost is $", sale
```

Program Output

```
The total cost is $80
```

Line 1 sets the price variable to 100, and line 2 sets the discount variable to 20. Line 3 sets the sale variable to the result of the expression price – discount. As you can see from the program output, the sale variable holds the value 80.

In the Spotlight:

Calculating Cell Phone Overage Fees

Suppose your cell phone calling plan allows you to use 700 minutes per month. If you use more than this limit in a month, you are charged an overage fee of 35 cents for each excess minute. Your phone shows you the number of excess minutes that you have used in the current month, but it does not show you how much your overage fee currently is. Until now, you've been doing the math the old-fashioned way (with pencil and paper, or with a calculator), but you would like to design a program that will simplify the task. You would like to be able to enter the number of excess minutes, and have the program perform the calculation for you.

First, you want to make sure that you understand the steps that the program must perform. It will be helpful if you closely look at the way you've been solving this problem, using only paper and pencil, or calculator:

Manual Algorithm (Using pencil and paper, or calculator)

1. You get the number of excess minutes that you have used.
2. You multiply the number of excess minutes by 0.35.
3. The result of the calculation is your current overage fee.

Ask yourself the following questions about this algorithm:

Question: What input do I need to perform this algorithm?
Answer: I need the number of excess minutes.

Question: What must I do with the input?
Answer: I must multiply the input (the number of excess minutes) by 0.35. The result of that calculation is the overage fee.

Question: What output must I produce?
Answer: The overage fee.

Now that you have identified the input, the process that must be performed, and the output, you can write the general steps of the program's algorithm:

Computer Algorithm

1. Get the number of excess minutes as input.
2. Calculate the overage fee by multiplying the number of excess minutes by 0.35.
3. Display the overage fee.

In Step 1 of the computer algorithm, the program gets the number of excess minutes from the user. Any time a program needs the user to enter a piece of data, it does two things: (1) it displays a message prompting the user for the piece of data, and (2) it reads the data that the user enters on the keyboard, and stores that data in a variable. In pseudocode, Step 1 of the algorithm will look like this:

```
Display "Enter the number of excess minutes."
Input excessMinutes
```

Notice that the `Input` statement stores the value entered by the user in a variable named `excessMinutes`.

In Step 2 of the computer algorithm, the program calculates the overage fee by multiplying the number of excess minutes by 0.35. The following pseudocode statement performs this calculation, and stores the result in a variable named `overageFee`:

```
Set overageFee = excessMinutes * 0.35
```

In Step 3 of the computer algorithm, the program displays the overage fee. Because the overage fee is stored in the `overageFee` variable, the program will display a message that shows the value of the `overageFee` variable. In pseudocode we will use the following statement:

```
Display "Your current overage fee is $", overageFee
```

Program 8 shows the entire pseudocode program, with example output. Figure 9 shows the flowchart for this program.

Program 8

```
1 Display "Enter the number of excess minutes."
2 Input excessMinutes
3 Set overageFee = excessMinutes * 0.35
4 Display "Your current overage fee is $", overageFee
```

Program Output (with Input Shown in Bold)

```
Enter the number of excess minutes.
100 [Enter]
Your current overage fee is $35
```

Figure 9 Flowchart for Program 8

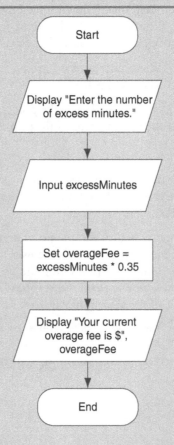

In the Spotlight:

Calculating a Percentage

Determining percentages is a common calculation in computer programming. In mathematics, the % symbol is used to indicate a percentage, but most programming languages don't use the % symbol for this purpose. In a program, you usually have to convert a percentage to a decimal number. For example, 50 percent would be written as 0.5 and 2 percent would be written as 0.02.

Let's step through the process of writing a program that calculates a percentage. Suppose a retail business is planning to have a storewide sale where the prices of all items will be 20 percent off. We have been asked to write a program to calculate the sale price of an item after the discount is subtracted. Here is the algorithm:

1. Get the original price of the item.
2. Calculate 20 percent of the original price. This is the amount of the discount.
3. Subtract the discount from the original price. This is the sale price.
4. Display the sale price.

In Step 1 we get the original price of the item. We will prompt the user to enter this data on the keyboard. Recall from the previous section that prompting the user is a two-step process: (1) display a message telling the user to enter the desired data, and (2) reading that data from the keyboard. We will use the following pseudocode statements to do this. Notice that the value entered by the user will be stored in a variable named originalPrice.

```
Display "Enter the item's original price."
Input originalPrice
```

In Step 2, we calculate the amount of the discount. To do this we multiply the original price by 20 percent. The following statement performs this calculation and stores the result in the discount variable.

```
Set discount = originalPrice * 0.2
```

In Step 3, we subtract the discount from the original price. The following statement does this calculation and stores the result in the salePrice variable.

```
Set salePrice = originalPrice − discount
```

Last, in Step 4, we will use the following statement to display the sale price:

```
Display "The sale price is $", salePrice
```

Program 9 shows the entire pseudocode program, with example output. Figure 10 shows the flowchart for this program.

Program 9

```
1 Display "Enter the item's original price."
2 Input originalPrice
3 Set discount = originalPrice * 0.2
4 Set salePrice = originalPrice − discount
5 Display "The sale price is $", salePrice
```

Program Output (with Input Shown in Bold)

```
Enter the item's original price.
100 [Enter]
The sale price is $80
```

Figure 10 Flowchart for Program 9

The Order of Operations

It is possible to build mathematical expressions with several operators. The following statement assigns the sum of 17, the variable x, 21, and the variable y to the variable answer.

```
Set answer = 17 + x + 21 + y
```

Some expressions are not that straightforward, however. Consider the following statement:

```
Set outcome = 12 + 6 / 3
```

What value will be stored in outcome? The number 6 is used as an operand for both the addition and division operators. The outcome variable could be assigned either 6 or 14, depending on when the division takes place. The answer is 14 because the *order of operations* dictates that the division operator works before the addition operator does.

In most programming languages, the order of operations can be summarized as follows:

1. Perform any operations that are enclosed in parentheses.
2. Perform any operations that use the exponent operator to raise a number to a power.
3. Perform any multiplications, divisions, or modulus operations as they appear from left to right.
4. Perform any additions or subtractions as they appear from left to right.

Mathematical expressions are evaluated from left to right. When two operators share an operand, the order of operations determines which operator works first. Multiplication and division are always performed before addition and subtraction, so the statement

```
Set outcome = 12 + 6 / 3
```

works like this:

1. 6 is divided by 3, yielding a result of 2
2. 12 is added to 2, yielding a result of 14

It could be diagrammed as shown in Figure 11.

Figure 11 The order of operations at work

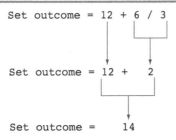

Table 2 shows some other sample expressions with their values.

Table 2 Some expressions and their values

Expression	Value
5 + 2 * 4	13
10 / 2 − 3	2
8 + 12 * 2 − 4	28
6 − 3 * 2 + 7 − 1	6

Grouping with Parentheses

Parts of a mathematical expression may be grouped with parentheses to force some operations to be performed before others. In the following statement, the variables a and b are added together, and their sum is divided by 4:

```
Set result = (a + b) / 4
```

Without the parentheses, however, b would be divided by 4 and the result added to a. Table 3 shows more expressions and their values.

Table 3 More expressions and their values

Expression	Value
(5 + 2) * 4	28
10 / (5 - 3)	5
8 + 12 * (6 - 2)	56
(6 - 3) * (2 + 7) / 3	9

In the Spotlight:

Calculating an Average

Determining the average of a group of values is a simple calculation: You add all of the values and then divide the sum by the number of values. Although this is a straightforward calculation, it is easy to make a mistake when writing a program that calculates an average. For example, let's assume that the variables a, b, and c each hold a value and we want to calculate the average of those values. If we are careless, we might write a statement such as the following to perform the calculation:

```
Set average = a + b + c / 3
```

Can you see the error in this statement? When it executes, the division will take place first. The value in c will be divided by 3, and then the result will be added to a + b. That is not the correct way to calculate an average. To correct this error we need to put parentheses around a + b + c, as shown here:

```
Set average = (a + b + c) / 3
```

Let's step through the process of writing a program that calculates an average. Suppose you have taken three tests in your computer science class, and you want to write a program that will display the average of the test scores. Here is the algorithm:

1. Get the first test score.
2. Get the second test score.
3. Get the third test score.
4. Calculate the average by adding the three test scores and dividing the sum by 3.
5. Display the average.

In Steps 1, 2, and 3 we will prompt the user to enter the three test scores. We will store those test scores in the variables test 1, test 2, and test 3. In Step 4 we will calculate the average of the three test scores. We will use the following statement to perform the calculation and store the result in the average variable:

```
Set average = (test1 + test2 + test3) / 3
```

Last, in Step 5, we display the average. Program 10 shows the pseudocode for this program, and Figure 12 shows the flowchart.

Program 10

```
1 Display "Enter the first test score."
2 Input test1
3 Display "Enter the second test score."
4 Input test2
5 Display "Enter the third test score."
6 Input test3
7 Set average = (test1 + test2 + test3) / 3
8 Display "The average score is ", average
```

Program Output (with Input Shown in Bold)

```
Enter the first test score.
90 [Enter]
Enter the second test score.
80 [Enter]
Enter the third test score.
100 [Enter]
The average score is 90
```

Figure 12 Flowchart for Program 10

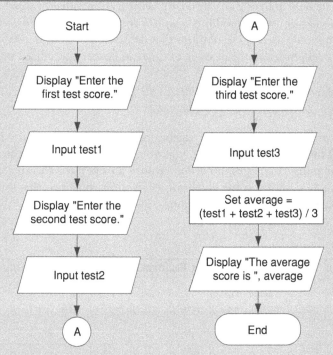

Notice that the flowchart uses a new symbol:

This is called a *connector symbol* and is used when a flowchart is broken into two or more smaller flowcharts. This is necessary when a flowchart does not fit on a single page, or must be divided into sections. A connector symbol, which is a small circle with a letter or number inside it, allows you to connect two flowcharts. In Figure 12 the A connector indicates that the second flowchart segment begins where the first flowchart segment ends.

Advanced Arithmetic Operators: Exponent and Modulus

In addition to the basic math operators for addition, subtraction, multiplication, and division, many languages provide an exponent operator and a modulus operator. The ^ symbol is commonly used as the exponent operator, and its purpose it to raise a number to a power. For example, the following pseudocode statement raises the `length` variable to the power of 2 and stores the result in the `area` variable:

```
Set area = length^2
```

The word MOD is used in many languages as the modulus operator. (Some languages use the % symbol for the same purpose.) The modulus operator performs division, but instead of returning the quotient, it returns the remainder. The following statement assigns 2 to `leftover`:

```
Set leftover = 17 MOD 3
```

This statement assigns 2 to `leftover` because 17 divided by 3 is 5 with a remainder of 2. You will not use the modulus operator frequently, but it is useful in some situations. It is commonly used in calculations that detect odd or even numbers, determine the day of the week, measure the passage of time, and other specialized operations.

Converting Math Formulas to Programming Statements

You probably remember from algebra class that the expression $2xy$ is understood to mean 2 times x times y. In math, you do not always use an operator for multiplication. Programming languages, however, require an operator for any mathematical operation. Table 4 shows some algebraic expressions that perform multiplication and the equivalent programming expressions.

Table 4 Algebraic expressions

Algebraic Expression	Operation Being Performed	Programming Expression
$6B$	6 times B	6 * B
(3)(12)	3 times 12	3 * 12
$4xy$	4 times x times y	4 * x * y

When converting some algebraic expressions to programming expressions, you may have to insert parentheses that do not appear in the algebraic expression. For example, look at the following formula:

$$x = \frac{a+b}{c}$$

To convert this to a programming statement, $a + b$ will have to be enclosed in parentheses:

```
Set x = (a + b) / c
```

Table 5 shows additional algebraic expressions and their pseudocode equivalents.

Table 5 Algebraic expressions and pseudocode statements

Algebraic Expression	Pseudocode Statement
$y = 3\dfrac{x}{2}$	`Set y = x / 2 * 3`
$z = 3bc + 4$	`Set z = 3 * b * c + 4`
$a = \dfrac{x+2}{a-1}$	`Set a = (x + 2) / (a - 1)`

In the Spotlight:
Converting a Math Formula to a Programming Statement

Suppose you want to deposit a certain amount of money into a savings account, and then leave it alone to draw interest for the next 10 years. At the end of 10 years you would like to have $10,000 in the account. How much do you need to deposit today to make that happen? You can use the following formula to find out:

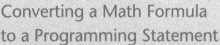

$$P = \frac{F}{(1+r)^n}$$

The terms in the formula are as follows:

- P is the present value, or the amount that you need to deposit today.
- F is the future value that you want in the account. (In this case, F is $10,000.)
- r is the annual interest rate.
- n is the number of years that you plan to let the money sit in the account.

It would be nice to write a computer program to perform the calculation, because then we can experiment with different values for the terms. Here is an algorithm that we can use:

1. Get the desired future value.
2. Get the annual interest rate.
3. Get the number of years that the money will sit in the account.
4. Calculate the amount that will have to be deposited.
5. Display the result of the calculation in Step 4.

In Steps 1 through 3, we will prompt the user to enter the specified values. We will store the desired future value in a variable named futureValue, the annual interest rate in a variable named rate, and the number of years in a variable named years.

In Step 4, we calculate the present value, which is the amount of money that we will have to deposit. We will convert the formula previously shown to the following pseudocode statement. The statement stores the result of the calculation in the presentValue variable.

```
Set presentValue = futureValue / (1 + rate)^years
```

In Step 5, we display the value in the presentValue variable. Program 11 shows the pseudocode for this program, and Figure 13 shows the flowchart.

Program 11

```
1 Display "Enter the desired future value."
2 Input futureValue
3 Display "Enter the annual interest rate."
4 Input rate
5 Display "How many years will you let the money grow?"
6 Input years
7 Set presentValue = futureValue / (1 + rate)^years
8 Display "You will need to deposit $", presentValue
```

Program Output (with Input Shown in Bold)

```
Enter the desired future value.
10000 [Enter]
Enter the annual interest rate.
0.05 [Enter]
How many years will you let the money grow?
10 [Enter]
You need to deposit $6139
```

Figure 13 Flowchart for Program 11

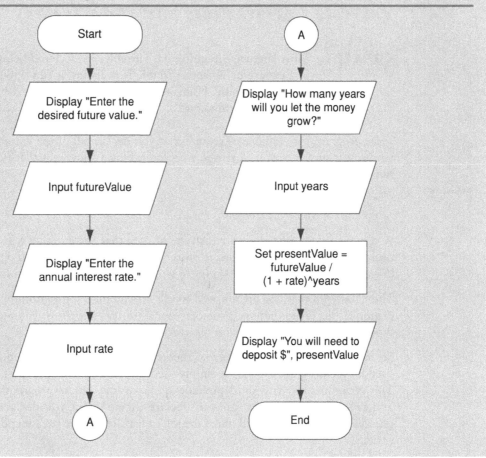

Checkpoint

19 What is an assignment statement?

20 When you assign a value to a variable, what happens to any value that is already stored in the variable?

21 Summarize the mathematical order of operations, as it works in most programming languages.

22 What is the purpose of the exponent operator?

23 What is the purpose of the modulus operator?

4 Variable Declarations and Data Types

CONCEPT: Most languages require that variables be declared before they are used in a program. When a variable is declared, it can optionally be initialized with a value. Using an uninitialized variable is the source of many errors in programming.

VideoNote

Variable Declarations

Most programming languages require that you *declare* all of the variables that you intend to use in a program. A *variable declaration* is a statement that typically specifies two things about a variable:

- The variable's name
- The variable's data type

A variable's *data type* is simply the type of data that the variable will hold. Once you declare a variable, it can be used to store values of only the specified data type. In most languages, an error occurs if you try to store values of other types in the variable.

The data types that you are allowed to use depend on the programming language. For example, the Java language provides four data types for integer numbers, two data types for real numbers, one data type for strings, and others.

So far, we haven't declared any of the variables that we have used in our example pseudocode programs. We have simply used the variables without first declaring them. This is permissible with short pseudocode programs, but as programs grow in length and complexity, it makes sense to declare them. When you declare variables in a pseudocode program, it will make the job of translating the pseudocode to actual code easier.

In most of the programs in this text, we will use only three data types when we declare variables: Integer, Real, and String. Here is a summary of each:

- A variable of the Integer data type can hold whole numbers. For example, an Integer variable can hold values such as 42, 0, and –99. An Integer variable cannot hold numbers with a fractional part, such as 22.1 or –4.9.
- A variable of the Real data type can hold either whole numbers or numbers with a fractional part. For example, a Real variable can hold values such as 3.5, –87.95, and 3.0.
- A variable of the String data type can hold any string of characters, such as someone's name, address, password, and so on.

We begin variable declarations with the word Declare, followed by a data type, followed by the variable's name. Here is an example:

```
Declare Integer length
```

This statement declares a variable named length, of the Integer data type. Here is another example:

```
Declare Real grossPay
```

This statement declares a variable named grossPay, of the Real data type. Here is one more example:

```
Declare String name
```

This statement declares a variable named name, of the String data type.

If we need to declare more than one variable of the same data type, we can use one declaration statement. For example, suppose we want to declare three variables, length, width, and height, all of the Integer data type. We can declare all three with one statement, as shown here:

```
Declare Integer length, width, height
```

NOTE: In addition to a String data type, many programming languages also provide a Character data type. The difference between a String variable and a Character variable is that a String variable can hold a sequence of characters of virtually any length, and a Character variable can hold only one character. We will keep things simple. We will use String variables to hold all character data.

Declaring Variables Before Using Them

The purpose of a variable declaration statement is to tell the compiler or interpreter that you plan to use a particular variable in the program. A variable declaration statement typically causes the variable to be created in memory. For this reason, you have to write a variable's declaration statement *before* any other statements in the program that use the variable. This makes perfect sense because you cannot store a value in a variable if the variable has not been created in memory.

For example, look at the following pseudocode. If this code were converted to actual code in a language like Java or C++, it would cause an error because the Input statement uses the age variable before the variable has been declared.

```
Display "What is your age?"
Input age                        This pseudocode has an error!
Declare Integer age
```

Program 12 shows the correct way to declare a variable. Notice that the declaration statement for the age variable appears before any other statements that use the variable.

Program 12

```
1 Declare Integer age
2 Display "What is your age?"
3 Input age
4 Display "Here is the value that you entered:"
5 Display age
```

Program Output (with Input Shown in Bold)

```
What is your age?
24 [Enter]
Here is the value that you entered:
24
```

Program 13 shows another example. This program declares a total of four variables: three to hold test scores and another to hold the average of those test scores.

Program 13

```
 1  Declare Real test1
 2  Declare Real test2
 3  Declare Real test3
 4  Declare Real average
 5
 6  Set test1 = 88.0
 7  Set test2 = 92.5
 8  Set test3 = 97.0
 9  Set average = (test1 + test2 + test3) / 3
10  Display "Your average test score is ", average
```

Program Output

```
Your average test score is 92.5
```

This program shows a common technique for declaring variables: they are all declared at the beginning of the program, before any other statements. This is one way of making sure that all variables are declared before they are used.

Notice that line 5 in this program is blank. This blank line does *not* affect the way the program works because most compilers and interpreters ignore blank lines. For the human reader, however, this blank line visually separates the variable declarations from the other statements. This makes the program appear more organized and easier for people to read.

Programmers commonly use blank lines and indentations in their code to create a sense of organization visually. This is similar to the way that authors visually arrange the text on the pages of a book. Instead of writing each chapter as one long series of sentences, they break it into paragraphs. This does not change the information in the book; it only makes it easier to read.

Although you are generally free to place blank lines and indentations anywhere in your code, you should not do this haphazardly. Programmers follow certain conventions when it comes to this. For example, you have just learned that one convention is to use a blank line to separate a group of variable declaration statements from the rest of the statements in a program. These conventions are known as *programming style*. As you progress through your study you will see many other programming style conventions.

Variable Initialization

When you declare a variable, you can optionally assign a value to it in the declaration statement. This is known as *initialization*. For example, the following statement declares a variable named price and assigns the value 49.95 to it:

```
Declare Real price = 49.95
```

We would say that this statement *initializes* the price variable with the value 49.95. The following statement shows another example:

```
Declare Integer length = 2, width = 4, height = 8
```

This statement declares and initializes three variables. The length variable is initialized with the value 2, width is initialized with the value 4, and height is initialized with the value 8.

Uninitialized Variables

An *uninitialized variable* is a variable that has been declared, but has not been initialized or assigned a value. Uninitialized variables are a common cause of logic errors in programs. For example, look at the following pseudocode:

```
Declare Real dollars
Display "I have ", dollars, " in my account."
```

In this pseudocode, we have declared the dollars variable, but we have not initialized it or assigned a value to it. Therefore, we do not know what value the variable holds. Nevertheless, we have used the variable in a Display statement.

You're probably wondering what a program like this would display. An honest answer would be "I don't know." This is because each language has its own way of handling uninitialized variables. Some languages assign a default value such as 0 to uninitialized variables. In many languages, however, uninitialized variables hold unpredictable values. This is because those languages set aside a place in memory for the variable, but do not alter the contents of that place in memory. As a result, an uninitialized variable holds the value that happens to be stored in its memory location. Programmers typically refer to unpredictable values such as this as "garbage."

Uninitialized variables can cause logic errors that are hard to find in a program. This is especially true when an uninitialized variable is used in a calculation. For example, look at the following pseudocode, which is a modified version of Program 13. Can you spot the error?

```
1  Declare Real test1
2  Declare Real test2
3  Declare Real test3
4  Declare Real average
5
6  Set test1 = 88.0
7  Set test2 = 92.5
8  Set average = (test1 + test2 + test3) / 3
9  Display "Your average test score is ", average
```

This pseudocode contains an error!

This program will not work properly because the `test3` variable is never assigned a value. The `test3` variable will contain garbage when it is used in the calculation in line 8. This means that the calculation will result in an unpredictable value, which will be assigned to the `average` variable. A beginning programmer might have trouble finding this error because he or she would initially assume that something is wrong with the math in line 8.

In the next section, we will discuss a debugging technique that will help uncover errors such as the one in Program 13. However, as a rule you should always make sure that your variables either (1) are initialized with the correct value when you declare them, or (2) receive the correct value from an assignment statement or an `Input` statement before they are used for any other purpose.

Numeric Literals and Data Type Compatibility

Many of the programs that you have seen so far have numbers written into their pseudocode. For example, the following statement, which appears in Program 6, has the number 2.75 written into it.

```
Set dollars = 2.75
```

And, the following statement, which appears in Program 7, has the number 100 written into it.

```
Set price = 100
```

A number that is written into a program's code is called a *numeric literal*. In most programming languages, if a numeric literal is written with a decimal point, such as 2.75, that numeric literal will be stored in the computer's memory as a `Real` and it will be treated as a `Real` when the program runs. If a numeric literal does not have a decimal point, such as 100, that numeric literal will be stored in the computer's memory as an `Integer` and it will be treated as an `Integer` when the program runs.

This is important to know when you are writing assignment statements or initializing variables. In many languages, an error will occur if you try to store a value of one data type in a variable of another data type. For example, look at the following pseudocode:

```
Declare Integer i
Set i = 3.7   ◄———— This is an error!
```

The assignment statement will cause an error because it attempts to assign a real number, 3.7, in an `Integer` variable. The following pseudocode will also cause an error.

```
Declare Integer i
Set i = 3.0   ◄———— This is an error!
```

Even though the numeric literal 3.0 does not have a fractional value (it is mathematically the same as the integer 3), it is still treated as a real number by the computer because it is written with a decimal point.

NOTE: Most languages do not allow you to assign real numbers to `Integer` variables because `Integer` variables cannot hold fractional amounts. In many languages, however, you are allowed to assign an integer value to a `Real` variable without causing an error. Here is an example:

```
Declare Real r
Set r = 77
```

Even though the numeric literal 77 is treated as an `Integer`, it can be assigned to a `Real` variable without the loss of data.

Integer Division

Be careful when dividing an integer by another integer. In many programming languages, when an integer is divided by an integer the result will also be an integer. This behavior is known as *integer division*. For example, look at the following pseudocode:

```
Set number = 3 / 2
```

This statement divides 3 by 2 and stores the result in the `number` variable. What will be stored in `number`? You would probably assume that 1.5 would be stored in `number` because that's the result your calculator shows when you divide 3 by 2. However, that's not what will happen in many programming languages. Because the numbers 3 and 2 are both treated as integers, the programming language that you are using might throw away the fractional part of the answer. (Throwing away the fractional part of a number is called *truncation*.) As a result, the statement will store 1 in the `number` variable, not 1.5.

If you are using a language that behaves this way and you want to make sure that a division operation yields a real number, at least one of the operands must be a real number or a `Real` variable.

NOTE: In Java, C++, C, and Python, the / operator throws away the fractional part of the result when both operands are integers. In these languages the result of the expression 3/2 would be 1. In Visual Basic, the / operator does not throw away the fractional part of the answer. In Visual Basic, the result of the expression 3/2 would be 1.5.

 Checkpoint

24 What two items do you usually specify with a variable declaration?

25 Does it matter where you write the variable declarations in a program?

26 What is variable initialization?

27 Do uninitialized variables pose any danger in a program?

28 What is an uninitialized variable?

5 Named Constants

CONCEPT: A named constant is a name that represents a value that cannot be changed during the program's execution.

Assume that the following statement appears in a banking program that calculates data pertaining to loans:

```
Set amount = balance * 0.069
```

In such a program, two potential problems arise. First, it is not clear to anyone other than the original programmer what 0.069 is. It appears to be an interest rate, but in some situations there are fees associated with loan payments. How can the purpose of this statement be determined without painstakingly checking the rest of the program?

The second problem occurs if this number is used in other calculations throughout the program and must be changed periodically. Assuming the number is an interest rate, what if the rate changes from 6.9 percent to 7.2 percent? The programmer would have to search through the source code for every occurrence of the number.

Both of these problems can be addressed by using named constants. A *named constant* is a name that represents a value that cannot be changed during the program's execution. The following is an example of how we will declare named constants in our pseudocode:

```
Constant Real INTEREST_RATE = 0.069
```

This creates a constant named INTEREST_RATE. The constant's value is the Real number 0.069. Notice that the declaration looks a lot like a variable declaration, except that we use the word Constant instead of Declare. Also, notice that the name of the constant is written in all uppercase letters. This is a standard practice in most programming languages because it makes named constants easily distinguishable from regular variable names. An initialization value must be given when declaring a named constant.

An advantage of using named constants is that they make programs more self-explanatory. The following statement:

```
Set amount = balance * 0.069
```

can be changed to read

```
Set amount = balance * INTEREST_RATE
```

A new programmer can read the second statement and know what is happening. It is evident that balance is being multiplied by the interest rate. Another advantage to this approach is that widespread changes can easily be made to the program. Let's say the interest rate appears in a dozen different statements throughout the program. When the rate changes, the initialization value in the declaration of the named constant is the only value that needs to be modified. If the rate increases to 7.2 percent, the declaration can be changed to the following:

```
Constant Real INTEREST_RATE = 0.072
```

The new value of 0.072 will then be used in each statement that uses the INTEREST_RATE constant.

NOTE: A named constant cannot be assigned a value with a Set statement. If a statement in a program attempts to change the value of a named constant, an error will occur.

6   Hand Tracing a Program

CONCEPT: Hand tracing is a simple debugging process for locating hard-to-find errors in a program.

Hand tracing is a debugging process where you imagine that you are the computer executing a program. (This process is also known as *desk checking*.) You step through each of the program's statements one by one. As you carefully look at a statement, you record the contents that each variable will have after the statement executes. This process is often helpful in finding mathematical mistakes and other logic errors.

To hand trace a program, you construct a chart that has a column for each variable, and a row for each line in the program. For example, Figure 14 shows how we would construct a hand trace chart for the program that you saw in the previous section. The chart has a column for each of the four variables: test1, test2, test3, and average. The chart also has nine rows, one for each line in the program.

Figure 14 A program with a hand trace chart

		test1	test2	test3	average
1	Declare Real test1				
2	Declare Real test2				
3	Declare Real test3				
4	Declare Real average			·	
5					
6	Set test1 = 88.0				
7	Set test2 = 92.5				
8	Set average = (test1 + test2 + test3) / 3				
9	Display "Your average test score is ", average				

To hand trace this program, you step through each statement, observing the operation that is taking place, and then record the value that each variable will hold *after* the statement executes. When the process is complete, the chart will appear as shown in Figure 15. We have written question marks in the chart to indicate that a variable is uninitialized.

Figure 15 Program with the hand trace chart completed

```
1  Declare Real test1
2  Declare Real test2
3  Declare Real test3
4  Declare Real average
5
6  Set test1 = 88.0
7  Set test2 = 92.5
8  Set average = (test1 + test2 + test3) / 3
9  Display "Your average test score is ", average
```

	test1	test2	test3	average
1	?	?	?	?
2	?	?	?	?
3	?	?	?	?
4	?	?	?	?
5	?	?	?	?
6	88	?	?	?
7	88	92.5	?	?
8	88	92.5	?	undefined
9	88	92.5	?	undefined

When we get to line 8 we will carefully do the math. This means we look at the values of each variable in the expression. At that point we discover that one of the variables, test3, is uninitialized. Because it is uninitialized, we have no way of knowing the value that it contains. Consequently, the result of the calculation will be undefined. After making this discovery, we can correct the problem by adding a line that assigns a value to test3.

Hand tracing is a simple process that focuses your attention on each statement in a program. Often this helps you locate errors that are not obvious.

7 Documenting a Program

CONCEPT: A program's external documentation describes aspects of the program for the user. The internal documentation is for the programmer, and explains how parts of the program work.

A program's documentation explains various things about the program. There are usually two types of program documentation: external and internal. *External documentation* is typically designed for the user. It consists of documents such as a reference guide that describes the program's features, and tutorials that teach the user how to operate the program.

Sometimes the programmer is responsible for writing all or part of a program's external documentation. This might be the case in a small organization, or in a company that has a relatively small programming staff. Some organizations, particularly large companies, will employ a staff of technical writers whose job is to produce external documentation. These documents might be in printed manuals, or in files that can be viewed on the computer. In recent years it has become common for software companies to provide all of a program's external documentation in PDF (Portable Document Format) files.

Internal documentation appears as *comments* in a program's code. Comments are short notes placed in different parts of a program, explaining how those parts of the program work. Although comments are a critical part of a program, they are ignored by the compiler or interpreter. Comments are intended for human readers of a program's code, not the computer.

Programming languages provide special symbols or words for writing comments. In several languages, including Java, C, and C++, you begin a comment with two forward slashes (//). Everything that you write on the same line, after the slashes, is ignored by the compiler. Here is an example of a comment in any of those languages:

```
// Get the number of hours worked.
```

Some languages use symbols other than the two forward slashes to indicate the beginning of a comment. For example, Visual Basic uses an apostrophe ('), and Python uses the # symbol. In this text, we will use two forward slashes (//) in pseudocode.

Block Comments and Line Comments

Programmers generally write two types of comments in a program: block comments and line comments. *Block comments* take up several lines and are used when lengthy explanations are required. For example, a block comment often appears at the beginning of a program, explaining what the program does, listing the name of the author, giving the date that the program was last modified, and any other necessary information. The following is an example of a block comment:

```
// This program calculates an employee's gross pay.
// Written by Matt Hoyle.
// Last modified on 12/14/2010
```

 NOTE: Some programming languages provide special symbols to mark the beginning and ending of a block comment.

Line comments are comments that occupy a single line, and explain a short section of the program. The following statements show an example:

```
// Calculate the interest.
Set interest = balance * INTEREST_RATE
// Add the interest to the balance.
Set balance = balance + interest
```

A line comment does not have to occupy an entire line. Anything appearing after the // symbol, to the end of the line, is ignored, so a comment can appear after an executable statement. Here is an example:

```
Input age     // Get the user's age.
```

As a beginning programmer, you might be resistant to the idea of liberally writing comments in your programs. After all, it's a lot more fun to write code that actually does something! It is crucial that you take the extra time to write comments, however. They will almost certainly save you time in the future when you have to modify or debug the program. Even large and complex programs can be made easy to read and understand if they are properly commented.

In the Spotlight:
Using Named Constants,
Style Conventions, and Comments

Suppose we have been given the following programming problem: Scientists have determined that the world's ocean levels are currently rising at about 1.5 millimeters per year. Write a program to display the following:

- The number of millimeters that the oceans will rise in five years
- The number of millimeters that the oceans will rise in seven years
- The number of millimeters that the oceans will rise in ten years

Here is the algorithm:

1. Calculate the amount that the oceans will rise in five years.
2. Display the result of the calculation in Step 1.
3. Calculate the amount that the oceans will rise in seven years.
4. Display the result of the calculation in Step 3.
5. Calculate the amount that the oceans will rise in ten years.
6. Display the result of the calculation in Step 5.

This program is straightforward. It performs three calculations and displays the results of each. The calculations should give the amount the oceans will rise in five, seven, and ten years. Each of these values can be calculated with the following formula:

Amount of yearly rise × Number of years

The amount of yearly rise is the same for each calculation, so we will create a constant to represent that value. Program 14 shows the pseudocode for the program.

Program 14

```
 1 // Declare the variables
 2 Declare Real fiveYears
 3 Declare Real sevenYears
 4 Declare Real tenYears
 5
 6 // Create a constant for the yearly rise
 7 Constant Real YEARLY_RISE = 1.5
 8
 9 // Display the amount of rise in five years
10 Set fiveYears = YEARLY_RISE * 5
11 Display "The ocean levels will rise ", fiveYears,
12     " millimeters in five years."
13
14 // Display the amount of rise in seven years
15 Set sevenYears = YEARLY_RISE * 7
16 Display "The ocean levels will rise ", sevenYears,
17     " millimeters in seven years."
18
19 // Display the amount of rise in ten years
20 Set tenYears = YEARLY_RISE * 10
21 Display "The ocean levels will rise ", tenYears,
22     " millimeters in ten years."
```

Program Output

```
The ocean levels will rise 7.5 millimeters in five years.
The ocean levels will rise 10.5 millimeters in seven years.
The ocean levels will rise 15 millimeters in ten years.
```

Three variables, fiveYears, sevenYears, and tenYears, are declared in lines 2 through 4. These variables will hold the amount that the ocean levels will rise in five, seven, and ten years.

Line 7 creates a constant, YEARLY_RISE, which is set to the value 1.5. This is the amount that the oceans rise per year. This constant will be used in each of the program's calculations.

Lines 10 through 12 calculate and display the amount that the oceans will rise in five years. The same values for seven years and ten years are calculated and displayed in lines 15 through 17 and 20 through 22.

This program illustrates the following programming style conventions:

- Several blank lines appear throughout the program (see lines 5, 8, 13, and 18). These blank lines do not affect the way the program works, but make the pseudocode easier to read.
- Line comments are used in various places to explain what the program is doing.
- Notice that each of the Display statements is too long to fit on one line. (See lines 11 and 12, 16 and 17, 21 and 22.) Most programming languages allow you to write long statements across several lines. When we do this in pseudocode, we will indent the second and subsequent lines. This will give a visual indication that the statement spans more than one line.

Figure 16 shows a flowchart for the program.

Figure 16 Flowchart for Program 14

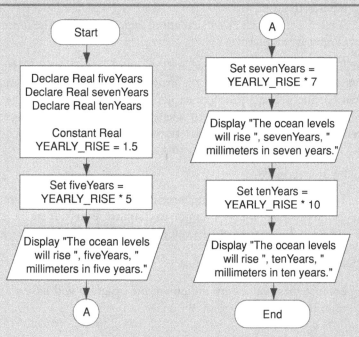

 **Checkpoint**

29 What is external documentation?

30 What is internal documentation?

31 What are the two general types of comments that programmers write in a program's code? Describe each.

8 Designing Your First Program

Sometimes, as a beginning student, you might have trouble getting started with a programming problem. In this section we will present a simple problem, go through the process of analyzing the program's requirements, and design the algorithm in pseudocode and a flowchart. Here is the programming problem:

Batting Average

In baseball, batting average is commonly used to measure a player's batting ability. You use the following formula to calculate a player's batting average:

$$Batting\ Average = Hits \div Times\ at\ Bat$$

In the formula, *Hits* is the number of successful hits made by the player, and *Times at Bat* is the number of times the player was at bat. For example, if a player is at bat 500 times during a season, and gets 150 hits, that player's batting average is .300. Design a program to calculate any player's batting average.

Recall from Section 2 that a program's actions can typically be divided into the following three phases:

1. Input is received.
2. Some process (such as a calculation) is performed on the input.
3. Output is produced.

Your first step is to determine what is required in each phase. Usually these requirements are not stated directly in the problem description. For example, the previously shown batting average problem explains what a batting average is, and merely instructs you to design a program to calculate any player's batting average. It is up to you to brainstorm the problem and determine the requirements of each phase. Let's take a closer look at each phase of the batting average problem.

1. **Input is received.**

   To determine a program's input requirements, you must determine the pieces of data that are required for the program to complete its task. If we look at the batting average formula, we see that two values are needed to perform the calculation:
   • The number of hits
   • The number of times at bat

   Because these values are unknown, the program will have to prompt the user to enter them.

Each piece of input will be stored in a variable. You will have to declare those variables when you design the program, so it is helpful in this phase to think about each variable's name and data type. In the batting average program we will use the name `hits` for the variable that stores the number of hits, and the name `atBat` for the variable that holds the number of times at bat. Both of these values will be whole numbers, so these variables will be declared as `Integers`.

2. **Some process (such as a calculation) is performed on the input.**

   Once the program has gathered the required input, it can proceed to use that input in any necessary calculations, or other operations. The batting average program will divide the number of hits by the number of times at bat. The result of the calculation is the player's batting average.

   Keep in mind that when a mathematical calculation is performed, you typically want to store the result of that calculation in a variable. So, you should think about the names and data types of any variables that are needed in this phase. In this example, we will use the name `battingAverage` for the variable that stores the player's batting average. Because this variable will store the result of a division, we will declare it as a `Real`.

3. **Output is produced.**

   A program's output will typically be the result of the process or processes that it has performed. The output of the batting average program will be the result of the calculation, which is stored in a variable named `battingAverage`. The program will display this number in a message that explains what it is.

Now that we have identified the input, processing, and output requirements, we can create the pseudocode and/or flowcharts. First, we will write the pseudocode variable declarations:

```
Declare Integer hits
Declare Integer atBat
Declare Real battingAverage
```

Next we will write the pseudocode for gathering input. Recall that a program typically does two things when it needs the user to enter a piece of input on the keyboard: (1) it displays a message prompting the user for the piece of data, and (2) it reads the user's input and stores that data in a variable. Here is the pseudocode for reading the two pieces of input required by the batting average program:

```
Display "Enter the player's number of hits."
Input hits

Display "Enter the player's number of times at bat."
Input atBat
```

Next we will write the pseudocode for calculating the batting average:

```
Set battingAverage = hits / atBat
```

And finally, we write the pseudocode for displaying the output:

```
Display "The player's batting average is ", battingAverage
```

Now we can put all of these pieces together to form a complete program. Program 15 shows the pseudocode program with comments, and Figure 17 shows the flowchart.

Program 15

```
 1 // Declare the necessary variables.
 2 Declare Integer hits
 3 Declare Integer atBat
 4 Declare Real battingAverage
 5
 6 // Get the number of hits.
 7 Display "Enter the player's number of hits."
 8 Input hits
 9
10 // Get the number of times at bat.
11 Display "Enter the player's number of times at bat."
12 Input atBat
13
14 // Calculate the batting average.
15 Set battingAverage = hits / atBat
16
17 // Display the batting average.
18 Display "The player's batting average is ", battingAverage
```

Program Output (with Input Shown in Bold)

```
Enter the player's number of hits.
150 [Enter]
Enter the player's number of times at bat.
500 [Enter]
The player's batting average is 0.3
```

Figure 17 Flowchart for Program 15

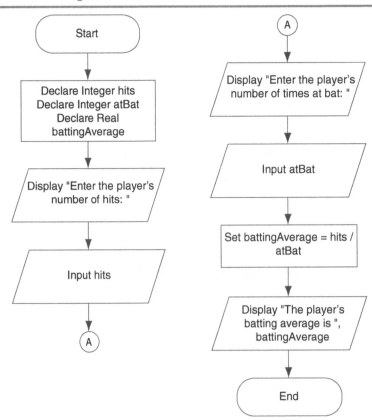

Summary

As a beginning student, whenever you have trouble getting started with a program design, determine the program's requirements as follows:

1. **Input:** Carefully study the problem and identify the pieces of data that the program needs to read as input. Once you know what data is needed as input, decide the names of the variables for those pieces of data, and their data types.
2. **Process:** What must the program do with the input that it will read? Determine the calculations and/or other processes that must be performed. At this time, decide the names and data types of any variables needed to hold the results of calculations.
3. **Output:** What output must the program produce? In most cases, it will be the results of the program's calculations and/or other processes.

Once you have determined these requirements, you will have an understanding of what the program must do. You will also have a list of variables and their data types. The next step is writing the algorithm in pseudocode, or drawing it as a flowchart.

Review Questions

Multiple Choice

1. A _____ error does not prevent the program from running, but causes it to produce incorrect results.

   a. syntax
   b. hardware
   c. logic
   d. fatal

2. A _____ is a single function that the program must perform in order to satisfy the customer.

   a. task
   b. software requirement
   c. prerequisite
   d. predicate

3. A(n) _____ is a set of well-defined logical steps that must be taken to perform a task.

   a. logarithm
   b. plan of action
   c. logic schedule
   d. algorithm

4. An informal language that has no syntax rules, and is not meant to be compiled or executed is called _____.

    a. faux code
    b. pseudocode
    c. Java
    d. a flowchart

5. A _____ is a diagram that graphically depicts the steps that take place in a program.

    a. flowchart
    b. step chart
    c. code graph
    d. program graph

6. A(n) _____ is a set of statements that execute in the order that they appear.

    a. serial program
    b. sorted code
    c. sequence structure
    d. ordered structure

7. A _____ is a sequence of characters that is used as data.

    a. sequence structure
    b. character collection
    c. string
    d. text block

8. A _____ is a storage location in memory that is represented by a name.

    a. variable
    b. register
    c. RAM slot
    d. byte

9. A _____ is any hypothetical person that is using a program and providing input for it.

    a. designer
    b. user
    c. guinea pig
    d. test subject

10. A(n) _____ is a message that tells (or asks) the user to enter a specific value.

    a. inquiry
    b. input statement
    c. directive
    d. prompt

11. A(n) _____ sets a variable to a specified value.

    a. variable declaration
    b. assignment statement
    c. math expression
    d. string literal

12. In the expression 12 + 7, the values on the right and left of the + symbol are called _____.

    a. operands
    b. operators
    c. arguments
    d. math expressions

13. A(n) _____ operator raises a number to a power.

    a. modulus
    b. multiplication
    c. exponent
    d. operand

14. A(n) _____ operator performs division, but instead of returning the quotient it returns the remainder.

    a. modulus
    b. multiplication
    c. exponent
    d. operand

15. A(n) _____ specifies a variable's name and data type.

    a. assignment
    b. variable specification
    c. variable certification
    d. variable declaration

16. Assigning a value to a variable in a declaration statement is called _____.

    a. allocation
    b. initialization
    c. certification
    d. programming style

17. A(n) _____ variable is one that has been declared, but has not been initialized or assigned a value.

    a. undefined
    b. uninitialized
    c. empty
    d. default

18. A(n) _____ is a variable whose content has a value that is read only and cannot be changed during the program's execution.

    a. static variable
    b. uninitialized variable
    c. named constant
    d. locked variable

19. A debugging process in which you imagine that you are the computer executing a program is called _____.

    a. imaginative computing
    b. role playing
    c. mental simulation
    d. hand tracing

20. Short notes placed in different parts of a program, explaining how those parts of the program work, are called _____.
    a. comments
    b. reference manuals
    c. tutorials
    d. external documentation

True or False

1. Programmers must be careful not to make syntax errors when writing pseudocode programs.

2. In a math expression, multiplication and division takes place before addition and subtraction.

3. Variable names can have spaces in them.

4. In most languages, the first character of a variable name cannot be a number.

5. The name gross_pay is written in the camelCase convention.

6. In languages that require variable declarations, a variable's declaration must appear before any other statements that use the variable.

7. Uninitialized variables are a common cause of errors.

8. The value of a named constant cannot be changed during the program's execution.

9. Hand tracing is the process of translating a pseudocode program into machine language by hand.

10. Internal documentation refers to books and manuals that document a program, and are intended for use within a company's programming department.

Short Answer

1. What does a professional programmer usually do first to gain an understanding of a problem?

2. What is pseudocode?

3. Computer programs typically perform what three steps?

4. What does the term *user-friendly* mean?

5. What two things must you normally specify in a variable declaration?

6. What value is stored in uninitialized variables?

Algorithm Workbench

1. Design an algorithm that prompts the user to enter his or her height and stores the user's input in a variable named height.

2. Design an algorithm that prompts the user to enter his or her favorite color and stores the user's input in a variable named color.

3. Write assignment statements that perform the following operations with the variables a, b, and c.

    a. Adds 2 to a and stores the result in b

    b. Multiplies b times 4 and stores the result in a

    c. Divides a by 3.14 and stores the result in b

    d. Subtracts 8 from b and stores the result in a

4. Assume the variables result, w, x, y, and z are all integers, and that w = 5, x = 4, y = 8, and z = 2. What value will be stored in result in each of the following statements?

    a. Set result = x + y

    b. Set result = z * 2

    c. Set result = y / x

    d. Set result = y - z

5. Write a pseudocode statement that declares the variable cost so it can hold real numbers.

6. Write a pseudocode statement that declares the variable total so it can hold integers. Initialize the variable with the value 0.

7. Write a pseudocode statement that assigns the value 27 to the variable count.

8. Write a pseudocode statement that assigns the sum of 10 and 14 to the variable total.

9. Write a pseudocode statement that subtracts the variable downPayment from the variable total and assigns the result to the variable due.

10. Write a pseudocode statement that multiplies the variable subtotal by 0.15 and assigns the result to the variable totalfee.

11. If the following pseudocode were an actual program, what would it display?

```
Declare Integer a = 5
Declare Integer b = 2
Declare Integer c = 3
Declare Integer result

Set result = a + b * c
Display result
```

12. If the following pseudocode were an actual program, what would it display?

```
Declare Integer num = 99
Set num = 5
Display num
```

Debugging Exercises

1. If the following pseudocode were an actual program, why would it not display the output that the programmer expects?

```
Declare String favoriteFood

Display "What is the name of your favorite food?"
Input favoriteFood

Display "Your favorite food is "
Display "favoriteFood"
```

2. If the programmer translates the following pseudocode to an actual programming language, a syntax error is likely to occur. Can you find the error?

```
Declare String 1stPrize

Display "Enter the award for first prize."
Input 1stPrize

Display "The first prize winner will receive ", 1stPrize
```

3. The following code will not display the results expected by the programmer. Can you find the error?

```
Declare Real lowest, highest, average

Display "Enter the lowest score."
Input lowest

Display "Enter the highest score."
Input highest

Set average = low + high / 2
Display "The average is ", average, "."
```

4. Find the error in the following pseudocode.

```
Display "Enter the length of the room."
Input length
Declare Integer length
```

5. Find the error in the following pseudocode.

```
Declare Integer value1, value2, value3, sum
Set sum = value1 + value2 + value3

Display "Enter the first value."
Input value1

Display "Enter the second value."
Input value2

Display "Enter the third value."
Input value3

Display "The sum of numbers is ", sum
```

6. Find the error in the following pseudocode.

```
Declare Real pi
Set 3.14159265 = pi
Display "The value of pi is ", pi
```

7. Find the error in the following pseudocode.

```
Constant Real GRAVITY = 9.81
Display "Rates of acceleration of an object in free fall:"
Display "Earth: ", GRAVITY, " meters per second every second."
Set GRAVITY = 1.63
Display "Moon: ", GRAVITY, " meters per second every second."
```

Programming Exercises

1. **Personal Information**

   Design a program that displays the following information:

   - Your name
   - Your address, with city, state, and ZIP
   - Your telephone number
   - Your college major

2. **Sales Prediction**

   A company has determined that its annual profit is typically 23 percent of total sales. Design a program that asks the user to enter the projected amount of total sales, and then displays the profit that will be made from that amount.

   Hint: Use the value 0.23 to represent 23 percent.

3. **Land Calculation**

   One acre of land is equivalent to 43,560 square feet. Design a program that asks the user to enter the total square feet in a tract of land and calculates the number of acres in the tract.

   Hint: Divide the amount entered by 43,560 to get the number of acres.

4. **Total Purchase**

   A customer in a store is purchasing five items. Design a program that asks for the price of each item, and then displays the subtotal of the sale, the amount of sales tax, and the total. Assume the sales tax is 6 percent.

5. **Distance Traveled**

   Assuming there are no accidents or delays, the distance that a car travels down the interstate can be calculated with the following formula:

   $$Distance = Speed \times Time$$

   A car is traveling at 60 miles per hour. Design a program that displays the following:

   - The distance the car will travel in 5 hours
   - The distance the car will travel in 8 hours
   - The distance the car will travel in 12 hours

6. **Sales Tax**

   Design a program that will ask the user to enter the amount of a purchase. The program should then compute the state and county sales tax. Assume the state sales tax is 4 percent and the county sales tax is 2 percent. The program should display the amount of the purchase, the state sales tax, the county sales tax, the total sales tax, and the total of the sale (which is the sum of the amount of purchase plus the total sales tax).

Hint: Use the value 0.02 to represent 2 percent, and 0.04 to represent 4 percent.

7. **Miles-per-Gallon**

A car's miles-per-gallon (MPG) can be calculated with the following formula:

MPG = Miles driven / Gallons of gas used

Design a program that asks the user for the number of miles driven and the gallons of gas used. It should calculate the car's miles-per-gallon and display the result on the screen.

VideoNote
The Tip, Tax, and Total Problem

8. **Tip, Tax, and Total**

Design a program that calculates the total amount of a meal purchased at a restaurant. The program should ask the user to enter the charge for the food, and then calculate the amount of a 15 percent tip and 7 percent sales tax. Display each of these amounts and the total.

9. **Celsius to Fahrenheit Temperature Converter**

Design a program that converts Celsius temperatures to Fahrenheit temperatures. The formula is as follows:

$$F = \frac{9}{5}C + 32$$

The program should ask the user to enter a temperature in Celsius, and then display the temperature converted to Fahrenheit.

10. **Stock Transaction Program**

Last month Joe purchased some stock in Acme Software, Inc. Here are the details of the purchase:

- The number of shares that Joe purchased was 1,000.
- When Joe purchased the stock, he paid $32.87 per share.
- Joe paid his stockbroker a commission that amounted to 2 percent of the amount he paid for the stock.

Two weeks later Joe sold the stock. Here are the details of the sale:

- The number of shares that Joe sold was 1,000.
- He sold the stock for $33.92 per share.
- He paid his stockbroker another commission that amounted to 2 percent of the amount he received for the stock.

Design a program that displays the following information:

- The amount of money Joe paid for the stock.
- The amount of commission Joe paid his broker when he bought the stock.
- The amount that Joe sold the stock for.
- The amount of commission Joe paid his broker when he sold the stock.
- Did Joe make money or lose money? Display the amount of profit or loss after Joe sold the stock and paid his broker (both times).

Answers to Checkpoint Questions

1 Any person, group, or organization that is asking you to write a program.

2 A single function that the program must perform in order to satisfy the customer.

3 A set of well-defined logical steps that must be taken to perform a task.

4 An informal language that has no syntax rules, and is not meant to be compiled or executed. Instead, programmers use pseudocode to create models, or "mock-ups" of programs.

5 A diagram that graphically depicts the steps that take place in a program.

6 Ovals are terminal symbols. Parallelograms are either output or input symbols. Rectangles are processing symbols.

7 Input, processing, and output.

8 A set of statements that execute in the order that they appear.

9 A string is a sequence of characters that is used as data. A string literal is a string that appears in the actual code of a program.

10 Quotation marks

11 A storage location in memory that is represented by a name.

12 • Variable names must be one word. They cannot contain spaces.
   • In most languages, punctuation characters cannot be used in variable names. It is usually a good idea to use only alphabetic letters and numbers in variable names.
   • In most languages, the first character of a variable name cannot be a number.

13 camelCase

14 • The program pauses and waits for the user to type something on the keyboard, and then press the [Enter] key.
   • When the [Enter] key is pressed, the data that was typed is stored in the temperature variable.

15 Any hypothetical person that is using a program and providing input for it.

16 A message that tells (or asks) the user to enter a specific value.

17 1. Display a prompt on the screen.
   2. Read a value from the keyboard.

18 The term *user-friendly* is commonly used in the software business to describe programs that are easy to use.

19 A statement that sets a variable to a specified value.

20 It is replaced.

21 1. Perform any operations that are enclosed in parentheses.
   2. Perform any operations that use the exponent operator to raise a number to a power.
   3. Perform any multiplications, divisions, or modulus operations as they appear from left to right.
   4. Perform any additions or subtractions as they appear from left to right.

22 It raises a number to a power.

23 It performs division, but instead of returning the quotient it returns the remainder.

24 The variable's name and data type.

25 Yes, you must write a variable declaration before any other statement that uses the variable.

26 The assignment of a value to a variable at the time the variable is declared.

27 Yes, they are a common cause of errors. If an uninitialized variable is used in an operation such as a calculation, a logic error will occur.

28 A variable that has been declared, but has not been initialized or assigned a value.

29 External documentation is typically designed for the user. It consists of documents such as a reference guide that describes the program's features, and tutorials that teach the user how to operate the program.

30 Internal documentation appears as comments in a program's code. Comments are short notes placed in different parts of a program, explaining how those parts of the program work.

31 Programmers generally write block comments and line comments. Block comments take up several lines and are used when lengthy explanations are required. Line comments are comments that occupy a single line, and explain a short section of the program.

Modules

TOPICS

Introduction to Modules

CONCEPT: A module is a group of statements that exist within a program for the purpose of performing a specific task.

A program is a set of instructions that a computer follows to perform a task. Consider a simple program that performs the task of calculating an employee's pay by multiplying the number of hours that the employee worked by the employee's hourly pay rate. A more realistic payroll program, however, would do much more than this. In a real-world application, the overall task of calculating an employee's pay would consist of several subtasks, such as the following:

- Getting the employee's hourly pay rate
- Getting the number of hours worked
- Calculating the employee's gross pay
- Calculating overtime pay
- Calculating withholdings for taxes and benefits
- Calculating the net pay
- Printing the paycheck

Most programs perform tasks that are large enough to be broken down into several subtasks. For this reason, programmers usually break down their programs into modules. A *module* is a group of statements that exist within a program for the purpose

From Chapter 3 of *Starting Out with Programming Logic and Design,* Third Edition. Tony Gaddis.
Copyright © 2013 by Pearson Education, Inc. Published by Pearson Addison-Wesley. All rights reserved.

of performing a specific task. Instead of writing a large program as one long sequence of statements, it can be written as several small modules, each one performing a specific part of the task. These small modules can then be executed in the desired order to perform the overall task.

This approach is sometimes called *divide and conquer* because a large task is divided into several smaller tasks that are easily performed. Figure 1 illustrates this idea by comparing two programs: one that uses a long, complex sequence of statements to perform a task, and another that divides a task into smaller tasks, each of which are performed by a separate module.

When using modules in a program, you generally isolate each task within the program in its own module. For example, a realistic pay calculating program might have the following modules:

- A module that gets the employee's hourly pay rate
- A module that gets the number of hours worked
- A module that calculates the employee's gross pay
- A module that calculates the overtime pay
- A module that calculates the withholdings for taxes and benefits
- A module that calculates the net pay
- A module that prints the paycheck

Although every modern programming language allows you to create modules, they are not always referred to as modules. Modules are commonly called *procedures, subroutines, subprograms, methods,* and *functions.* (A function is a special type of module.)

Benefits of Using Modules

A program benefits in the following ways when it is modularized:

Simpler Code

A program's code tends to be simpler and easier to understand when it is modularized. Several small modules are much easier to read than one long sequence of statements.

Code Reuse

Modules also reduce the duplication of code within a program. If a specific operation is performed in several places in a program, a module can be written once to perform that operation, and then be executed any time it is needed. This benefit of using modules is known as *code reuse* because you are writing the code to perform a task once and then reusing it each time you need to perform the task.

Better Testing

When each task within a program is contained in its own module, testing and debugging become simpler. Programmers can test each module in a program individually, to determine whether it correctly performs its operation. This makes it easier to isolate and fix errors.

Figure 1 Using modules to divide and conquer a large task

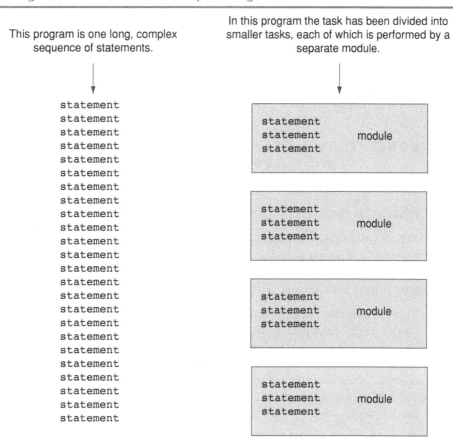

Faster Development

Suppose a programmer or a team of programmers is developing multiple programs. They discover that each of the programs performs several common tasks, such as asking for a username and a password, displaying the current time, and so on. It doesn't make sense to write the code for these tasks multiple times. Instead, modules can be written for the commonly needed tasks, and those modules can be incorporated into each program that needs them.

Easier Facilitation of Teamwork

Modules also make it easier for programmers to work in teams. When a program is developed as a set of modules that each performs an individual task, then different programmers can be assigned the job of writing different modules.

 Checkpoint

1 What is a module?

2 What is meant by the phrase "divide and conquer"?

3 How do modules help you reuse code in a program?

4 How can modules make the development of multiple programs faster?

5 How can modules make it easier for programs to be developed by teams of programmers?

2 Defining and Calling a Module

CONCEPT: The code for a module is known as a module definition. To execute the module, you write a statement that calls it.

Module Names

Before we discuss the process of creating and using modules, we should mention a few things about module names. Just as you name the variables that you use in a program, you also name the modules. A module's name should be descriptive enough so that anyone reading your code can reasonably guess what the module does.

Because modules perform actions, most programmers prefer to use verbs in module names. For example, a module that calculates gross pay might be named `calculateGrossPay`. This name would make it evident to anyone reading the code that the module calculates something. What does it calculate? The gross pay, of course. Other examples of good module names would be `getHours`, `getPayRate`, `calculateOvertime`, `printCheck`, and so on. Each module name describes what the module does.

When naming a module, most languages require that you follow the same rules that you follow when naming variables. This means that module names cannot contain spaces, cannot typically contain punctuation characters, and usually cannot begin with a number. These are only general rules, however. The specific rules for naming a module will vary slightly with each programming language.

VideoNote

Defining and Calling a Module

Defining and Calling a Module

To create a module you write its *definition*. In most languages, a module definition has two parts: a header and a body. The *header* indicates the starting point of the module, and the *body* is a list of statements that belong to the module. Here is the general format that we will follow when we write a module definition in pseudocode:

```
Module name()
    statement
    statement        } These statements are the body of the module.
    etc.
End Module
```

The first line is the module header. In our pseudocode the header begins with the word `Module`, followed by the name of the module, followed by a set of parentheses. It is a common practice in most programming languages to put a set of parentheses after a module name. Later in this chapter, you will see the actual purpose of the parentheses, but for now, just remember that they come after the module name.

Beginning at the line after the module header, one or more statements will appear. These statements are the module's body, and are performed any time the module is executed. The last line of the definition, after the body, reads End Module. This line marks the end of the module definition.

Let's look at an example. Keep in mind that this is not a complete program. We will show the entire pseudocode program in a moment.

```
Module showMessage()
    Display "Hello world."
End Module
```

This pseudocode defines a module named showMessage. As its name implies, the purpose of this module is to show a message on the screen. The body of the showMessage module contains one statement: a Display statement that displays the message "Hello world."

Notice in the previous example that the statement in the body of the module is indented. Indenting the statements in the body of a module is not usually required,[1] but it makes your code much easier to read. By indenting the statements inside a module, you visually set them apart. As a result, you can tell at a glance which statements are inside the module. This practice is a programming style convention that virtually all programmers follow.

Calling a Module

A module definition specifies what a module does, but it does not cause the module to execute. To execute a module, we must *call* it. In pseudocode we will use the word Call to call a module. This is how we would call the showMessage module:

```
Call showMessage()
```

When a module is called, the computer jumps to that module and executes the statements in the module's body. Then, when the end of the module is reached, the computer jumps back to the part of the program that called the module, and the program resumes execution at that point.

To fully demonstrate how module calling works, we will look at Program 1.

Program 1

```
1 Module main()
2    Display "I have a message for you."
3    Call showMessage()
4    Display "That's all, folks!"
5 End Module
6
```

---

[1]The Python language requires you to indent the statements inside a module.

```
7 Module showMessage()
8    Display "Hello world"
9 End Module
```

Program Output

```
I have a message for you.
Hello world
That's all, folks!
```

First, notice that Program 1 has two modules: a module named `main` appears in lines 1 through 5, and the `showMessage` module appears in lines 7 through 9. Many programming languages require that programs have a *main module*. The main module is the program's starting point, and it generally calls other modules. When the end of the main module is reached, the program stops executing. In this text, any time you see a pseudocode program with a module named `main`, we are using that module as the program's starting point. Likewise, when the end of the `main` module is reached, the program will stop executing. This is shown in Figure 2.

Figure 2 The `main` module

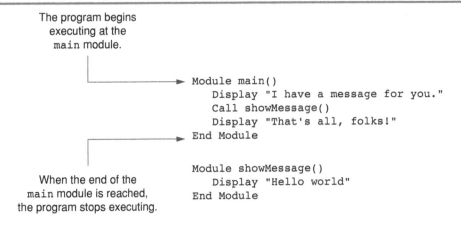

 NOTE: Many languages, including Java, C, and C++, require that the main module actually be named `main`, as we have shown in Program 1.

Let's step through the program. When the program runs, the `main` module starts and the statement in line 2 displays "I have a message for you." Then, line 3 calls the `showMessage` module. As shown in Figure 3, the computer jumps to the `showMessage` module and executes the statements in its body. There is only one statement in the body of the `showMessage` module: the `Display` statement in line 8. This statement displays "Hello world" and then the module ends. As shown in Figure 4, the computer jumps back to the part of the program that called `showMessage`, and resumes execution from that point. In this case, the program resumes execution at line 4, which displays "That's all folks!" The main module ends at line 5, so the program stops executing.

Figure 3 Calling the showMessage module

The computer jumps to the showMessage module and executes the statements in its body.

```
Module main()
    Display "I have a message for you."
    Call showMessage()
    Display "That's all, folks!"
End Module


Module showMessage()
    Display "Hello world"
End Module
```

Figure 4 The showMessage module returns

When the showMessage module ends, the computer jumps back to the part of the program that called it, and resumes execution from that point.

```
Module main()
    Display "I have a message for you."
    Call showMessage()
    Display "That's all, folks!"
End Module


Module showMessage()
    Display "Hello world"
End Module
```

When the computer encounters a module call, such as the one in line 3 of Program 1, it has to perform some operations "behind the scenes" so it will know where to return after the module ends. First, the computer saves the memory address of the location that it should return to. This is typically the statement that appears immediately after the module call. This memory location is known as the *return point*. Then, the computer jumps to the module and executes the statements in its body. When the module ends, the computer jumps back to the return point and resumes execution.

NOTE: When a program calls a module, programmers commonly say that the *control* of the program transfers to that module. This simply means that the module takes control of the program's execution.

Flowcharting a Program with Modules

In a flowchart, a module call is shown with a rectangle that has vertical bars at each side, as shown in Figure 5. The name of the module that is being called is written on the symbol. The example shown in Figure 5 shows how we would represent a call to the showMessage module.

Figure 5 Module call symbol

Programmers typically draw a separate flowchart for each module in a program. For example, Figure 6 shows how Program 1 would be flowcharted. Notice that the figure shows two flowcharts: one for the `main` module and another for the `showMessage` module.

Figure 6 Flowchart for Program 1

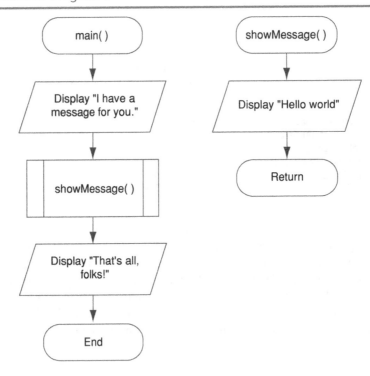

When drawing a flowchart for a module, the starting terminal symbol usually shows the name of the module. The ending terminal symbol in the `main` module reads `End` because it marks the end of the program's execution. The ending terminal symbol for all other modules reads `Return` because it marks the point where the computer returns to the part of the program that called the module.

Top-Down Design

In this section, we have discussed and demonstrated how modules work. You've seen how the computer jumps to a module when it is called, and returns to the part of the program that called the module when the module ends. It is important that you understand these mechanical aspects of modules.

Just as important as understanding how modules work is understanding how to design a modularized program. Programmers commonly use a technique known as *top-down design* to break down an algorithm into modules. The process of top-down design is performed in the following manner:

- The overall task that the program is to perform is broken down into a series of subtasks.
- Each of the subtasks is examined to determine whether it can be further broken down into more subtasks. This step is repeated until no more subtasks can be identified.
- Once all of the subtasks have been identified, they are written in code.

This process is called top-down design because the programmer begins by looking at the topmost level of tasks that must be performed, and then breaks down those tasks into lower levels of subtasks.

NOTE: The top-down design process is sometimes called *stepwise refinement*.

Hierarchy Charts

Flowcharts are good tools for graphically depicting the flow of logic inside a module, but they do not give a visual representation of the relationships between modules. Programmers commonly use *hierarchy charts* for this purpose. A hierarchy chart, which is also known as a *structure chart*, shows boxes that represent each module in a program. The boxes are connected in a way that illustrates their relationship to one another. Figure 7 shows an example of a hierarchy chart for a pay calculating program.

Figure 7 A hierarchy chart

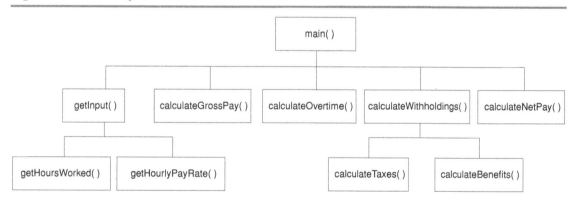

The chart shown in Figure 7 shows the main module as the topmost module in the hierarchy. The main module calls five other modules: getInput, calculateGrossPay, calculateOvertime, calculateWithholdings, and calculateNetPay. The getInput module calls two additional modules: getHoursWorked and getHourlyPayRate. The calculateWithholdings module also calls two modules: calculateTaxes and calculateBenefits.

Notice that the hierarchy chart does not show the steps that are taken inside a module. Because hierarchy charts do not reveal any details about how modules work, they do not replace flowcharts or pseudocode.

In the Spotlight:
Defining and Calling Modules

Professional Appliance Service, Inc. offers maintenance and repair services for household appliances. The owner wants to give each of the company's service technicians a small handheld computer that displays step-by-step instructions for many of the repairs that they perform. To see how this might work, the owner has asked you to develop a program that displays the following instructions for disassembling an ACME laundry dyer:

Step 1: Unplug the dryer and move it away from the wall.
Step 2: Remove the six screws from the back of the dryer.
Step 3: Remove the dryer's back panel.
Step 4: Pull the top of the dryer straight up.

During your interview with the owner, you determine that that the program should display the steps one at a time. You decide that after each step is displayed, the user will be asked to press a key to see the next step. Here is the algorithm for the program:

1. Display a starting message, explaining what the program does.
2. Ask the user to press a key to see Step 1.
3. Display the instructions for Step 1.
4. Ask the user to press a key to see the next step.
5. Display the instructions for Step 2.
6. Ask the user to press a key to see the next step.
7. Display the instructions for Step 3.
8. Ask the user to press a key to see the next step.
9. Display the instructions for Step 4.

This algorithm lists the top level of tasks that the program needs to perform, and becomes the basis of the program's main module. Figure 8 shows the program's structure in a hierarchy chart.

Figure 8 Hierarchy chart for the program

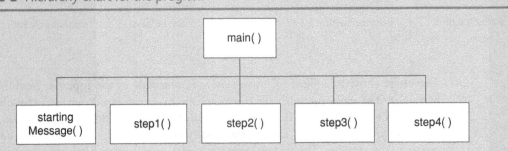

As you can see from the hierarchy chart, the main module will call several other modules. Here are summaries of those modules:

- startingMessage—This module will display the starting message that tells the technician what the program does.
- step1—This module will display the instructions for Step 1.
- step2—This module will display the instructions for Step 2.
- step3—This module will display the instructions for Step 3.
- step4—This module will display the instructions for Step 4.

Between calls to these modules, the main module will instruct the user to press a key to see the next step in the instructions. Program 2 shows the pseudocode for the program. Figure 9 shows the flowchart for the main module, and Figure 10 shows the flowcharts for the startingMessage, step1, step2, step3, and step4 modules.

Program 2

```
 1 Module main()
 2     // Display the starting message.
 3     Call startingMessage()
 4     Display "Press a key to see Step 1."
 5     Input
 6
 7     // Display Step 1.
 8     Call step1()
 9     Display "Press a key to see Step 2."
10     Input
11
12     // Display Step 2.
13     Call step2()
14     Display "Press a key to see Step 3."
15     Input
16
17     // Display Step 3.
18     Call step3()
19     Display "Press a key to see Step 4."
20     Input
21
22     // Display Step 4.
23     Call step4()
24 End Module
25
26 // The startingMessage module displays
27 // the program's starting message.
28 Module startingMessage()
29     Display "This program tells you how to"
30     Display "disassemble an ACME laundry dryer."
31     Display "There are 4 steps in the process."
32 End Module
33
34 // The step1 module displays the instructions
35 // for Step 1.
```

```
36 Module step1()
37    Display "Step 1: Unplug the dryer and"
38    Display "move it away from the wall."
39 End Module
40
41 // The step2 module displays the instructions
42 // for Step 2.
43 Module step2()
44    Display "Step 2: Remove the six screws"
45    Display "from the back of the dryer."
46 End Module
47
48 // The step3 module displays the instructions
49 // for Step 3.
50 Module step3()
51    Display "Step 3: Remove the dryer's"
52    Display "back panel."
53 End Module
54
55 // The step4 module displays the instructions
56 // for Step 4.
57 Module step4()
58    Display "Step 4: Pull the top of the"
59    Display "dryer straight up."
60 End Module
```

Program Output

```
This program tells you how to
disassemble an ACME laundry dryer.
There are 4 steps in the process.
Press a key to see Step 1.
[Enter]
Step 1: Unplug the dryer and
move it away from the wall.
Press a key to see Step 2.
[Enter]
Step 2: Remove the six screws
from the back of the dryer.
Press a key to see Step 3.
[Enter]
Step 3: Remove the dryer's
back panel.
Press a key to see Step 4.
[Enter]
Step 4: Pull the top of the
dryer straight up.
```

NOTE: Lines 5, 10, 15, and 20 show an `Input` statement with no variable specified. In our pseudocode, this is the way we will read a keystroke from the keyboard without saving the character that was pressed. Most programming languages provide a way to do this.

Figure 9 Flowchart for the `main` module in Program 2

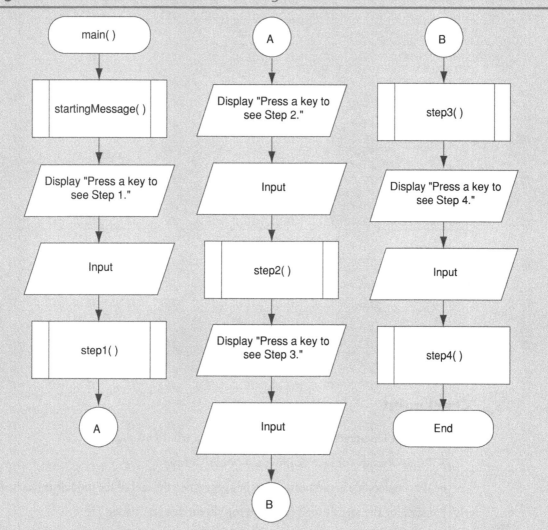

Figure 10 Flowcharts for the other modules in Program 2

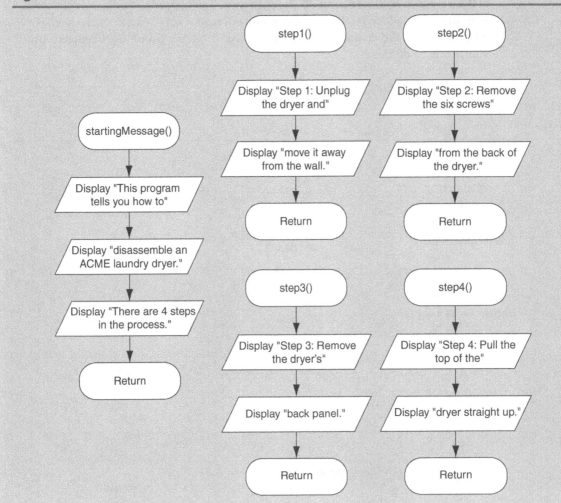

 Checkpoint

6 In most languages, a module definition has what two parts?

7 What does the phrase "calling a module" mean?

8 When a module is executing, what happens when the end of the module is reached?

9 Describe the steps involved in the top-down design process.

 Local Variables

CONCEPT: A local variable is declared inside a module and cannot be accessed by statements that are outside the module. Different modules can have local variables with the same names because the modules cannot see each other's local variables.

In most programming languages, a variable that is declared inside a module is called a *local variable*. A local variable belongs to the module in which it is declared, and only statements inside that module can access the variable. (The term *local* is meant to indicate that the variable can be used only locally, within the module in which it is declared.)

An error will occur if a statement in one module tries to access a local variable that belongs to another module. For example, look at the pseudocode in Program 3.

Program 3

```
 1 Module main()
 2    Call getName()
 3    Display "Hello ", name    ◄──────── This will cause an error!
 4 End Module
 5
 6 Module getName()
 7    Declare String name   ◄──────── This is local variable.
 8    Display "Enter your name."
 9    Input name
10 End Module
```

The name variable is declared in line 7, inside the getName module. Because it is declared inside the getName module, it is a local variable belonging to that module. Line 8 prompts the user to enter his or her name, and the Input statement in line 9 stores the user's input in the name variable.

The main module calls the getName module in line 2. Then, the Display statement in line 3 tries to access the name variable. This results in an error because the name variable is local to the getName module, and statements in the main module cannot access it.

Scope and Local Variables

Programmers commonly use the term *scope* to describe the part of a program in which a variable may be accessed. A variable is visible only to statements inside the variable's scope.

A local variable's scope usually begins at the variable's declaration and ends at the end of the module in which the variable is declared. The variable cannot be accessed by statements that are outside this region. This means that a local variable cannot be accessed by code that is outside the module, or inside the module but before the variable's declaration. For example, look at the following code. It has an error because the Input statement tries to store a value in the name variable, but the statement is outside the variable's scope. Moving the variable declaration to a line before the Input statement will fix this error.

```
Module getName()
   Display "Enter your name."
   Input name   ◄────────────────  This statement will cause an error because
   Declare String name             the name variable has not been declared yet.
End Module
```

Duplicate Variable Names

In most programming languages, you cannot have two variables with the same name in the same scope. For example, look at the following module:

```
Module getTwoAges()
   Declare Integer age
   Display "Enter your age."
   Input age

   Declare Integer age        ←──────── This will cause an error!
   Display "Enter your pet's age."      A variable named age has
   Input age                            already been declared.
End Module
```

This module declares two local variables named age. The second variable declaration will cause an error because a variable named age has already been declared in the module. Renaming one of the variables will fix this error.

> **TIP:** You cannot have two variables with the same name in the same module because the compiler or interpreter would not know which variable to use when a statement tries to access one of them. All variables that exist within the same scope must have unique names.

Although you cannot have two local variables with the same name in the same module, it is usually okay for a local variable in one module to have the same name as a local variable in a different module. For example, suppose a program has two modules: getPersonAge and getPetAge. It would be legal for both modules to have a local variable named age.

 Checkpoint

10 What is a local variable? How is access to a local variable restricted?

11 What is a variable's scope?

12 Is it usually permissible to have more than one variable with the same name in the same scope? Why or why not?

13 Is it usually permissible for a local variable in one module to have the same name as a local variable in a different module?

 ## Passing Arguments to Modules

CONCEPT: An argument is any piece of data that is passed into a module when the module is called. A parameter is a variable that receives an argument that is passed into a module.

VideoNote

Passing Arguments to a Module

Sometimes it is useful not only to call a module, but also to send one or more pieces of data into the module. Pieces of data that are sent into a module are known as *arguments*. The module can use its arguments in calculations or other operations.

If you want a module to receive arguments when it is called, you must equip the module with one or more parameter variables. A *parameter variable,* often simply called a *parameter,* is a special variable that receives an argument when a module is called. Here is an example of a pseudocode module that has a parameter variable:

```
Module doubleNumber(Integer value)
   Declare Integer result
   Set result = value * 2
   Display result
End Module
```

This module's name is doubleNumber. Its purpose is to accept an integer number as an argument and display the value of that number doubled. Look at the module header and notice the words Integer value that appear inside the parentheses. This is the declaration of a parameter variable. The parameter variable's name is value and its data type is Integer. The purpose of this variable is to receive an Integer argument when the module is called. Program 4 demonstrates the module in a complete program.

Program 4

```
1 Module main()
2    Call doubleNumber(4)
3 End Module
4
5 Module doubleNumber(Integer value)
6    Declare Integer result
7    Set result = value * 2
8    Display result
9 End Module
```

Program Output

```
8
```

When this program runs, the main module will begin executing. The statement in line 2 calls the doubleNumber module. Notice that the number 4 appears inside the parentheses. This is an argument that is being passed to the doubleNumber module. When this statement executes, the doubleNumber module will be called with the number 4 copied into the value parameter variable. This is shown in Figure 11.

Figure 11 The argument 4 is copied into the value parameter variable

```
Module main()                        The argument 4 is copied into
   Call doubleNumber(4)              the value parameter variable.
End Module


Module doubleNumber(Integer value)
   Declare Integer result
   Set result = value * 2
   Display result
End Module
```

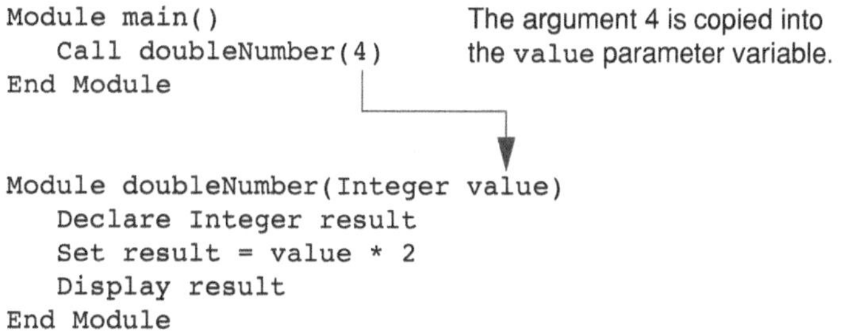

Let's step through the doubleNumber module. As we do, remember that the value parameter variable will contain the number that was passed into it as an argument. In this program, that number is 4.

Line 6 declares a local Integer variable named result. Then, line 7 assigns the value of the expression value * 2 to result. Because the value variable contains 4, this line assigns 8 to result. Line 8 displays the contents of the result variable. The module ends at line 9.

For example, if we had called the module as follows:

```
Call doubleNumber(5)
```

the module would have displayed 10.

We can also pass the contents of a variable as an argument. For example, look at Program 5. The main module declares an Integer variable named number in line 2. Lines 3 and 4 prompt the user to enter a number, and line 5 reads the user's input into the number variable. Notice that in line 6 number is passed as an argument to the doubleNumber module, which causes the number variable's contents to be copied into the value parameter variable. This is shown in Figure 12.

Program 5

```
 1 Module main()
 2     Declare Integer number
 3     Display "Enter a number and I will display"
 4     Display "that number doubled."
 5     Input number
 6     Call doubleNumber(number)
 7 End Module
 8
 9 Module doubleNumber(Integer value)
10     Declare Integer result
11     Set result = value * 2
12     Display result
13 End Module
```

Program Output (with Input Shown in Bold)

```
Enter a number and I will display
that number doubled.
20 [Enter]
40
```

Argument and Parameter Compatibility

When you pass an argument to a module, most programming languages require that the argument and the receiving parameter variable be of the same data type. If you try to pass an argument of one type into a parameter variable of another type, an error usually occurs. For example, Figure 13 shows that you cannot pass a real number or a Real variable into an Integer parameter.

Figure 12 The contents of the number variable passed as an argument

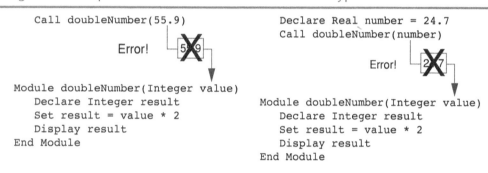

```
Module main()
    Declare Integer number
    Display "Enter a number and I will display"
    Display "that number doubled."
    Input number
    Call doubleNumber(number)
End Module

                              ┌──┐
                              │20│    The contents of the number
                              └──┘    variable are copied into the
                                 ▼    value parameter variable.

Module doubleNumber(Integer value)
    Declare Integer result
    Set result = value * 2
    Display result
End Module
```

Figure 13 Arguments and parameter variables must be of the same type

```
    Call doubleNumber(55.9)                Declare Real number = 24.7
                                           Call doubleNumber(number)

    Error!    ┌──┐                         Error!    ┌──┐
              │5 9│                                  │2 7│
              └──┘                                   └──┘
                 ▼                                      ▼
Module doubleNumber(Integer value)         Module doubleNumber(Integer value)
    Declare Integer result                     Declare Integer result
    Set result = value * 2                     Set result = value * 2
    Display result                             Display result
End Module                                  End Module
```

> **NOTE:** Some languages allow you to pass an argument into a parameter variable of a different type as long as no data will be lost. For example, some languages allow you to pass integer arguments into real parameters because real variables can hold whole numbers. If you pass a real argument, such as 24.7, into an integer parameter, the fractional part of the number would be lost.

Parameter Variable Scope

Earlier in this chapter, you learned that a variable's scope is the part of the program in which the variable may be accessed. A variable is visible only to statements inside the variable's scope. A parameter variable's scope is usually the entire module in which the parameter is declared. No statement outside the module can access the parameter variable.

Passing Multiple Arguments

Most languages allow you to write modules that accept multiple arguments. Program 6 shows a pseudocode module named showSum, that accepts two Integer arguments. The module adds the two arguments and displays their sum.

Program 6

```
 1 Module main()
 2    Display "The sum of 12 and 45 is:"
 3    Call showSum(12, 45)
 4 End Module
 5
 6 Module showSum(Integer num1, Integer num2)
 7    Declare Integer result
 8    Set result = num1 + num2
 9    Display result
10 End Module
```

Program Output

```
The sum of 12 and 45 is:
57
```

Notice that two parameter variables, num1 and num2, are declared inside the parentheses in the module header. This is often referred to as a *parameter list*. Also notice that a comma separates the declarations.

The statement in line 3 calls the showSum module and passes two arguments: 12 and 45. The arguments are passed into the parameter variables in the order that they appear in the module call. In other words, the first argument is passed into the first parameter variable, and the second argument is passed into the second parameter variable. So, this statement causes 12 to be passed into the num1 parameter and 45 to be passed into the num2 parameter, as shown in Figure 14.

Figure 14 Two arguments passed into two parameters

```
Module main()
   Display "The sum of 12 and 45 is:"
   Call showSum(12, 45)
End Module



Module showSum(Integer num1, Integer num2)
   Declare Integer result
   Set result = num1 + num2
   Display result
End Module
```

Suppose we were to reverse the order in which the arguments are listed in the module call, as shown here:

```
Call showSum(45, 12)
```

This would cause 45 to be passed into the num1 parameter and 12 to be passed into the num2 parameter. The following pseudocode code shows one more example. This time we are passing variables as arguments.

```
Declare Integer value1 = 2
Declare Integer value2 = 3
Call showSum(value1, value2)
```

When the showSum method executes as a result of this code, the num1 parameter will contain 2 and the num2 parameter will contain 3.

In the Spotlight:

Passing an Argument to a Module

Your friend Michael runs a catering company. Some of the ingredients that his recipes require are measured in cups. When he goes to the grocery store to buy those ingredients, however, they are sold only by the fluid ounce. He has asked you to write a simple program that converts cups to fluid ounces.

You design the following algorithm:

1. Display an introductory screen that explains what the program does.
2. Get the number of cups.
3. Convert the number of cups to fluid ounces and display the result.

This algorithm lists the top level of tasks that the program needs to perform, and becomes the basis of the program's main module. Figure 15 shows the program's structure in a hierarchy chart.

Figure 15 Hierarchy chart for the program

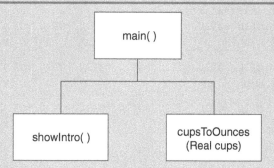

As shown in the hierarchy chart, the main module will call two other modules.

Here are summaries of those modules:

- showIntro—This module will display a message on the screen that explains what the program does.
- cupsToOunces—This module will accept the number of cups as an argument and calculate and display the equivalent number of fluid ounces.

In addition to calling these modules, the main module will ask the user to enter the number of cups. This value will be passed to the cupsToOunces module. Program 7 shows the pseudocode for the program, and Figure 16 shows a flowchart.

Program 7

```
1 Module main()
2     // Declare a variable for the
3     // number of cups needed.
4     Declare Real cupsNeeded
5
6     // Display an intro message.
7     Call showIntro()
8
9     // Get the number of cups.
10    Display "Enter the number of cups."
11    Input cupsNeeded
12
13    // Convert cups to ounces.
14    Call cupsToOunces(cupsNeeded)
15 End Module
16
17 // The showIntro module displays an
18 // introductory screen.
19 Module showIntro()
20    Display "This program converts measurements"
21    Display "in cups to fluid ounces. For your"
22    Display "reference the formula is:"
23    Display "    1 cup = 8 fluid ounces."
24 End Module
25
26 // The cupsToOunces module accepts a number
27 // of cups and displays the equivalent number
28 // of ounces.
29 Module cupsToOunces(Real cups)
30    // Declare variables.
31    Declare Real ounces
32
33    // Convert cups to ounces.
34    Set ounces = cups * 8
35
36    // Display the result.
37    Display "That converts to ",
38            ounces, " ounces."
39 End Module
```

Program Output (with Input Shown in Bold)

```
This program converts measurements
in cups to fluid ounces. For your
reference the formula is:
    1 cup = 8 fluid ounces.
Enter the number of cups.
2 [Enter]
That converts to 16 ounces.
```

Figure 16 Flowchart for Program 7

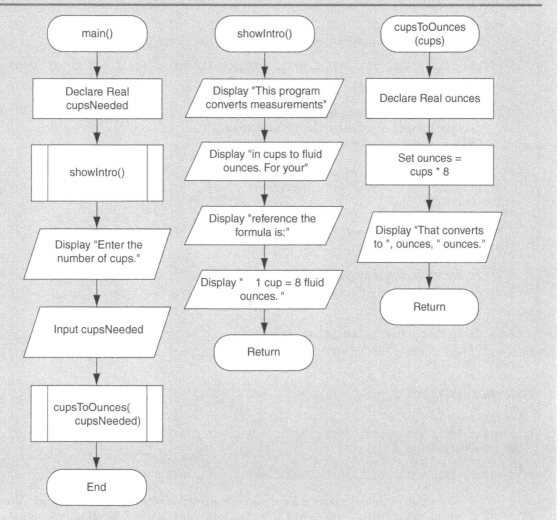

Passing Arguments by Value and by Reference

Many programming languages provide two different ways to pass arguments: by value and by reference. Before studying these techniques in detail, we should mention that different languages have their own way of doing each. It is important to learn the fundamental concepts behind these techniques and how to model them in pseudocode. When you begin to use these techniques in an actual language, you will need to learn the details of how they are carried out in that language.

Passing Arguments by Value

All of the example programs that we have looked at so far pass arguments by value. Arguments and parameter variables are separate items in memory. Passing an argument *by value* means that only a copy of the argument's value is passed into the parameter variable. If the contents of the parameter variable are changed inside the module, it has no effect on the argument in the calling part of the program. For example, look at Program 8.

Program 8

```
 1 Module main()
 2    Declare Integer number = 99
 3
 4    // Display the value stored in number.
 5    Display "The number is ", number
 6
 7    // Call the changeMe module, passing
 8    // the number variable as an argument.
 9    Call changeMe(number)
10
11    // Display the value of number again.
12    Display "The number is", number
13 End Module
14
15 Module changeMe(Integer myValue)
16    Display "I am changing the value."
17
18    // Set the myValue parameter variable
19    // to 0.
20    Set myValue = 0
21
22    // Display the value in myValue.
23    Display "Now the number is ", myValue
24 End Module
```

Program Output

```
The number is 99
I am changing the value.
Now the number is 0
The number is 99
```

The main module declares a local variable named number in line 2, and initializes it to the value 99. As a result, the Display statement in line 5 displays "The number is 99." The number variable's value is then passed as an argument to the changeMe module in line 9. This means that in the changeMe module the value 99 will be copied into the myValue parameter variable.

Inside the changeMe module, in line 20, the myValue parameter variable is set to 0. As a result, the Display statement in line 23 displays "Now the number is 0." The module ends, and control of the program returns to the main module.

The next statement to execute is the Display statement in line 12. This statement displays "The number is 99." Even though the parameter variable myValue was changed in the changeMe method, the argument (the number variable in main) was not modified.

Passing an argument is a way that one module can communicate with another module. When the argument is passed by value, the communication channel works in only one direction: the calling module can communicate with the called module. The called module, however, cannot use the argument to communicate with the calling module.

Passing Arguments by Reference

Passing an argument *by reference* means that the argument is passed into a special type of parameter known as a *reference variable*. When a reference variable is used as a parameter in a module, it allows the module to modify the argument in the calling part of the program.

A reference variable acts as an alias for the variable that was passed into it as an argument. It is called a reference variable because it references the other variable. Anything that you do to the reference variable is actually done to the variable it references.

Reference variables are useful for establishing two-way communication between modules. When a module calls another module and passes a variable by reference, communication between the modules can take place in the following ways:

- The calling module can communicate with the called module by passing an argument.
- The called module can communicate with the calling module by modifying the value of the argument via the reference variable.

In pseudocode we will declare that a parameter is a reference variable by writing the word Ref before the parameter variable's name in the module header. For example, look at the following pseudocode module:

```
Module setToZero(Integer Ref value)
    Set value = 0
End Module
```

The word Ref indicates that value is a reference variable. The module stores 0 in the value parameter. Because value is a reference variable, this action is actually performed on the variable that was passed to the module as an argument. Program 9 demonstrates this module.

Program 9

```
 1 Module main()
 2    // Declare and initialize some variables.
 3    Declare Integer x = 99
 4    Declare Integer y = 100
 5    Declare Integer z = 101
 6
 7    // Display the values in those variables.
 8    Display "x is set to ", x
 9    Display "y is set to ", y
10    Display "z is set to ", z
11
12    // Pass each variable to setToZero.
13    Call setToZero(x)
14    Call setToZero(y)
15    Call setToZero(z)
16
17    // Display the values now.
18    Display "----------------"
19    Display "x is set to ", x
```

```
20     Display "y is set to ", y
21     Display "z is set to ", z
22 End Module
23
24 Module setToZero(Integer Ref value)
25     Set value = 0
26 End Module
```

Program Output

```
x is set to 99
y is set to 100
z is set to 101
----------------
x is set to 0
y is set to 0
z is set to 0
```

In the main module the variable x is initialized with 99, the variable y is initialized with 100, and the variable z is initialized with 101. Then, in lines 13 through 15 those variables are passed as arguments to the setToZero module. Each time setToZero is called, the variable that is passed as an argument is set to 0. This is shown when the values of the variables are displayed in lines 19 through 21.

NOTE: In an actual program you should never use variable names like x, y, and z. This particular program is meant for demonstration purposes, however, and these simple names are adequate.

NOTE: Normally, only variables may be passed by reference. If you attempt to pass a non-variable argument into a reference variable parameter, an error will result. Using the setToZero module as an example, the following statement will generate an error:

```
// This is an error!
setToZero(5);
```

In the Spotlight:

Passing an Argument by Reference

In the previous *In the Spotlight* case study, we developed a program that your friend Michael can use in his catering business. The program does exactly what Michael wants it to do: it converts cups to fluid ounces. After studying the program that we initially wrote, however, you believe that you can improve the design. As shown in the following pseudocode, the main module contains the code that reads the user's input. This code should really be treated as a separate subtask, and put in its own module. If this change is made, the program will be like the new hierarchy chart shown in Figure 17.

```
Module main()
    // Declare a variable for the
    // number of cups needed.
    Declare Real cupsNeeded

    // Display an intro message.
    Call showIntro()

    // Get the number of cups.
    Display "Enter the number of cups."     } This code can be put
    Input cupsNeeded                          in its own module.

    // Convert cups to ounces.
    Call cupsToOunces(cupsNeeded)
End Module
```

Figure 17 Revised hierarchy chart

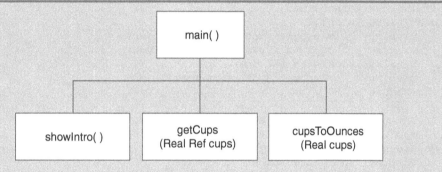

This version of the hierarchy chart shows a new module: getCups. Here is the pseudocode for the getCups module:

```
Module getCups(Real Ref cups)
    Display "Enter the number of cups."
    Input cups
End Module
```

The getCups module has a parameter, cups, which is a reference variable. The module prompts the user to enter the number of cups and then stores the user's input in the cups parameter. When the main module calls getCups, it will pass the local variable cupsNeeded as an argument. Because it will be passed by reference, it will contain the user's input when the module returns. Program 10 shows the revised pseudocode for the program, and Figure 18 shows a flowchart.

NOTE: In this case study, we improved the design of an existing program without changing the behavior of the program. In a nutshell, we "cleaned up" the design. Programmers call this *refactoring*.

Program 10

```
 1 Module main()
 2     // Declare a variable for the
 3     // number of cups needed.
 4     Declare Real cupsNeeded
 5
 6     // Display an intro message.
 7     Call showIntro()
 8
 9     // Get the number of cups.
10     Call getCups(cupsNeeded)
11
12     // Convert cups to ounces.
13     Call cupsToOunces(cupsNeeded)
14 End Module
15
16 // The showIntro module displays an
17 // introductory screen.
18 Module showIntro()
19     Display "This program converts measurements"
20     Display "in cups to fluid ounces. For your"
21     Display "reference the formula is:"
22     Display "    1 cup = 8 fluid ounces."
23 End Module
24
25 // The getCups module gets the number of cups
26 // and stores it in the reference variable cups.
27 Module getCups(Real Ref cups)
28     Display "Enter the number of cups."
29     Input cups
30 End Module
31
32 // The cupsToOunces module accepts a number
33 // of cups and displays the equivalent number
34 // of ounces.
35 Module cupsToOunces(Real cups)
36     // Declare variables.
37     Declare Real ounces
38
39     // Convert cups to ounces.
40     Set ounces = cups * 8
41
42     // Display the result.
43     Display "That converts to ",
44             ounces, " ounces."
45 End Module
```

Program Output (with Input Shown in Bold)

```
This program converts measurements
in cups to fluid ounces. For your
reference the formula is:
    1 cup = 8 fluid ounces.
Enter the number of cups.
2 [Enter]
That converts to 16 ounces.
```

Figure 18 Flowchart for Program 10

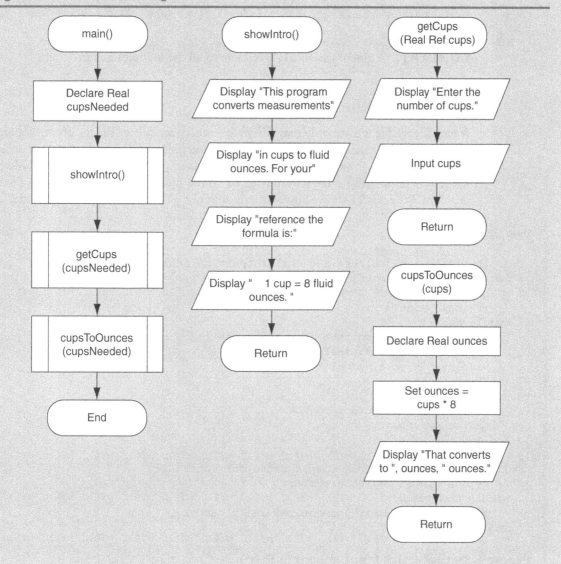

Checkpoint

14 What are the pieces of data that are passed into a module called?

15 What are the variables that receive pieces of data in a module called?

16 Does it usually matter whether an argument's data type is different from the data type of the parameter that it is being passed to?

17 Typically, what is a parameter variable's scope?

18 Explain the difference between passing by value and passing by reference.

5 Global Variables and Global Constants

CONCEPT: A global variable is accessible to all the modules in a program.

Global Variables

A *global variable* is a variable that is visible to every module in the program. A global variable's scope is the entire program, so all of the modules in the program can access a global variable. In most programming languages, you create a global variable by writing its declaration statement outside of all the modules, usually at the top of the program. Program 11 shows how you can declare a global variable in pseudocode.

Program 11

```
 1 // The following declares a global Integer variable.
 2 Declare Integer number
 3
 4 // The main module
 5 Module main()
 6    // Get a number from the user and store it
 7    // in the global variable number.
 8    Display "Enter a number."
 9    Input number
10
11    // Call the showNumber module.
12    Call showNumber()
13 End Module
14
15 // The showNumber module displays the contents
16 // of the global variable number.
17 Module showNumber()
18    Display "The number you entered is ", number
19 End Module
```

Program Output (with Input Shown in Bold)
```
Enter a number.
22 [Enter]
The number you entered is 22
```

Line 2 declares an Integer variable named number. Because the declaration does not appear inside a module, the number variable is a global variable. All of the modules that are defined in the program have access to the variable. When the Input statement in line 9 (inside the main module) executes, the value entered by the user is stored in the global variable number. When the Display statement in line 18 (inside the showNumber module) executes, it is the value of the same global variable that is displayed.

Most programmers agree that you should restrict the use of global variables, or not use them at all. The reasons are as follows:

- Global variables make debugging difficult. Any statement in a program can change the value of a global variable. If you find that the wrong value is being stored in a global variable, you have to track down every statement that accesses it to determine where the bad value is coming from. In a program with thousands of lines of code, this can be difficult.
- Modules that use global variables are usually dependent on those variables. If you want to use such a module in a different program, most likely you will have to redesign it so it does not rely on the global variable.
- Global variables make a program hard to understand. A global variable can be modified by any statement in the program. If you are to understand any part of the program that uses a global variable, you have to be aware of all the other parts of the program that access the global variable.

In most cases, you should declare variables locally and pass them as arguments to the modules that need to access them.

Global Constants

Although you should try to avoid the use of global variables, it is permissible to use global constants in a program. A *global constant* is a named constant that is available to every module in the program. Because a global constant's value cannot be changed during the program's execution, you do not have to worry about many of the potential hazards that are associated with the use of global variables.

Global constants are typically used to represent unchanging values that are needed throughout a program. For example, suppose a banking program uses a named constant to represent an interest rate. If the interest rate is used in several modules, it is easier to create a global constant, rather than a local named constant in each module. This also simplifies maintenance. If the interest rate changes, only the declaration of the global constant has to be changed, instead of several local declarations.

In the Spotlight:
Using Global Constants

Marilyn works for Integrated Systems, Inc., a software company that has a reputation for providing excellent fringe benefits. One of its benefits is a quarterly bonus that is paid to all employees. Another benefit is a retirement plan for each employee. The company contributes 5 percent of each employee's gross pay and bonuses to his or her retirement plan. Marilyn wants to design a program that will calculate the company's contribution to an employee's retirement account for a year. She wants the program to show the amount of contribution for the employee's gross pay and for the bonuses separately.

Here is an algorithm for the program:

1. Get the employee's annual gross pay.
2. Get the amount of bonuses paid to the employee.
3. Calculate and display the contribution for the gross pay.
4. Calculate and display the contribution for the bonuses.

Figure 19 shows a hierarchy chart for the program. The pseudocode for the program is shown in Program 12, and a set of flowcharts is shown in Figure 20.

Figure 19 Hierarchy chart

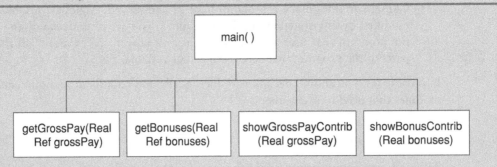

Program 12

```
1 // Global constant for the rate of contribution.
2 Constant Real CONTRIBUTION_RATE = 0.05
3
4 // main module
5 Module main()
6     // Local variables
7     Declare Real annualGrossPay
8     Declare Real totalBonuses
9
10     // Get the annual gross pay.
11     Call getGrossPay(annualGrossPay)
12
13     // Get the total of the bonuses.
14     Call getBonuses(totalBonuses)
15
16     // Display the contribution for
17     // the gross pay.
18     Call showGrossPayContrib(annualGrossPay)
19
20     // Display the contribution for
21     // the bonuses.
22     Call showBonusContrib(totalBonuses)
23 End Module
24
25 // The getGrossPay module gets the
26 // gross pay and stores it in the
27 // grossPay reference variable.
28 Module getGrossPay(Real Ref grossPay)
29     Display "Enter the total gross pay."
```

```
30     Input grossPay
31 End Module
32
33 // The getBonuses module gets the
34 // amount of bonuses and stores it
35 // in the bonuses reference variable.
36 Module getBonuses(Real Ref bonuses)
37     Display "Enter the amount of bonuses."
38     Input bonuses
39 End Module
40
41 // The showGrossPayContrib module
42 // accepts the gross pay as an argument
43 // and displays the retirement contribution
44 // for gross pay.
45 Module showGrossPayContrib(Real grossPay)
46     Declare Real contrib
47     Set contrib = grossPay * CONTRIBUTION_RATE
48     Display "The contribution for the gross pay"
49     Display "is $", contrib
50 End Module
51
52 // The showBonusContrib module accepts
53 // the bonus amount as an argument and
54 // displays the retirement contribution
55 // for bonuses.
56 Module showBonusContrib(Real bonuses)
57     Declare Real contrib
58     Set contrib = bonuses * CONTRIBUTION_RATE
59     Display "The contribution for the bonuses"
60     Display "is $", contrib
61 End Module
```

Program Output (with Input Shown in Bold)

```
Enter the total gross pay.
80000.00 [Enter]
Enter the amount of bonuses.
20000.00 [Enter]
The contribution for the gross pay
is $4000
The contribution for the bonuses
is $1000
```

A global constant named CONTRIBUTION_RATE is declared in line 2, and initialized with the value 0.05. The constant is used in the calculation in line 47 (in the showGrossPayContrib module) and again in line 58 (in the showBonusContrib module). Marilyn decided to use this global constant to represent the 5 percent contribution rate for two reasons:

- It makes the program easier to read. When you look at the calculations in lines 47 and 58, it is apparent what is happening.
- Occasionally the contribution rate changes. When this happens, it will be easy to update the program by changing the declaration statement in line 2.

Figure 20 Flowchart for Program 12

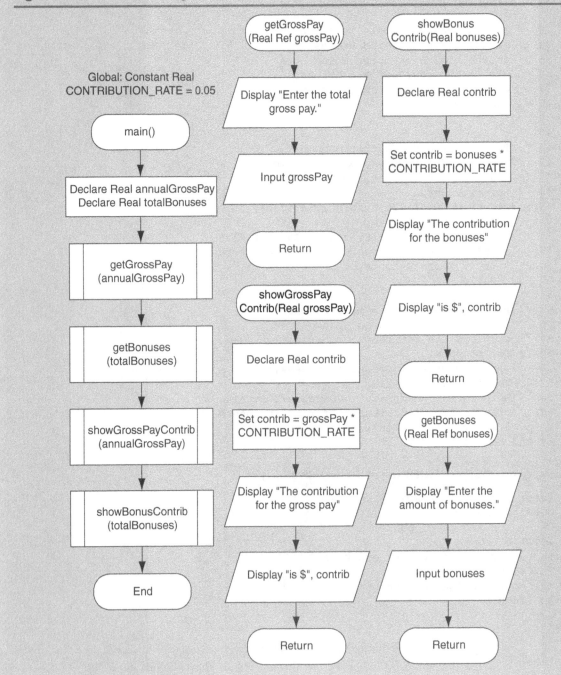

Checkpoint

19 What is the scope of a global variable?

20 Give one good reason that you should not use global variables in a program.

21 What is a global constant? Is it permissible to use global constants in a program?

Review Questions

Multiple Choice

1. A group of statements that exist within a program for the purpose of performing a specific task is a(n) _____.

   a. block
   b. parameter
   c. module
   d. expression

2. A benefit of using modules that helps to reduce the duplication of code within a program is _____.

   a. code reuse
   b. divide and conquer
   c. debugging
   d. facilitation of teamwork

3. The first line of a module definition is known as the _____.

   a. body
   b. introduction
   c. initialization
   d. header

4. You _____ the module to execute it.

   a. define
   b. call
   c. import
   d. export

5. A _____ point is the memory address of the location in the program that the computer will return to when a module ends.

   a. termination
   b. module definition
   c. return
   d. reference

6. A design technique that programmers use to break down an algorithm into modules is known as _____.

   a. top-down design
   b. code simplification
   c. code refactoring
   d. hierarchical subtasking

7. A _____ is a diagram that gives a visual representation of the relationships between modules in a program.

   a. flowchart
   b. module relationship chart
   c. symbol chart
   d. hierarchy chart

8. A _____ is a variable that is declared inside a module.

    a. global variable
    b. local variable
    c. hidden variable
    d. none of the above; you cannot declare a variable inside a module

9. A(n) _____ is the part of a program in which a variable may be accessed.

    a. declaration space
    b. area of visibility
    c. scope
    d. mode

10. A(n) _____ is a piece of data that is sent into a module.

    a. argument
    b. parameter
    c. header
    d. packet

11. A(n) _____ is a special variable that receives a piece of data when a module is called.

    a. argument
    b. parameter
    c. header
    d. packet

12. When _____, only a copy of the argument's value is passed into the parameter variable.

    a. passing an argument by reference
    b. passing an argument by name
    c. passing an argument by value
    d. passing an argument by data type

13. When _____, the module can modify the argument in the calling part of the program.

    a. passing an argument by reference
    b. passing an argument by name
    c. passing an argument by value
    d. passing an argument by data type

14. A variable that is visible to every module in the program is a _____.

    a. local variable
    b. universal variable
    c. program-wide variable
    d. global variable

15. When possible, you should avoid using _____ variables in a program.

    a. local
    b. global
    c. reference
    d. parameter

True or False

1. The phrase "divide and conquer" means that all of the programmers on a team should be divided and work in isolation.

2. Modules make it easier for programmers to work in teams.

3. Module names should be as short as possible.

4. Calling a module and defining a module mean the same thing.

5. A flowchart shows the hierarchical relationships between modules in a program.

6. A hierarchy chart does not show the steps that are taken inside a module.

7. A statement in one module can access a local variable in another module.

8. In most programming languages, you cannot have two variables with the same name in the same scope.

9. Programming languages typically require that arguments be of the same data type as the parameters that they are passed to.

10. Most languages do not allow you to write modules that accept multiple arguments.

11. When an argument is passed by reference, the module can modify the argument in the calling part of the program.

12. Passing an argument by value is a means of establishing two-way communication between modules.

Short Answer

1. How do modules help you to reuse code in a program?

2. Name and describe the two parts that a module definition has in most languages.

3. When a module is executing, what happens when the end of the module is reached?

4. What is a local variable? What statements are able to access a local variable?

5. In most languages, where does a local variable's scope begin and end?

6. What is the difference between passing an argument by value and passing it by reference?

7. Why do global variables make a program difficult to debug?

Algorithm Workbench

1. Design a module named `timesTen`. The module should accept an `Integer` argument. When the module is called, it should display the product of its argument multiplied times 10.

2. Examine the following pseudocode module header, and then write a statement that calls the module, passing 12 as an argument.

```
Module showValue(Integer quantity)
```

3. Look at the following pseudocode module header:

```
Module myModule(Integer a, Integer b, Integer c)
```

Now look at the following call to myModule:

```
Call myModule(3, 2, 1)
```

When this call executes, what value will be stored in a? What value will be stored in b? What value will be stored in c?

4. Assume that a pseudocode program contains the following module:

```
Module display(Integer arg1, Real arg2, String arg3)
    Display "Here are the values:"
    Display arg1, " ", arg2, " ", arg3
End Module
```

Assume that the same program has a main module with the following variable declarations:

```
Declare Integer age
Declare Real income
Declare String name
```

Write a statement that calls the display module and passes these variables to it.

5. Design a module named getNumber, which uses a reference parameter variable to accept an Integer argument. The module should prompt the user to enter a number and then store the input in the reference parameter variable.

6. What will the following pseudocode program display?

```
Module main()
    Declare Integer x = 1
    Declare Real y = 3.4
    Display x, " ", y
    Call changeUs(x, y)
    Display x, " ", y
End Module

Module changeUs(Integer a, Real b)
    Set a = 0
    Set b = 0
    Display a, " ", b
End Module
```

7. What will the following pseudocode program display?

```
Module main()
    Declare Integer x = 1
    Declare Real y = 3.4
    Display x, " ", y
    Call changeUs(x, y)
    Display x, " ", y
End Module

Module changeUs(Integer Ref a, Real Ref b)
    Set a = 0
    Set b = 0.0
    Display a, " ", b
End Module
```

Debugging Exercises

1. Find the error in the following pseudocode.

```
Module main()
    Declare Real mileage
    Call getMileage()
    Display "You've driven a total of ", mileage, " miles."
End Module

Module getMileage()
    Display "Enter your vehicle's mileage."
    Input mileage
End Module
```

2. Find the error in the following pseudocode.

```
Module main()
   Call getCalories()
End Module

Module getCalories()
   Declare Real calories
   Display "How many calories are in the first food?"
   Input calories

   Declare Real calories
   Display "How many calories are in the second food?"
   Input calories
End Module
```

3. Find the potential error in the following pseudocode.

```
Module main()
    Call squareNumber(5)
End Module

Module squareNumber(Integer Ref number)
    Set number = number^2
    Display number
End Module
```

4. Find the error in the following pseudocode.

```
Module main()
    Call raiseToPower(2, 1.5)
End Module

Module raiseToPower(Real value, Integer power)
    Declare Real result
    Set result = value^power
    Display result
End Module
```

Programming Exercises

VideoNote
Kilometer Converter

1. Kilometer Converter

   Design a modular program that asks the user to enter a distance in kilometers, and then converts that distance to miles. The conversion formula is as follows:

   $$Miles = Kilometers \times 0.6214$$

2. **Sales Tax Program Refactoring**

   Design a Sales Tax program that calculates and displays the county and state sales tax on a purchase. Create a modular design for it.

3. **How Much Insurance?**

   Many financial experts advise that property owners should insure their homes or buildings for at least 80 percent of the amount it would cost to replace the structure. Design a modular program that asks the user to enter the replacement cost of a building and then displays the minimum amount of insurance he or she should buy for the property.

4. **Automobile Costs**

   Design a modular program that asks the user to enter the monthly costs for the following expenses incurred from operating his or her automobile: loan payment, insurance, gas, oil, tires, and maintenance. The program should then display the total monthly cost of these expenses, and the total annual cost of these expenses.

5. **Property Tax**

   A county collects property taxes on the assessment value of property, which is 60 percent of the property's actual value. For example, if an acre of land is valued at $10,000, its assessment value is $6,000. The property tax is then 64¢ for each $100 of the assessment value. The tax for the acre assessed at $6,000 will be $38.40. Design a modular program that asks for the actual value of a piece of property and displays the assessment value and property tax.

6. **Body Mass Index**

   Design a modular program that calculates and displays a person's body mass index (BMI). The BMI is often used to determine whether a person with a sedentary lifestyle is overweight or underweight for his or her height. A person's BMI is calculated with the following formula:

   $$BMI = Weight \times 703/Height^2$$

7. **Calories from Fat and Carbohydrates**

   A nutritionist who works for a fitness club helps members by evaluating their diets. As part of her evaluation, she asks members for the number of fat grams and carbohydrate grams that they consumed in a day. Then, she calculates the number of calories that result from the fat, using the following formula:

   $$Calories\ from\ Fat = Fat\ Grams \times 9$$

   Next, she calculates the number of calories that result from the carbohydrates, using the following formula:

   $$Calories\ from\ Carbs = Carb\ Grams \times 4$$

   The nutritionist asks you to design a modular program that will make these calculations.

8. **Stadium Seating**

   There are three seating categories at a stadium. For a softball game, Class A seats cost $15, Class B seats cost $12, and Class C seats cost $9. Design a modular program that asks how many tickets for each class of seats were sold, and then displays the amount of income generated from ticket sales.

9. **Paint Job Estimator**

   A painting company has determined that for every 115 square feet of wall space, one gallon of paint and eight hours of labor will be required. The company charges $20.00 per hour for labor. Design a modular program that asks the user to enter the square feet of wall space to be painted and the price of the paint per gallon. The program should display the following data:

   - The number of gallons of paint required
   - The hours of labor required
   - The cost of the paint
   - The labor charges
   - The total cost of the paint job

10. **Monthly Sales Tax**

    A retail company must file a monthly sales tax report listing the total sales for the month, and the amount of state and county sales tax collected. The state sales tax rate is 4 percent and the county sales tax rate is 2 percent. Design a modular program that asks the user to enter the total sales for the month. From this figure, the application should calculate and display the following:

    - The amount of county sales tax
    - The amount of state sales tax
    - The total sales tax (county plus state)

    In the pseudocode, represent the county tax rate (0.02) and the state tax rate (0.04) as named constants.

Answers to Checkpoint Questions

1 A module is a group of statements that exist within a program for the purpose of performing a specific task.

2 A large task is divided into several smaller tasks that are easily performed.

3 If a specific operation is performed in several places in a program, a module can be written once to perform that operation, and then be executed any time it is needed.

4 Modules can be written for the common tasks that are needed by the different programs. Those modules can then be incorporated into each program that needs them.

5 When a program is developed as a set of modules that each perform an individual task, then different programmers can be assigned the job of writing different modules.

6 In most languages, a module definition has two parts: a header and a body. The header indicates the starting point of the module, and the body is a list of statements that belong to the module.

7 To call a module means to execute the module.

8 When the end of the module is reached, the computer jumps back to the part of the program that called the module, and the program resumes execution at that point.

9 • The overall task that the program is to perform is broken down into a series of subtasks.
  • Each of the subtasks is examined to determine whether it can be further broken down into more subtasks. This step is repeated until no more subtasks can be identified.
  • Once all of the subtasks have been identified, they are written in code.

10 A local variable is a variable that is declared inside a module. It belongs to the module in which it is declared, and only statements inside the same module can access it.

11 The part of a program in which a variable may be accessed.

12 No, it is not permissible. The compiler or interpreter would not know which variable to use when a statement tries to access one of them.

13 Yes, it is permissible.

14 Arguments

15 Parameters

16 Yes, an error will usually occur if an argument's data type is different from the data type of the parameter it is being passed to.

17 A parameter variable's scope is usually the entire module in which the parameter is declared.

18 Passing an argument by value means that only a copy of the argument's value is passed into the parameter variable. If the contents of the parameter variable are changed inside the module, it has no effect on the argument in the calling part of the program. Passing an argument by reference means that the argument is passed into a special type of parameter known as a reference variable. When a reference variable is used as a parameter in a module, it allows the module to modify the argument in the calling part of the program.

19 The entire program

20 Here are three:
  • Global variables make debugging difficult. Any statement in a program can change the value of a global variable. If you find that the wrong value is being stored in a global variable, you have to track down every statement that accesses it to determine where the bad value is coming from. In a program with thousands of lines of code, this can be difficult.
  • Modules that use global variables are usually dependent on those variables. If you want to use such a module in a different program, you will most likely have to redesign it so it does not rely on the global variable.
  • Global variables make a program hard to understand. A global variable can be modified by any statement in the program. If you are to understand any part of the program that uses a global variable, you have to be aware of all the other parts of the program that access the global variable.

21 A global constant is a named constant that is available to every module in the program. It is permissible to use global constants. Because a global constant's value cannot be changed during the program's execution, you do not have to worry about its value being altered.

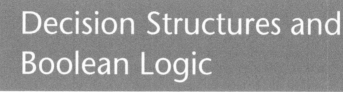

Decision Structures and Boolean Logic

1   Introduction to Decision Structures

CONCEPT: A decision structure allows a program to perform actions only under certain conditions.

VideoNote

The Single Alternative Decision Structure

A control structure is a logical design that controls the order in which a set of statements executes. The sequence structure, the simplest type of control structure, is a set of statements that execute in the order that they appear. For example, the following pseudocode is a sequence structure because the statements execute from top to bottom.

```
Declare Integer age
Display "What is your age?"
Input age
Display "Here is the value that you entered:"
Display age
```

Even with modules, each module maybe written as a sequence structure. For example, the following module is a sequence structure because the statements in it execute in the order that they appear, from the beginning of the module to the end.

From Chapter 4 of *Starting Out with Programming Logic and Design,* Third Edition. Tony Gaddis.

```
Module doubleNumber(Integer value)
    Declare Integer result
    Set result = value * 2
    Display result
End Module
```

Although the sequence structure is heavily used in programming, it cannot handle every type of task. Some problems simply cannot be solved by performing a set of ordered steps, one after the other. For example, consider a pay calculating program that determines whether an employee has worked overtime. If the employee has worked more than 40 hours, he or she gets paid extra for all the hours over 40. Otherwise, the overtime calculation should be skipped. Programs like this require a different type of control structure: one that can execute a set of statements only under certain circumstances. This can be accomplished with a *decision structure*. (Decision structures are also known as *selection structures*.)

In a decision structure's simplest form, a specific action is performed only if a certain condition exists. If the condition does not exist, the action is not performed. The flowchart shown in Figure 1 shows how the logic of an everyday decision can be diagrammed as a decision structure. The diamond symbol represents a true/false condition. If the condition is true, we follow one path, which leads to an action being performed. If the condition is false, we follow another path, which skips the action.

Figure 1 A simple decision structure for an everyday task

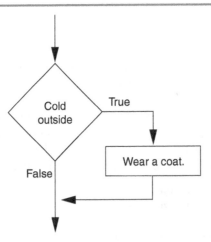

In the flowchart, the diamond symbol indicates some condition that must be tested. In this case, we are determining whether the condition *Cold outside* is true or false. If this condition is true, the action *Wear a coat* is performed. If the condition is false, the action is skipped. The action is *conditionally executed* because it is performed only when a certain condition is true.

Programmers call the type of decision structure shown in Figure 1 a *single alternative decision structure*. This is because it provides only one alternative path of execution. If the condition in the diamond symbol is true, we take the alternative path. Otherwise, we exit the structure.

Combining Structures

You cannot use decision structures alone to create a complete program. You use a decision structure to handle any part of a program that needs to test a condition and conditionally execute an action depending on the outcome of the condition. For other parts of a program you need to use other structures. For example, Figure 2 shows a complete flowchart that combines a decision structure with two sequence structures. (Figure 2 is not a flowchart of a computer algorithm, but of a human action.)

The flowchart in the figure starts with a sequence structure. Assuming you have an outdoor thermometer in your window, the first step is *Go to the window,* and the next step is *Read thermometer.* A decision structure appears next, testing the condition *Cold outside.* If this is true, the action *Wear a coat* is performed. Another sequence structure appears next. The step *Open the door* is performed, followed by *Go outside.*

Quite often, structures must be nested inside of other structures. For example, look at the partial flowchart in Figure 3. It shows a decision structure with a sequence structure nested inside it. (Once again, this is a flowchart showing human actions, not program statements.) The decision structure tests the condition *Cold outside.* If that condition is true, the steps in the sequence structure are executed.

Figure 2 Combining sequence structures with a decision structure

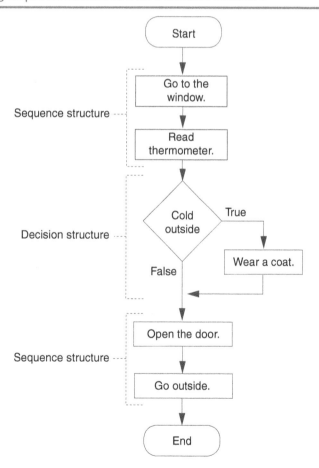

Figure 3 A sequence structure nested inside a decision structure

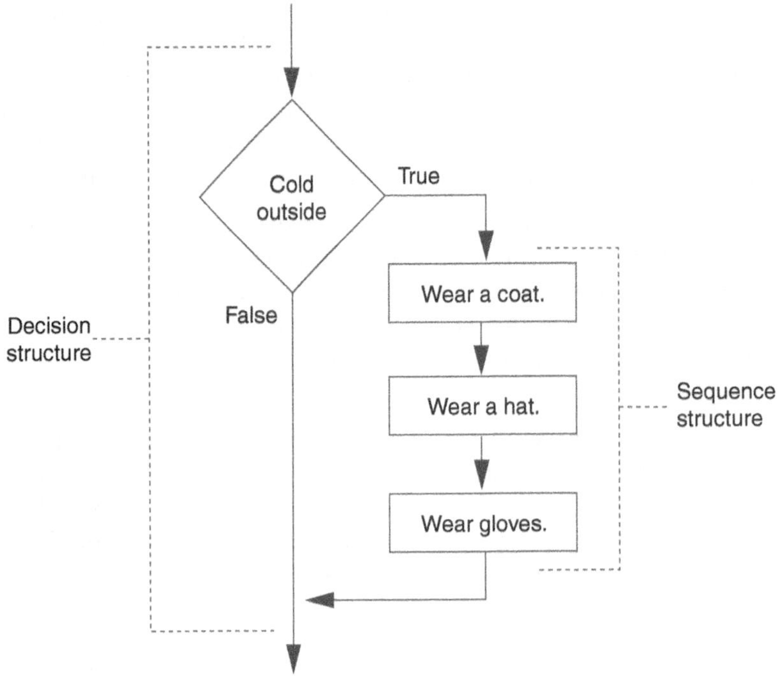

Writing a Decision Structure in Pseudocode

In pseudocode we use the If-Then statement to write a single alternative decision structure. Here is the general format of the If-Then statement:

```
If condition Then
     statement
     statement
     etc.
End If
```
These statements are conditionally executed.

For simplicity, we will refer to the line that begins with the word If as the *If clause,* and we will refer to the line that reads End If as the *End If clause.* In the general format, the *condition* is any expression that can be evaluated as either true or false. When the If-Then statement executes, the *condition* is tested. If it is true, the statements that appear between the If clause and the End If clause are executed. The End If clause marks the end of the If-Then statement.

Boolean Expressions and Relational Operators

All programming languages allow you to create expressions that can be evaluated as either true or false. These are called *Boolean expressions,* named in honor of the English mathematician George Boole. In the 1800s Boole invented a system of mathematics in which the abstract concepts of true and false can be used in computations. The condition that is tested by an If-Then statement must be a Boolean expression.

Typically, the Boolean expression that is tested by an If-Then statement is formed with a relational operator. A *relational operator* determines whether a specific relationship exists between two values. For example, the greater than operator (>) determines whether one value is greater than another. The equal to operator (==) determines whether two values are equal. Table 1 lists the relational operators that are commonly available in most programming languages.

Table 1 Relational operators

Operator	Meaning
>	Greater than
<	Less than
>=	Greater than or equal to
<=	Less than or equal to
==	Equal to
!=	Not equal to

The following is an example of an expression that uses the greater than (>) operator to compare two variables, length and width:

```
length > width
```

This expression determines whether the value of length is greater than the value of width. If length is greater than width, the value of the expression is true. Otherwise, the value of the expression is false. Because the expression can be only true or false, it is a Boolean expression. The following expression uses the less than operator to determine whether length is less than width:

```
length < width
```

Table 2 shows examples of several Boolean expressions that compare the variables x and y.

Table 2 Boolean expressions using relational operators

Expression	Meaning
x > y	Is x greater than y?
x < y	Is x less than y?
x >= y	Is x greater than or equal to y?
x <= y	Is x less than or equal to y?
x == y	Is x equal to y?
x != y	Is x not equal to y?

The >= and <= Operators

Two of the operators, >= and <=, test for more than one relationship. The >= operator determines whether the operand on its left is greater than *or* equal to the operand on its right. For example, assuming that a is 4, b is 6, and c is 4, both of the expressions b >= a and a >= c are true, and the expression a >= 5 is false.

The <= operator determines whether the operand on its left is less than *or* equal to the operand on its right. Once again, assuming that a is 4, b is 6, and c is 4, both a <= c and b <= 10 are true, but b <= a is false.

The == Operator

The == operator determines whether the operand on its left is equal to the operand on its right. If both operands have the same value, the expression is true. Assuming that a is 4, the expression a == 4 is true and the expression a == 2 is false.

In this text, we use two = characters as the equal to operator to avoid confusion with the assignment operator, which is one = character. Several programming languages, most notably Java, Python, C, and C++, also follow this practice.

> **WARNING!** When programming in a language that uses == as the equal to operator, take care not to confuse this operator with the assignment operator, which is one = sign. In languages such as Java, Python, C, and C++ the == operator determines whether a variable is equal to another value, but the = operator assigns the value to a variable.

The != Operator

The != operator is the not equal to operator. It determines whether the operand on its left is not equal to the operand on its right, which is the opposite of the == operator. As before, assuming a is 4, b is 6, and c is 4, both a != b and b != c are true because a is not equal to b and b is not equal to c. However, a != c is false because a is equal to c.

Note that != is the same character sequence used by several languages for the not equal to operator, including Java, C, and C++. Some languages, such as Visual Basic, use <> as the not equal to operator.

Putting It All Together

Let's look at the following example of the If-Then statement in pseudocode:

```
If sales > 50000 Then
    Set bonus = 500.0
End If
```

This statement uses the > operator to determine whether sales is greater than 50,000. If the expression sales > 50000 is true, the variable bonus is assigned 500.0. If the expression is false, however, the assignment statement is skipped. Figure 4 shows a flowchart for this section of code.

The following example conditionally executes a set of statements. Figure 5 shows a flowchart for this section of code.

```
If sales > 50000 Then
    Set bonus = 500.0
    Set commissionRate = 0.12
    Display "You've met your sales quota!"
End If
```

Figure 4 Example decision structure

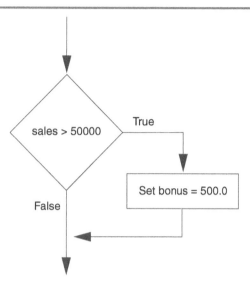

Figure 5 Example decision structure

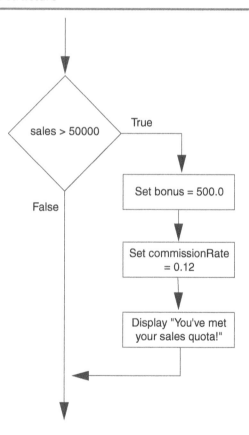

The following pseudocode uses the == operator to determine whether two values are equal. The expression balance == 0 will be true if the balance variable is set to 0. Otherwise the expression will be false.

```
If balance == 0 Then
    // Statements appearing here will
    // be executed only if balance is
    // equal to 0.
End If
```

The following pseudocode uses the != operator to determine whether two values are *not* equal. The expression choice != 5 will be true if the choice variable is not set to 5. Otherwise the expression will be false.

```
If choice != 5 Then
    // Statements appearing here will
    // be executed only if choice is
    // not equal to 5.
End If
```

Programming Style and the If-Then Statement

As shown in Figure 6, you should use the following conventions when you write an If-Then statement:

- Make sure the If clause and the End If clause are aligned.
- Indent the conditionally executed statements that appear between the If clause and the End If clause.

By indenting the conditionally executed statements you visually set them apart from the surrounding code. This makes your program easier to read and debug. Most programmers use this style of writing If-Then statements in both pseudocode and actual code.

Figure 6 Programming style with an If-Then statement

```
                    If sales > 50000 Then
Align the If             Set bonus = 500.0
and End If              Set commissionRate = 0.12          Indent the
clauses.                Display "You've met your sales quota!"   conditionally
                    End If                                 executed
                                                           statements.
```

In the Spotlight:

Using the If-Then Statement

Kathryn teaches a science class and her students are required to take three tests. She wants to write a program that her students can use to calculate their average test score. She also wants the program to congratulate the student enthusiastically if the average is greater than 95. Here is the algorithm:

1. Get the first test score.
2. Get the second test score.
3. Get the third test score.
4. Calculate the average.
5. Display the average.
6. If the average is greater than 95, congratulate the user.

Program 1 shows the pseudocode, and Figure 7 shows a flowchart for the program.

Program 1

```
 1 // Declare variables
 2 Declare Real test1, test2, test3, average
 3
 4 // Get test 1
 5 Display "Enter the score for test #1."
 6 Input test1
 7
 8 // Get test 2
 9 Display "Enter the score for test #2."
10 Input test2
11
12 // Get test 3
13 Display "Enter the score for test #3."
14 Input test3
15
16 // Calculate the average score.
17 Set average = (test1 + test2 + test3) / 3
18
19 // Display the average.
20 Display "The average is ", average
21
22 // If the average is greater than 95
23 // congratulate the user.
24 If average > 95 Then
25    Display "Congratulations! Great average!"
26 End If
```

Program Output (with Input Shown in Bold)

```
Enter the score for test #1.
82 [Enter]
Enter the score for test #2.
76 [Enter]
Enter the score for test #3.
91 [Enter]
The average is 83
```

Program Output (with Input Shown in Bold)

```
Enter the score for test #1.
93 [Enter]
Enter the score for test #2.
99 [Enter]
Enter the score for test #3.
96 [Enter]
The average is 96
Congratulations! Great average!
```

Figure 7 Flowchart for Program 1

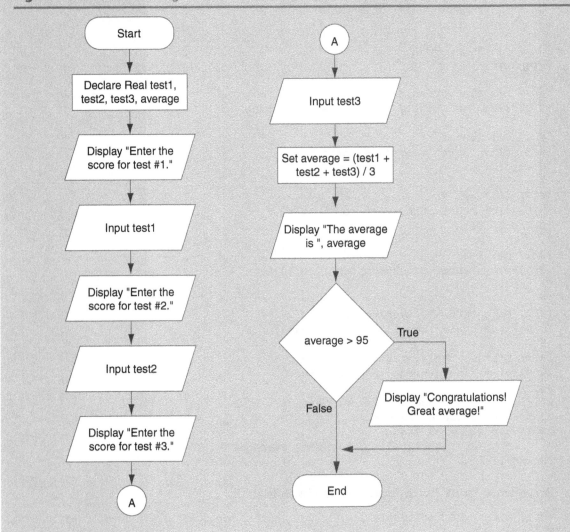

 **Checkpoint**

1 What is a control structure?

2 What is a decision structure?

3 What is a single alternative decision structure?

4 What is a Boolean expression?

5 What types of relationships between values can you test with relational operators?

6 Write a pseudocode If-Then statement that assigns 0 to x if y is equal to 20.

7 Write a pseudocode If-Then statement that assigns 0.2 to commission if sales is greater than or equal to 10,000.

2 Dual Alternative Decision Structures

CONCEPT: A dual alternative decision structure will execute one group of statements if its Boolean expression is true, or another group if its Boolean expression is false.

VideoNote

The Dual Alternative Decision Structure

A *dual alternative decision structure* has two possible paths of execution—one path is taken if a condition is true, and the other path is taken if the condition is false. Figure 8 shows a flowchart for a dual alternative decision structure.

Figure 8 A dual alternative decision structure

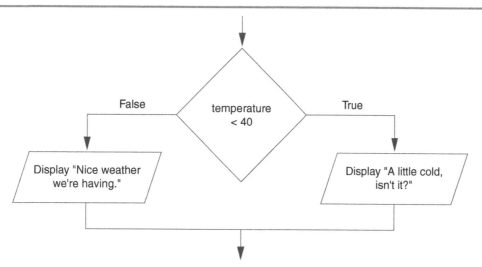

The decision structure in the flowchart tests the condition `temperature < 40`. If this condition is true, the statement `Display "A little cold, isn't it?"` is performed. If the condition is false, the statement `Display "Nice weather we're having."` is performed.

In pseudocode we write a dual alternative decision structure as an `If-Then-Else` statement. Here is the general format of the `If-Then-Else` statement:

```
If condition Then
    statement
    statement          These statements are executed if the condition is true.
    etc.
Else
    statement
    statement          These statements are executed if the condition is false.
    etc.
End If
```

In the general format, the *condition* is any Boolean expression. If the expression is true, the statements that appear next are executed, up to the line that reads `Else`. If the expression is false, the statements that appear between `Else` and `End If` are executed. The line that reads `End If` marks the end of the `If-Then-Else` statement.

135

The following pseudocode shows an example of an `If-Then-Else` statement. This pseudocode matches the flowchart that was shown in Figure 8.

```
If temperature < 40 Then
    Display "A little cold, isn't it?"
Else
    Display "Nice weather we're having."
End If
```

We will refer to the line that reads `Else` as the *Else clause*. When you write an `If-Then-Else` statement, use the following style conventions:

- Make sure the `If` clause, the `Else` clause, and the `End If` clause are aligned.
- Indent the conditionally executed statements that appear between the `If` clause and the `Else` clause, and between the `Else` clause and the `End If` clause.

This is shown in Figure 9.

Figure 9 Programming style with an `If-Then-Else` statement

Align the `If`, `Else`, and `End If` clauses.

```
If temperature < 40 Then
    Display "A little cold, isn't it?"
Else
    Display "Nice weather we're having."
End If
```

Indent the conditionally executed statements.

In the Spotlight:

Using the `If-Then-Else` Statement

Chris owns an auto repair business and has several employees. If an employee works over 40 hours in a week, Chris pays that employee 1.5 times his or her regular hourly pay rate for all hours over 40. Chris has asked you to design a simple payroll program that calculates an employee's gross pay, including any overtime wages. You design the following algorithm:

1. Get the number of hours worked.
2. Get the hourly pay rate.
3. If the employee worked more than 40 hours, calculate the gross pay with overtime. Otherwise, calculate the gross pay as usual.
4. Display the gross pay.

You go through the top-down design process and create the hierarchy chart shown in Figure 10. As shown in the hierarchy chart, the `main` module will call four other modules. The following are summaries of those modules:

- `getHoursWorked`—This module will ask the user to enter the number of hours worked.
- `getPayRate`—This module will ask the user to enter the hourly pay rate.
- `calcPayWithOT`—This module will calculate an employee's pay with overtime.
- `calcRegularPay`—This module will calculate the gross pay for an employee with no overtime.

The `main` module, which executes when the program is run, will call these modules and then display the gross pay. The pseudocode for the program is shown in Program 2. Figures 11 and 12 show flowcharts for each of the modules.

Figure 10 Hierarchy chart

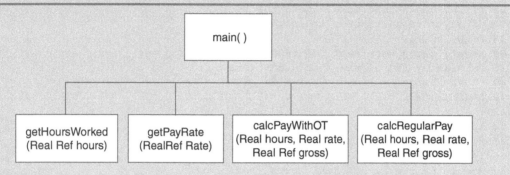

Program 2

```
1 // Global constants
2 Constant Integer BASE_HOURS = 40
3 Constant Real OT_MULTIPLIER = 1.5
4
5 Module main()
6     // Local variables
7     Declare Real hoursWorked, payRate, grossPay
8
9     // Get the number of hours worked.
10    Call getHoursWorked(hoursWorked)
11
12    // Get the hourly pay rate.
13    Call getPayRate(payRate)
14
15    // Calculate the gross pay.
16    If hoursWorked > BASE_HOURS Then
17        Call calcPayWithOT(hoursWorked, payRate,
18                         grossPay)
19    Else
20        Call calcRegularPay(hoursWorked, payRate,
21                         grossPay)
22    End If
23
24    // Display the gross pay.
25    Display "The gross pay is $", grossPay
26 End Module
27
28 // The getHoursWorked module gets the number
29 // of hours worked and stores it in the
```

```
30 // hours parameter.
31 Module getHoursWorked(Real Ref hours)
32     Display "Enter the number of hours worked."
33     Input hours
34 End Module
35
36 // The getPayRate module gets the hourly
37 // pay rate and stores it in the rate
38 // parameter.
39 Module getPayRate(Real Ref rate)
40     Display "Enter the hourly pay rate."
41     Input rate
42 End Module
43
44 // The calcPayWithOT module calculates pay
45 // with overtime. The gross pay is stored
46 // in the gross parameter.
47 Module calcPayWithOT(Real hours, Real rate,
48                      Real Ref gross)
49     // Local variables
50     Declare Real overtimeHours, overtimePay
51
52     // Calculate the number of overtime hours.
53     Set overtimeHours = hours - BASE_HOURS
54
55     // Calculate the overtime pay
56     Set overtimePay = overtimeHours * rate *
57                       OT_MULTIPLIER
58
59     // Calculate the gross pay.
60     Set gross = BASE_HOURS * rate + overtimePay
61 End Module
62
63 // The calcRegularPay module calculates
64 // pay with no overtime and stores it in
65 // the gross parameter.
66 Module calcRegularPay(Real hours, Real rate,
67                       Real Ref gross)
68     Set gross = hours * rate
69 End Module
```

Program Output (with Input Shown in Bold)

```
Enter the number of hours worked.
40 [Enter]
Enter the hourly pay rate.
20 [Enter]
The gross pay is $800
```

Program Output (with Input Shown in Bold)

```
Enter the number of hours worked.
50 [Enter]
Enter the hourly pay rate.
20 [Enter]
The gross pay is $1100
```

Notice that two global constants are declared in lines 2 and 3. The BASE_HOURS constant is set to 40, which is the number of hours an employee can work in a week without getting paid overtime. The OT_MULTIPLIER constant is set to 1.5, which is the pay rate multiplier for overtime hours. This means that the employee's hourly pay rate is multiplied by 1.5 for all overtime hours.

Figure 11 Flowchart for the main module

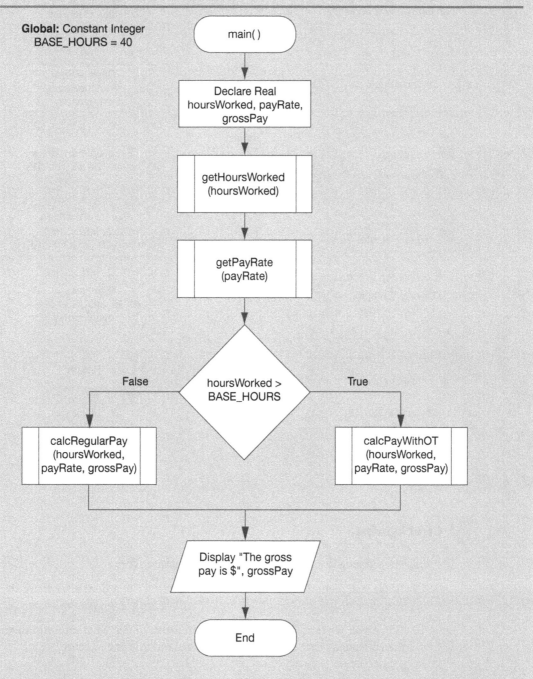

Figure 12 Flowcharts for the other modules

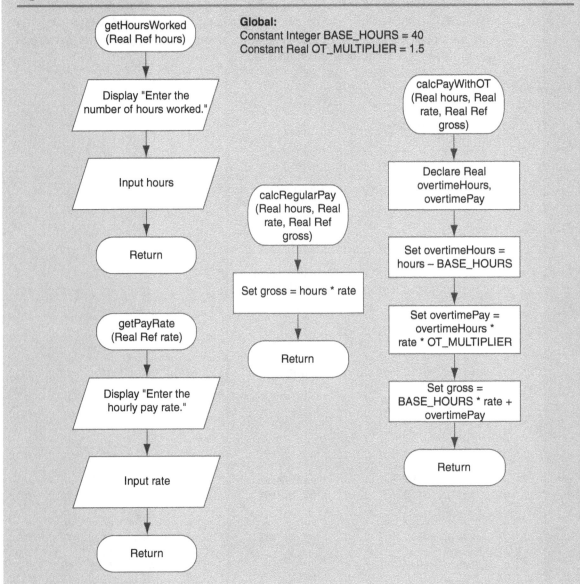

Global:
Constant Integer BASE_HOURS = 40
Constant Real OT_MULTIPLIER = 1.5

Checkpoint

8 How does a dual alternative decision structure work?

9 What statement do you use in pseudocode to write a dual alternative decision structure?

10 When you write an If-Then-Else statement, under what circumstances do the statements that appear between Else and End If execute?

3 Comparing Strings

CONCEPT: Most programming languages allow you to compare strings. This allows you to create decision structures that test the value of a string.

You saw in the preceding examples how numbers can be compared. Most programming languages also allow you to compare strings. For example, look at the following pseudocode:

```
Declare String name1 = "Mary"
Declare String name2 = "Mark"
If name1 == name2 Then
    Display "The names are the same"
Else
    Display "The names are NOT the same"
End If
```

The == operator tests name1 and name2 to determine whether they are equal. Because the strings "Mary" and "Mark" are not equal, the Else clause will display the message "The names are NOT the same."

You can compare String variables with string literals as well. Assume month is a String variable. The following pseudocode sample uses the != operator to determine whether month is not equal to "October."

```
If month != "October" Then
    statement
End If
```

The pseudocode in Program 3 demonstrates how two strings can be compared. The program prompts the user to enter a password and then determines whether the string entered is equal to "prospero."

Program 3

```
 1 // A variable to hold a password.
 2 Declare String password
 3
 4 // Prompt the user to enter the password.
 5 Display "Enter the password."
 6 Input password
 7
 8 // Determine whether the correct password
 9 // was entered.
10 If password == "prospero" Then
11     Display "Password accepted."
12 Else
13     Display "Sorry, that is not the correct password."
14 End If
```

Program Output (with Input Shown in Bold)

```
Enter the password.
ferdinand [Enter]
Sorry, that is not the correct password.
```

Program Output (with Input Shown in Bold)

```
Enter the password.
prospero [Enter]
Password accepted.
```

 NOTE: In most languages, string comparisons are case sensitive. For example, the strings "saturday" and "Saturday" are not equal because the "s" is lowercase in the first string, but uppercase in the second string.

Other String Comparisons

In addition to determining whether strings are equal or not equal, many languages allow you to determine whether one string is greater than or less than another string. This is a useful capability because programmers commonly need to design programs that sort strings in some order.

Recall that computers do not actually store characters, such as A, B, C, and so on, in memory. Instead, they store numeric codes that represent the characters. ASCII (the American Standard Code for Information Interchange) is the most commonly used character coding system. Here are some facts about it:

- The uppercase characters "A" through "Z" are represented by the numbers 65 through 90.
- The lowercase characters "a" through "z" are represented by the numbers 97 through 122.
- When the digits "0" through "9" are stored in memory as characters, they are represented by the numbers 48 through 57. (For example, the string "abc123" would be stored in memory as the codes 97, 98, 99, 49, 50, and 51.)
- A blank space is represented by the number 32.

In addition to establishing a set of numeric codes to represent characters in memory, ASCII also establishes an order for characters. The character "A" comes before the character "B," which comes before the character "C," and so on.

When a program compares characters, it actually compares the codes for the characters. For example, look at the following pseudocode:

```
If "a" < "b" Then
    Display "The letter a is less than the letter b."
End If
```

This If statement determines whether the ASCII code for the character "a" is less than the ASCII code for the character "b." The expression "a" < "b" is true because the code for "a" is less than the code for "b." So, if this were part of an actual program it would display the message "The letter a is less than the letter b."

Let's look at how strings containing more than one character are typically compared. Suppose we have the strings "Mary" and "Mark" stored in memory, as follows:

```
Declare String name1 = "Mary"
Declare String name2 = "Mark"
```

Figure 13 shows how the strings "Mary" and "Mark" would actually be stored in memory, using ASCII codes.

Figure 13 Character codes for the strings "Mary" and "Mark"

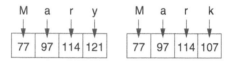

When you use relational operators to compare these strings, they are compared character-by-character. For example, look at the following pseudocode:

```
Declare String name1 = "Mary"
Declare String name2 = "Mark"
If name1 > name2 Then
    Display "Mary is greater than Mark"
Else
    Display "Mary is not greater than Mark"
End If
```

The > operator compares each character in the strings "Mary" and "Mark," beginning with the first, or leftmost, characters. This is shown in Figure 14.

Figure 14 Comparing each character in a string

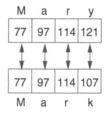

Here is how the comparison typically takes place:

1. The "M" in "Mary" is compared with the "M" in "Mark." Because these are the same, the next characters are compared.
2. The "a" in "Mary" is compared with the "a" in "Mark." Because these are the same, the next characters are compared.

3. The "r" in "Mary" is compared with the "r" in "Mark." Because these are the same, the next characters are compared.

4. The "y" in "Mary" is compared with the "k" in "Mark." Because these are not the same, the two strings are not equal. The character "y" has a higher ASCII code (121) than "k" (107), so it is determined that the string `Mary` is greater than the string `Mark.`

If one of the strings in a comparison is shorter than the other, many languages compare only the corresponding characters. If the corresponding characters are identical, then the shorter string is considered less than the longer string. For example, suppose the strings `High` and `Hi` were being compared. The string `Hi` would be considered less than `High` because it is shorter.

The pseudocode in Program 4 shows a simple demonstration of how two strings can be compared with the < operator. The user is prompted to enter two names and the program displays those two names in alphabetical order.

Program 4

```
1 // Declare variables to hold two names.
2 Declare String name1
3 Declare String name2
4
5 // Prompt the user for two names.
6 Display "Enter a name (last name first)."
7 Input name1
8 Display "Enter another name (last name first)."
9 Input name2
10
11 // Display the names in alphabetical order.
12 Display "Here are the names, listed alphabetically:"
13 If name1 < name2 Then
14     Display name1
15     Display name2
16 Else
17     Display name2
18     Display name1
19 End If
```

Program Output (with Input Shown in Bold)

```
Enter a name (last name first).
Jones, Richard [Enter]
Enter another name (last name first).
Costa, Joan [Enter]
Here are the names, listed alphabetically:
Costa, Joan
Jones, Richard
```

 **Checkpoint**

11 If the following pseudocode were an actual program, what would it display?

```
If "z" < "a" Then
    Display "z is less than a."
Else
    Display "z is not less than a."
End If
```

12 If the following pseudocode were an actual program, what would it display?

```
Declare String s1 = "New York"
Declare String s2 = "Boston"
If s1 > s2 Then
    Display s2
    Display s1
Else
    Display s1
    Display s2
End If
```

4 Nested Decision Structures

CONCEPT: To test more than one condition, a decision structure can be nested inside another decision structure.

In Section 1, we mentioned that programs are usually designed as combinations of different control structures. In that section you saw an example of a sequence struc-ture nested inside a decision structure (see Figure 3). You can also nest decision structures inside of other decision structures. In fact, this is a common requirement in programs that need to test more than one condition.

For example, consider a program that determines whether a bank customer qualifies for a loan. To qualify, two conditions must exist: (1) the customer must earn at least $30,000 per year, and (2) the customer must have been employed at his or her current job for at least two years. Figure 15 shows a flowchart for an algorithm that could be used in such a program. Assume that the `salary` variable contains the customer's annual salary, and the `yearsOnJob` variable contains the number of years that the customer has worked on his or her current job.

If we follow the flow of execution, we see that the condition `salary >= 30000` is tested. If this condition is false, there is no need to perform further tests; we know that the customer does not qualify for the loan. If the condition is true, however, we need to test the second condition. This is done with a nested decision structure that tests the condition `yearsOnJob >= 2`. If this condition is true, then the customer qualifies for the loan. If this condition is false, then the customer does not qualify. Program 5 shows the pseudocode for the complete program.

Figure 15 A nested decision structure

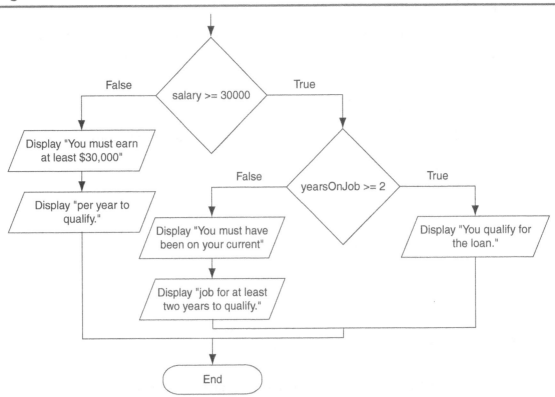

Program 5

```
 1  // Declare variables
 2  Declare Real salary, yearsOnJob
 3
 4  // Get the annual salary.
 5  Display "Enter your annual salary."
 6  Input salary
 7
 8  // Get the number of years on the current job.
 9  Display "Enter the number of years on your"
10  Display "current job."
11  Input yearsOnJob
12
13  // Determine whether the user qualifies.
14  If salary >= 30000 Then
15      If yearsOnJob >= 2 Then
16          Display "You qualify for the loan."
17      Else
18          Display "You must have been on your current"
19          Display "job for at least two years to qualify."
20      End If
21  Else
22      Display "You must earn at least $30,000"
23      Display "per year to qualify."
24  End If
```

Program Output (with Input Shown in Bold)

```
Enter your annual salary.
35000 [Enter]
Enter the number of years on your
current job.
1 [Enter]
You must have been on your current
job for at least two years to qualify.
```

Program Output (with Input Shown in Bold)

```
Enter your annual salary.
25000 [Enter]
Enter the number of years on your
current job.
5 [Enter]
You must earn at least $30,000
per year to qualify.
```

Program Output (with Input Shown in Bold)

```
Enter your annual salary.
35000 [Enter]
Enter the number of years on your
current job.
5 [Enter]
You qualify for the loan.
```

Look at the `If-Then-Else` statement that begins in line 14. It tests the condition `salary >= 30000`. If this condition is true, the `If-Then-Else` statement that begins in line 15 is executed. Otherwise the program jumps to the `Else` clause in line 21 and executes the two `Display` statements in lines 22 and 23. The program then leaves the decision structure and the program ends.

Programming Style and Nested Decision Structures

For debugging purposes, it's important to use proper alignment and indentation in a nested decision structure. This makes it easier to see which actions are performed by each part of the structure. For example, in most languages the following pseudocode is functionally equivalent to lines 14 through 24 in Program 5. Although this pseudocode is logically correct, it would be very difficult to debug because it is not properly indented.

```
If salary >= 30000 Then
If yearsOnJob >= 2 Then            Don't write
Display "You qualify for the loan."   pseudocode
Else                               like this!
Display "You must have been on your current"
Display "job for at least two years to qualify."
End If
```

```
Else
Display "You must earn at least $30,000"
Display "per year to qualify.
End If
```

Proper indentation and alignment also makes it easier to see which If, Else, and End If clauses belong together, as shown in Figure 16.

Figure 16 Alignment of If, Else, and End If clauses

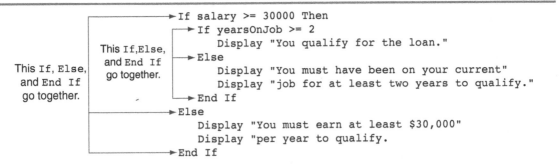

Testing a Series of Conditions

In the previous example you saw how a program can use nested decision structures to test more than one condition. It is not uncommon for a program to have a series of conditions to test, and then perform an action depending on which condition is true. One way to accomplish this is to have a decision structure with numerous other decision structures nested inside it. For example, consider the program presented in the following *In the Spotlight* section.

In the Spotlight:
Multiple Nested Decision Structures

Dr. Suarez teaches a literature class and uses the following 10 point grading scale for all of his exams:

Test Score	Grade
90 and above	A
80–89	B
70–79	C
60–69	D
Below 60	F

He has asked you to write a program that will allow a student to enter a test score and then display the grade for that score. Here is the algorithm that you will use:

1. Ask the user to enter a test score.
2. Determine the grade in the following manner:

If the score is less than 60, then the grade is "F."
Otherwise, if the score is less than 70, then the grade is "D."
Otherwise, if the score is less than 80, then the grade is "C."
Otherwise, if the score is less than 90, then the grade is "B."
Otherwise, the grade is "A."

You decide that the process of determining the grade will require several nested decision structures, as shown in Figure 17. Program 6 shows the pseudocode for the complete program. The code for the nested decision structures is in lines 9 through 25.

Figure 17 Nested decision structure to determine a grade

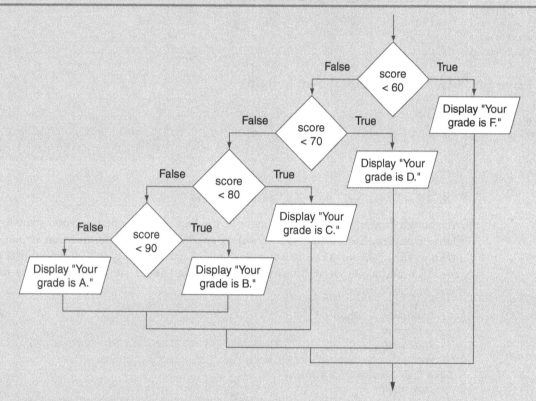

Program 6

```
1 // Variable to hold the test score
2 Declare Real score
3
4 // Get the test score.
5 Display "Enter your test score."
6 Input score
7
8 // Determine the grade.
9 If score < 60 Then
10    Display "Your grade is F."
11 Else
12    If score < 70 Then
13        Display "Your grade is D."
14    Else
15        If score < 80 Then
```

```
16          Display "Your grade is C."
17       Else
18          If score < 90 Then
19             Display "Your grade is B."
20          Else
21             Display "Your grade is A."
22          End If
23       End If
24    End If
25 End If
```

Program Output (with Input Shown in Bold)

```
Enter your test score.
78 [Enter]
Your grade is C.
```

Program Output (with Input Shown in Bold)

```
Enter your test score.
84 [Enter]
Your grade is B.
```

The If-Then-Else If Statement

Even though Program 6 is a simple example, the logic of the nested decision struc-ture is fairly complex. Most languages provide a special version of the decision structure known as the If-Then-Else If statement, which makes this type of logic simpler to write. In pseudocode we will write the If-Then-Else If statement using the following general format:

```
If condition_1 Then
     statement
     statement          If condition_1 is true these statements are executed,
     etc.               and the rest of the structure is ignored.
Else If condition_2 Then
     statement
     statement          If condition_2 is true these statements are executed,
     etc.               and the rest of the structure is ignored.

Insert as many Else If clauses as necessary

Else
     statement
     statement          These statements are executed if none of the
     etc.               conditions above are true.
End If
```

When the statement executes, *condition_1* is tested. If *condition_1* is true, the state-ments that immediately follow are executed, up to the Else If clause. The rest of the structure is ignored. If *condition_1* is false, however, the program jumps to the very next Else If clause and tests *condition_2*. If it is true, the statements that immediately follow are executed, up to the next Else If clause. The rest of the structure is then ignored. This process continues until a condition is found to be true, or no more Else

If clauses are left. If none of the conditions are true, the statements following the Else clause are executed.

The pseudocode in Program 7 shows an example of the If-Then-Else If statement. This program works the same as Program 6. Instead of using a nested decision structure, this program uses the If-Then-Else If statement in lines 9 through 19.

Program 7

```
 1 // Variable to hold the test score
 2 Declare Real score
 3
 4 // Get the test score.
 5 Display "Enter your test score."
 6 Input score
 7
 8 // Determine the grade.
 9 If score < 60 Then
10     Display "Your grade is F."
11 Else If score < 70 Then
12     Display "Your grade is D."
13 Else If score < 80 Then
14     Display "Your grade is C."
15 Else If score < 90 Then
16     Display "Your grade is B."
17 Else
18     Display "Your grade is A."
19 End If
```

Program Output (with Input Shown in Bold)

```
Enter your test score.
78 [Enter]
Your grade is C.
```

Program Output (with Input Shown in Bold)

```
Enter your test score.
84 [Enter]
Your grade is B.
```

Notice the alignment and indentation that are used with the If-Then-Else If statement: The If, Else If, Else, and End If clauses are all aligned, and the conditionally executed statements are indented.

You never have to use the If-Then-Else If statement because its logic can be coded with nested If-Then-Else statements. However, a long series of nested If-Then-Else statements has two particular disadvantages when you are debugging code:

- The code can grow complex and become difficult to understand.
- Because indenting is important in nested statements, a long series of nested If-Then-Else statements can become too long to be displayed on the computer screen without horizontal scrolling. Also, long statements tend to "wrap around" when printed on paper, making the code even more difficult to read.

The logic of an `If-Then-Else If` statement is usually easier to follow than a long series of nested `If-Then-Else` statements. And, because all of the clauses are aligned in an `If-Then-Else If` statement, the lengths of the lines in the statement tend to be shorter.

 Checkpoint

13 How does a dual alternative decision structure work?

14 What statement do you use in pseudocode to write a dual alternative decision structure?

15 When you write an `If-Then-Else` statement, under what circumstances do the statements that appear between the `Else` clause and the `End If` clause execute?

16 Convert the following pseudocode to an `If-Then-Else If` statement:

```
If number == 1 Then
    Display "One"
Else
    If number == 2 Then
        Display "Two"
    Else
        If number == 3 Then
            Display "Three"
        Else
            Display "Unknown"
        End If
    End If
End If
```

5 The Case Structure

CONCEPT: The case structure lets the value of a variable or an expression determine which path of execution the program will take.

VideoNote

The Case
Structure

The *case structure* is a *multiple alternative decision structure*. It allows you to test the value of a variable or an expression and then use that value to determine which statement or set of statements to execute. Figure 18 shows an example of how a case structure looks in a flowchart.

In the flowchart, the diamond symbol contains the name of a variable. If the variable contains the value 1, the statement `Display "January"` is executed. If the variable contains the value 2 the statement `Display "February"` is executed. If the variable contains the value 3 the statement `Display "March"` is executed. If the variable contains none of these values, the statement labeled `Default` is executed. In this case, the statement `Display "Error: Invalid month"` is executed.

To write a case structure in pseudocode we will use a `Select Case` statement. The general format follows Figure 18.

Figure 18 A case structure

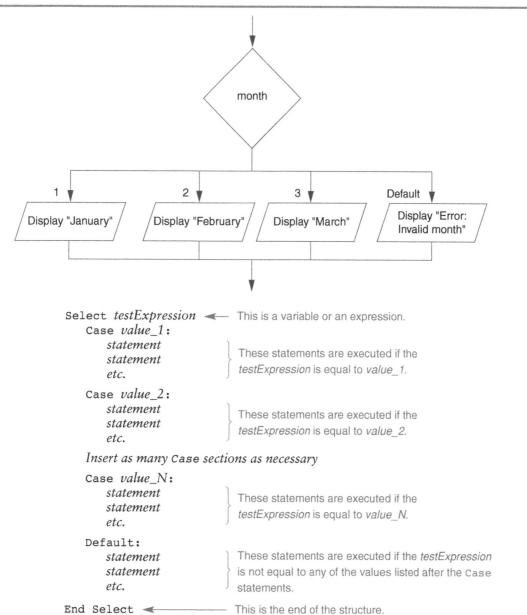

The first line of the structure starts with the word Select, followed by a *testExpression*. The *testExpression* is usually a variable, but in many languages it can also be anything that gives a value (such as a math expression). Inside the structure there is one or more blocks of statements that begin with a Case statement. Notice that the word Case is followed by a value.

When the Select Case statement executes, it compares the value of the *testExpression* with the values that follow each of the Case statements (from top to bottom). When it finds a Case value that matches the *testExpression*'s value, the program branches to the Case statement. The statements that immediately follow the Case statement are executed, and then the program jumps out of the structure. If the *testExpression* does not match any of the Case values, the program branches to the Default statement and executes the statements that immediately follow it.

For example, the following pseudocode performs the same operation as the flowchart shown in Figure 18:

```
Select month
    Case 1:
        Display "January"
    Case 2:
        Display "February"
    Case 3:
        Display "March"
    Default:
        Display "Error: Invalid month"
End Select
```

In this example, the *testExpression* is the month variable. If the value in the month variable is 1, the program will branch to the Case 1: section and execute the Display "January" statement that immediately follows it. If the value in the month variable is 2, the program will branch to the Case 2: section and execute the Display "February" statement that immediately follows it. If the value in the month variable is 3, the program will branch to the Case 3: section and execute the Display "March" statement that immediately follows it. If the value in the month variable is not 1, 2, or 3, the program will branch to the Default: section; and if the value in the month variable is 1, the program will branch to the Case 1: section and execute the Display "Error: Invalid month" statement that immediately follows it.

NOTE: In many languages the case structure is called a switch statement.

Case structures are never required because the same logic can be achieved with nested decision structures. For example, Figure 19 shows nested decision structures that are equivalent to the case structure in Figure 18. In situations where they can be used, however, case structures are more straightforward.

Figure 19 Nested decision structures

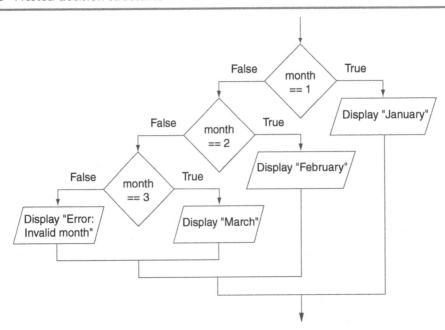

In the Spotlight:
Using a Case Structure

Lenny, who owns Lenny's Stereo and Television, has asked you to write a program that will let a customer pick one of three TV models and then displays the price and size of the selected model. Here is the algorithm:

1. Get the TV model number.
2. If the model is 100, then display the information for that model.
     Otherwise, if the model is 200, then display the information for that model.
         Otherwise, if the model is 300, then display the information for that model.

At first, you consider designing a nested decision structure to determine the model number and display the correct information. But you realize that a case structure will work just as well because a single value, the model number, will be used to determine the action that the program will perform. The model number can be stored in a variable, and that variable can be tested by the case structure. Assuming that the model number is stored in a variable named modelNumber, Figure 20 shows a flowchart for the case structure. Program 8 shows the pseudocode for the program.

Figure 20 Flowchart for the case structure

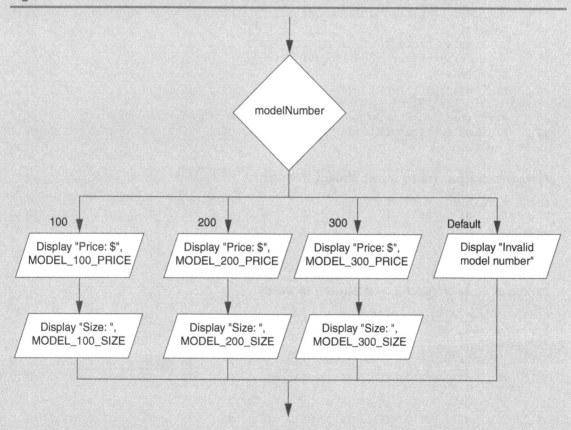

Program 8

```
 1 // Constants for the TV prices
 2 Constant Real MODEL_100_PRICE = 199.99
 3 Constant Real MODEL_200_PRICE = 269.99
 4 Constant Real MODEL_300_PRICE = 349.99
 5
 6 // Constants for the TV sizes
 7 Constant Integer MODEL_100_SIZE = 24
 8 Constant Integer MODEL_200_SIZE = 27
 9 Constant Integer MODEL_300_SIZE = 32
10
11 // Variable for the model number
12 Declare Integer modelNumber
13
14 // Get the model number.
15 Display "Which TV are you interested in?"
16 Display "The 100, 200, or 300?"
17 Input modelNumber
18
19 // Display the price and size.
20 Select modelNumber
21    Case 100:
22       Display "Price: $", MODEL_100_PRICE
23       Display "Size: ", MODEL_100_SIZE
24    Case 200:
25       Display "Price: $", MODEL_200_PRICE
26       Display "Size: ", MODEL_200_SIZE
27    Case 300:
28       Display "Price $", MODEL_300_PRICE
29       Display "Size: ", MODEL_300_SIZE
30    Default:
31       Display "Invalid model number"
32 End Select
```

Program Output (with Input Shown in Bold)

```
Which TV are you interested in?
The 100, 200, or 300?
100 [Enter]
Price: $199.99
Size: 24
```

Program Output (with Input Shown in Bold)

```
Which TV are you interested in?
The 100, 200, or 300?
200 [Enter]
Price: $269.99
Size: 27
```

Program Output (with Input Shown in Bold)

```
Which TV are you interested in?
The 100, 200, or 300?
300 [Enter]
Price: $349.99
Size: 32
```

Program Output (with Input Shown in Bold)

```
Which TV are you interested in?
The 100, 200, or 300?
500 [Enter]
Invalid model number
```

 NOTE: The details of writing a case structure differ from one language to another. Because of the specific rules that each language uses for writing case structures, you might not be able to use the case structure for every multiple alternative decision. In such an event, you can use the `If-Then-Else If` statement or a nested decision structure.

Checkpoint

17 What is a multiple alternative decision structure?

18 How do you write a multiple alternative decision structure in pseudocode?

19 What does the case structure test, in order to determine which set of statements to execute?

20 You need to write a multiple alternative decision structure, but the language you are using will not allow you to perform the test you need in a `Select Case` statement. What can you do to achieve the same results?

6 Logical Operators

CONCEPT: The logical **AND** operator and the logical **OR** operator allow you to connect multiple Boolean expressions to create a compound expression. The logical **NOT** operator reverses the truth of a Boolean expression.

Programming languages provide a set of operators known as *logical operators*, which you can use to create complex Boolean expressions. Table 3 describes these operators.

Table 4 shows examples of several compound Boolean expressions that use logical operators.

Table 3 Logical operators

Operator	Meaning
AND	The AND operator connects two Boolean expressions into one compound expression. Both subexpressions must be true for the compound expression to be true.
OR	The OR operator connects two Boolean expressions into one compound expression. One or both subexpressions must be true for the compound expression to be true. It is only necessary for one of the subexpressions to be true, and it does not matter which.
NOT	The NOT operator is a unary operator, meaning it works with only one operand. The operand must be a Boolean expression. The NOT operator reverses the truth of its operand. If it is applied to an expression that is true, the operator returns false. If it is applied to an expression that is false, the operator returns true.

Table 4 Compound Boolean expressions using logical operators

Expression	Meaning
x > y AND a < b	Is x greater than y AND is a less than b?
x == y OR x == z	Is x equal to y OR is x equal to z?
NOT (x > y)	Is the expression x > y NOT true?

> **NOTE:** In many languages, most notably C, C++, and Java, the AND operator is written as &&, the OR operator is written as ||, and the NOT operator is written as !.

The AND Operator

The AND operator takes two Boolean expressions as operands and creates a compound Boolean expression that is true only when both subexpressions are true. The following is an example of an If-Then statement that uses the AND operator:

```
If temperature < 20 AND minutes > 12 Then
    Display "The temperature is in the danger zone."
End If
```

In this statement, the two Boolean expressions temperature < 20 and minutes > 12 are combined into a compound expression. The Display statement will be executed only if temperature is less than 20 AND minutes is greater than 12. If either of the Boolean subexpressions is false, the compound expression is false and the message is not displayed.

Table 5 shows a truth table for the AND operator. The truth table lists expressions showing all the possible combinations of true and false connected with the AND operator. The resulting values of the expressions are also shown.

Table 5 Truth table for the AND operator

Expression	Value of the Expression
true AND false	false
false AND true	false
false AND false	false
true AND true	true

As the table shows, both sides of the AND operator must be true for the operator to return a true value.

The OR Operator

The OR operator takes two Boolean expressions as operands and creates a compound Boolean expression that is true when either of the subexpressions is true. The following is an example of an If-Then statement that uses the OR operator:

```
If temperature < 20 OR temperature > 100 Then
    Display "The temperature is in the danger zone."
End If
```

The Display statement will execute only if temperature is less than 20 OR temperature is greater than 100. If either subexpression is true, the compound expression is true. Table 6 shows a truth table for the OR operator.

Table 6 Truth table for the OR operator

Expression	Value of the Expression
true OR false	true
false OR true	true
false OR false	false
true OR true	true

All it takes for an OR expression to be true is for one side of the OR operator to be true. It doesn't matter if the other side is false or true.

Short-Circuit Evaluation

In many languages both the AND and OR operators perform *short-circuit evaluation*. Here's how it works with the AND operator: If the expression on the left side of the AND operator is false, the expression on the right side will not be checked. Because the compound expression will be false if only one of the subexpressions is false, it would waste CPU time to check the remaining expression. So, when the AND operator finds that the expression on its left is false, it short-circuits and does not evaluate the expression on its right.

Here's how short-circuit evaluation works with the OR operator: If the expression on the left side of the OR operator is true, the expression on the right side will not be checked. Because it is only necessary for one of the expressions to be true, it would waste CPU time to check the remaining expression.

The NOT Operator

The NOT operator is a unary operator that takes a Boolean expression as its operand and reverses its logical value. In other words, if the expression is true, the NOT operator returns false, and if the expression is false, the NOT operator returns true. The following is an If-Then statement using the NOT operator:

```
If NOT(temperature > 100) Then
    Display "This is below the maximum temperature."
End If
```

First, the expression (temperature > 100) is tested and a value of either true or false is the result. Then the NOT operator is applied to that value. If the expression (temperature > 100) is true, the NOT operator returns false. If the expression (temperature > 100) is false, the NOT operator returns true. The previous code is equivalent to asking: "Is the temperature not greater than 100?"

> **NOTE:** In this example, we have put parentheses around the expression temperature > 100. The reason for this is that, in many languages, the NOT operator has higher precedence than the relational operators. Suppose we wrote the expression as follows:
>
> ```
> NOT temperature > 100
> ```
>
> In many languages this expression would not work correctly because the NOT operator would be applied to the temperature variable, not the expression temperature > 100. To make sure that the operator is applied to the expression, we enclose it in parentheses.

Table 7 shows a truth table for the NOT operator.

Table 7 Truth table for the NOT operator

Expression	Value of the Expression
NOT true	false
NOT false	true

The Loan Qualifier Program Revisited

In some situations the AND operator can be used to simplify nested decision structures. For example, recall that the loan qualifier program in Program 5 uses the following nested If-Then-Else statements:

```
If salary >= 30000 Then
    If yearsOnJob >= 2 Then
        Display "You qualify for the loan."
    Else
        Display "You must have been on your current"
        Display "job for at least two years to qualify."
    End If
Else
    Display "You must earn at least $30,000"
    Display "per year to qualify."
End If
```

The purpose of this decision structure is to determine that a person's salary is at least $30,000 and that he or she has been at his or her current job for at least two years. Program 9 shows a way to perform a similar task with simpler code.

Program 9

```
1  // Declare variables
2  Declare Real salary, yearsOnJob
3
4  // Get the annual salary.
5  Display "Enter your annual salary."
6  Input salary
7
8  // Get the number of years on the current job.
9  Display "Enter the number of years on your ",
10         "current job."
11 Input yearsOnJob
12
13 // Determine whether the user qualifies.
14 If salary >= 30000 AND yearsOnJob >= 2 Then
15    Display "You qualify for the loan."
16 Else
17    Display "You do not qualify for this loan."
18 End If
```

Program Output (with Input Shown in Bold)

```
Enter your annual salary.
35000 [Enter]
Enter the number of years on your current job.
1 [Enter]
You do not qualify for this loan.
```

Program Output (with Input Shown in Bold)

```
Enter your annual salary.
25000 [Enter]
Enter the number of years on your current job.
5 [Enter]
You do not qualify for this loan.
```

Program Output (with Input Shown in Bold)

```
Enter your annual salary.
35000 [Enter]
Enter the number of years on your current job.
5 [Enter]
You qualify for the loan.
```

The If-Then-Else statement in lines 14 through 18 tests the compound expression salary >= 30000 AND yearsOnJob >= 2. If both subexpressions are true, the compound expression is true and the message "You qualify for the loan" is displayed. If either of the subexpressions is false, the compound expression is false and the message "You do not qualify for this loan" is displayed.

NOTE: A careful observer will realize that Program 9 is similar to Program 5, but it is not equivalent. If the user does not qualify for the loan, Program 9 displays only the message "You do not qualify for this loan," whereas Program 5 displays one of two possible messages explaining why the user did not qualify.

Yet Another Loan Qualifier Program

Suppose the bank is losing customers to a competing bank that isn't as strict about whom it loans money to. In response, the bank decides to change its loan requirements. Now, customers have to meet only one of the previous conditions, not both. Program 10 shows the pseudocode for the new loan qualifier program. The compound expression that is tested by the If-Then-Else statement in line 14 now uses the OR operator.

Program 10

```
 1 // Declare variables
 2 Declare Real salary, yearsOnJob
 3
 4 // Get the annual salary.
 5 Display "Enter your annual salary."
 6 Input salary
 7
 8 // Get the number of years on the current job.
 9 Display "Enter the number of years on your"
10 Display "current job."
11 Input yearsOnJob
12
13 // Determine whether the user qualifies.
14 If salary >= 30000 OR yearsOnJob >= 2 Then
15     Display "You qualify for the loan."
16 Else
17     Display "You do not qualify for this loan."
18 End If
```

Program Output (with Input Shown in Bold)

```
Enter your annual salary.
35000 [Enter]
Enter the number of years on your
current job.
1 [Enter]
You qualify for the loan.
```

Program Output (with Input Shown in Bold)

```
Enter your annual salary.
25000 [Enter]
Enter the number of years on your
current job.
5 [Enter]
You qualify for the loan.
```

Program Output (with Input Shown in Bold)

```
Enter your annual salary.
12000 [Enter]
Enter the number of years on your
current job.
1 [Enter]
You do not qualify for this loan.
```

Checking Numeric Ranges with Logical Operators

Sometimes you will need to design an algorithm that determines whether a numeric value is within a specific range of values or outside a specific range of values. When determining whether a number is inside a range, it is best to use the AND operator. For example, the following If-Then statement checks the value in x to determine whether it is in the range of 20 through 40:

```
If x >= 20 AND x <= 40 Then
    Display "The value is in the acceptable range."
End If
```

The compound Boolean expression being tested by this statement will be true only when x is greater than or equal to 20 AND less than or equal to 40. The value in x must be within the range of 20 through 40 for this compound expression to be true.

When determining whether a number is outside a range, it is best to use the OR operator. The following statement determines whether x is outside the range of 20 through 40:

```
If x < 20 OR x > 40 Then
    Display "The value is outside the acceptable range."
End If
```

It is important not to get the logic of the logical operators confused when testing for a range of numbers. For example, the compound Boolean expression in the following pseudocode would never test true:

```
// This is an error!
If x < 20 AND x > 40 Then
    Display "The value is outside the acceptable range."
End If
```

Obviously, x cannot be less than 20 and at the same time be greater than 40.

 Checkpoint

21 What is a compound Boolean expression?

22 The following truth table shows various combinations of the values true and false connected by a logical operator. Complete the table by circling T or F to indicate whether the result of such a combination is true or false.

Logical Expression	Result (circle T or F)	
True AND False	T	F
True AND True	T	F

(continues next page)

Logical Expression	Result (circle T or F)	
False AND True	T	F
False AND False	T	F
True OR False	T	F
True OR True	T	F
False OR True	T	F
False OR False	T	F
NOT True	T	F
NOT False	T	F

23 Assume the variables a = 2, b = 4, and c = 6. Circle the T or F for each of the following conditions to indicate whether its value is true or false.

a == 4 OR b > 2	T	F
6 <= c AND a > 3	T	F
1 != b AND c != 3	T	F
a >= -1 OR a <= b	T	F
NOT (a > 2)	T	F

24 Explain how short-circuit evaluation works with the AND and OR operators.

25 Write an If-Then statement that displays the message "The number is valid" if the variable speed is within the range 0 through 200.

26 Write an If-Then statement that displays the message "The number is not valid" if the variable speed is outside the range 0 through 200.

Boolean Variables

CONCEPT: A Boolean variable can hold one of two values: true or false. Boolean variables are commonly used as flags, which indicate whether specific conditions exist.

You have probably worked with Integer, Real, and String variables. In addition to numeric and string data types, most programming languages provide a Boolean data type. The Boolean data type allows you to create variables that may hold one of two possible values: True or False. Here is an example of the way we declare Boolean variables in this text:

```
Declare Boolean isHungry
```

Most programming languages have key words such as True and False that can be assigned to Boolean variables. Here are examples of how we assign values to a Boolean variable:

```
Set isHungry = True
Set isHungry = False
```

Boolean variables are most commonly used as flags. A *flag* is a variable that signals when some condition exists in the program. When the flag variable is set to False, it indicates the condition does not exist. When the flag variable is set to `True`, it means the condition does exist.

For example, suppose a salesperson has a quota of $50,000. Assuming the `sales` variable holds the amount that the salesperson has sold, the following pseudocode determines whether the quota has been met:

```
If sales >= 50000 Then
    Set salesQuotaMet = True
Else
    Set salesQuotaMet = False
End If
```

As a result of this code, the `salesQuotaMet` variable can be used as a flag to indicate whether the sales quota has been met. Later in the program we might test the flag in the following way:

```
If salesQuotaMet Then
    Display "You have met your sales quota!"
End If
```

This code displays the message "You have met your sales quota!" if the `Boolean` variable `salesQuotaMet` equals `True`. Notice that we did not have to use the `==` operator to explicitly compare the `salesQuotaMet` variable with the value `True`. This code is equivalent to the following:

```
If salesQuotaMet == True Then
    Display "You have met your sales quota!"
End If
```

 ## Checkpoint

27 What values can you store in a Boolean variable?

28 What is a flag variable?

Review Questions

Multiple Choice

1. A _____ structure can execute a set of statements only under certain circumstances.

   a. sequence
   b. circumstantial
   c. decision
   d. Boolean

2. A _____ structure provides one alternative path of execution.

   a. sequence
   b. single alternative decision
   c. one path alternative
   d. single execution decision

3. In pseudocode, the `If-Then` statement is an example of a _____.

   a. sequence structure
   b. decision structure
   c. pathway structure
   d. class structure

4. A(n) _____ expression has a value of either true or false.

   a. binary
   b. decision
   c. unconditional
   d. Boolean

5. The symbols >, <, and == are all _____ operators.

   a. relational
   b. logical
   c. conditional
   d. ternary

6. A(n) _____ structure tests a condition and then takes one path if the condition is true, or another path if the condition is false.

   a. `If-Then` statement
   b. single alternative decision
   c. dual alternative decision
   d. sequence

7. You use a(n) _____ statement in pseudocode to write a single alternative decision structure.

   a. `Test-Jump`
   b. `If-Then`
   c. `If-Then-Else`
   d. `If-Call`

8. You use a(n) _____ statement in pseudocode to write a dual alternative decision structure.

   a. `Test-Jump`
   b. `If-Then`
   c. `If-Then-Else`
   d. `If-Call`

9. A _____ structure allows you to test the value of a variable or an expression and then use that value to determine which statement or set of statements to execute.

   a. variable test decision
   b. single alternative decision
   c. dual alternative decision
   d. multiple alternative decision

10. A(n) _____ section of a `Select Case` statement is branched to if none of the case values match the expression listed after the `Select` statement.

    a. `Else`
    b. `Default`
    c. `Case`
    d. `Otherwise`

11. `AND`, `OR`, and `NOT` are _____ operators.

    a. relational
    b. logical
    c. conditional
    d. ternary

12. A compound Boolean expression created with the _____ operator is true only if both of its subexpressions are true.

    a. `AND`
    b. `OR`
    c. `NOT`
    d. `BOTH`

13. A compound Boolean expression created with the _____ operator is true if either of its subexpressions is true.

    a. `AND`
    b. `OR`
    c. `NOT`
    d. `EITHER`

14. The _____ operator takes a Boolean expression as its operand and reverses its logical value.

    a. `AND`
    b. `OR`
    c. `NOT`
    d. `EITHER`

15. A _____ is a Boolean variable that signals when some condition exists in the program.

    a. flag
    b. signal
    c. sentinel
    d. siren

True or False

1. You can write any program using only sequence structures.

2. A program can be made of only one type of control structure. You cannot combine structures.

3. A single alternative decision structure tests a condition and then takes one path if the condition is true, or another path if the condition is false.

4. A decision structure can be nested inside another decision structure.

5. A compound Boolean expression created with the AND operator is true only when both subexpressions are true.

Short Answer

1. Explain what is meant by the term *conditionally executed*.

2. You need to test a condition and then execute one set of statements if the condition is true. If the condition is false, you need to execute a different set of statements. What structure will you use?

3. If you need to test the value of a variable and use that value to determine which statement or set of statements to execute, which structure would be the most straightforward to use?

4. Briefly describe how the AND operator works.

5. Briefly describe how the OR operator works.

6. When determining whether a number is inside a range, which logical operator is it best to use?

7. What is a flag and how does it work?

Algorithm Workbench

1. Design an If-Then statement (or a flowchart with a single alternative decision structure) that assigns 20 to the variable y and assigns 40 to the variable z if the variable x is greater than 100.

2. Design an If-Then statement (or a flowchart with a single alternative decision structure) that assigns 0 to the variable b and assigns 1 to the variable c if the variable a is less than 10.

3. Design an If-Then-Else statement (or a flowchart with a dual alternative decision structure) that assigns 0 to the variable b if the variable a is less than 10. Otherwise, it should assign 99 to the variable b.

4. The following pseudocode contains several nested If-Then-Else statements. Unfortunately, it was written without proper alignment and indentation. Rewrite the code and use the proper conventions of alignment and indentation.

```
If score < 60 Then
Display "Your grade is F."
Else
If score < 70 Then
Display "Your grade is D."
Else
If score < 80 Then
Display "Your grade is C."
Else
```

```
If score < 90 Then
Display "Your grade is B."
Else
Display "Your grade is A."
End If
End If
End If
End If
```

5. Design nested decision structures that perform the following: If amount1 is greater than 10 and amount2 is less than 100, display the greater of amount1 and amount2.

6. Rewrite the following If-Then-Else If statement as a Select Case statement.

```
If selection == 1 Then
    Display "You selected A."
Else If selection == 2 Then
    Display "You selected 2."
Else If selection == 3 Then
    Display "You selected 3."
Else If selection == 4 Then
    Display "You selected 4."
Else
    Display "Not good with numbers, eh?"
End If
```

7. Design an If-Then-Else statement (or a flowchart with a dual alternative decision structure) that displays "Speed is normal" if the speed variable is within the range of 24 to 56. If speed holds a value outside this range, display "Speed is abnormal."

8. Design an If-Then-Else statement (or a flowchart with a dual alternative decision structure) that determines whether the points variable is outside the range of 9 to 51. If the variable holds a value outside this range it should display "Invalid points." Otherwise, it should display "Valid points."

9. Design a case structure that tests the month variable and does the following:
   - If the month variable is set to 1, it displays "January has 31 days."
   - If the month variable is set to 2, it displays "February has 28 days."
   - If the month variable is set to 3, it displays "March has 31 days."
   - If the month variable is set to anything else, it displays "Invalid selection."

10. Write an If-Then statement that sets the variable hours to 10 when the flag variable minimum is set.

Debugging Exercises

1. Part of the following pseudocode is incompatible with the Java, Python, C, and C++ languages. Identify the problem. How would you fix the problem if you were to translate this pseudocode into one of the aforementioned languages?

```
Module checkEquality(Integer num1, Integer num2)
    If num1 = num2 Then
       Display "The values are equal."
    Else
       Display "The values are NOT equal."
    End If
End Module
```

2. The intended purpose of the following module is to set the `temp` parameter to the value 32.0 if it is not already equal to 32.0. This will not work as the programmer expects, however. Find the problem.

```
Module resetTemperature(Real Ref temp)
    If NOT temp == 32.0 Then
        Set temp = 32.0
    End If
End Module
```

3. The intended purpose of the following module is to determine whether the `value` parameter is within a specified range. The module will not work, however. Find the problem.

```
Module checkRange(Integer value, Integer lower, Integer upper)
    If value < lower AND value > upper Then
        Display "The value is outside the range."
    Else
        Display "The value is within the range."
    End If
End Module
```

Programming Exercises

1. Roman Numerals

Design a program that prompts the user to enter a number within the range of 1 through 10. The program should display the Roman numeral version of that number. If the number is outside the range of 1 through 10, the program should display an error message.

2. Areas of Rectangles

VideoNote

The Areas of Rectangles Problem

The area of a rectangle is the rectangle's length times its width. Design a program that asks for the length and width of two rectangles. The program should tell the user which rectangle has the greater area, or whether the areas are the same.

3. Mass and Weight

Scientists measure an object's mass in kilograms and its weight in Newtons. If you know the amount of mass of an object, you can calculate its weight, in Newtons, with the following formula:

$$Weight = Mass \times 9.8$$

Design a program that asks the user to enter an object's mass, and then calculates its weight. If the object weighs more than 1,000 Newtons, display a message indicating that it is too heavy. If the object weighs less than 10 Newtons, display a message indicating that it is too light.

4. Magic Dates

The date June 10, 1960, is special because when it is written in the following format, the month times the day equals the year:

6/10/60

Design a program that asks the user to enter a month (in numeric form), a day, and a two-digit year. The program should then determine whether the month times the day equals the year. If so, it should display a message saying the date is magic. Otherwise, it should display a message saying the date is not magic.

5. **Color Mixer**

The colors red, blue, and yellow are known as the primary colors because they cannot be made by mixing other colors. When you mix two primary colors, you get a secondary color, as shown here:

- When you mix red and blue, you get purple.
- When you mix red and yellow, you get orange.
- When you mix blue and yellow, you get green.

Design a program that prompts the user to enter the names of two primary colors to mix. If the user enters anything other than "red," "blue," or "yellow," the program should display an error message. Otherwise, the program should display the name of the secondary color that results.

6. **Book Club Points**

Serendipity Booksellers has a book club that awards points to its customers based on the number of books purchased each month. The points are awarded as follows:

- If a customer purchases 0 books, he or she earns 0 points.
- If a customer purchases 1 book, he or she earns 5 points.
- If a customer purchases 2 books, he or she earns 15 points.
- If a customer purchases 3 books, he or she earns 30 points.
- If a customer purchases 4 or more books, he or she earns 60 points.

Design a program that asks the user to enter the number of books that he or she has purchased this month and displays the number of points awarded.

7. **Software Sales**

A software company sells a package that retails for $99. Quantity discounts are given according to the following table:

Quantity	Discount
10–19	20%
20–49	30%
50–99	40%
100 or more	50%

Design a program that asks the user to enter the number of packages purchased. The program should then display the amount of the discount (if any) and the total amount of the purchase after the discount.

8. **Change for a Dollar Game**

Design a change-counting game that gets the user to enter the number of coins required to make exactly one dollar. The program should ask the user to enter the number of pennies, nickels, dimes, and quarters. If the total value of the coins entered is equal to one dollar, the program should congratulate the user for winning the game. Otherwise, the program should display a message indicating whether the amount entered was more than or less than one dollar.

9. **Shipping Charges**

The Fast Freight Shipping Company charges the following rates:

Weight of Package	Rate per Pound
2 pounds or less	$1.10
Over 2 pounds but not more than 6 pounds	$2.20
Over 6 pounds but not more than 10 pounds	$3.70
Over 10 pounds	$3.80

Design a program that asks the user to enter the weight of a package and then displays the shipping charges.

10. **Body Mass Index Program Enhancement**

Design a program that calculates a person's body mass index (BMI). The BMI is often used to determine whether a person with a sedentary lifestyle is overweight or underweight for his or her height. A person's BMI is calculated with the following formula:

$$BMI = Weight \times 703 / Height^2$$

In the formula, weight is measured in pounds and height is measured in inches. Enhance the program so it displays a message indicating whether the person has optimal weight, is underweight, or is overweight. A sedentary person's weight is considered to be optimal if his or her BMI is between 18.5 and 25. If the BMI is less than 18.5, the person is considered to be underweight. If the BMI value is greater than 25, the person is considered to be overweight.

11. **Time Calculator**

Design a program that asks the user to enter a number of seconds, and works as follows:

- There are 60 seconds in a minute. If the number of seconds entered by the user is greater than or equal to 60, the program should display the number of minutes in that many seconds.
- There are 3,600 seconds in an hour. If the number of seconds entered by the user is greater than or equal to 3,600, the program should display the number of hours in that many seconds.
- There are 86,400 seconds in a day. If the number of seconds entered by the user is greater than or equal to 86,400, the program should display the number of days in that many seconds.

Answers to Checkpoint Questions

1 A logical design that controls the order in which a set of statements executes.

2 It is a program structure that can execute a set of statements only under certain circumstances.

3 A decision structure that provides a single alternative path of execution. If the condition that is being tested is true, the program takes the alternative path.

4 An expression that can be evaluated as either true or false.

5 You can determine whether one value is greater than, less than, greater than or equal to, less than or equal to, equal to, or not equal to another value.

6 ```
If y == 20 Then
    Set x = 0
End If
```

7 ```
If sales >= 10000 Then
    Set commission = 0.2
End If
```

8 A dual alternative decision structure has two possible paths of execution—one path is taken if a condition is true, and the other path is taken if the condition is false.

9 `If-Then-Else`

10 When the condition is false.

11 z is not less than a.

12 Boston
New York

13 A dual alternative decision structure has two possible paths of execution—one path is taken if a condition is true, and the other path is taken if the condition is false.

14 `If-Then-Else`

15 If the condition is false.

16 ```
If number == 1 Then
    Display "One"
Else If number == 2 Then
    Display "Two"
Else If number == 3 Then
    Display "Three"
Else
    Display "Unknown"
End If
```

17 A structure that tests the value of a variable or an expression and then uses that value to determine which statement or set of statements to execute.

18 With a `Select Case` statement.

19 A variable or an expression.
```

20 In such an event, you can use the `If-Then-Else If` statement, or a nested decision structure.

21 It is an expression that is created by using a logical operator to combine two Boolean subexpressions.

22 F
T
F
F
T
T
T
F
F
T

23 T
F
T
T
T

24 The AND operator: If the expression on the left side of the AND operator is false, the expression on the right side will not be checked.
The OR operator: If the expression on the left side of the OR operator is true, the expression on the right side will not be checked.

25
```
If speed >= 0 AND speed <= 200 Then
    Display "The number is valid"
End If
```

26
```
If speed < 0 OR speed > 200 Then
    Display "The number is not valid"
End If
```

27 True or false

28 A variable that signals when some condition exists in the program.

Repetition Structures

1 Introduction to Repetition Structures

CONCEPT: A repetition structure causes a statement or set of statements to execute repeatedly.

Programmers commonly have to write code that performs the same task over and over. For example, suppose you have been asked to write a program that calculates a 10 percent sales commission for several salespeople. Although it would not be a good design, one approach would be to write the code to calculate one salesperson's commission, and then repeat that code for each salesperson. For example, look at the following pseudocode:

```
// Variables for sales and commission.
Declare Real sales, commission

// Constant for the commission rate.
Constant Real COMMISSION_RATE = 0.10

// Get the amount of sales.
Display "Enter the amount of sales."
Input sales

// Calculate the commission.
Set commission = sales * COMMISSION_RATE

// Display the commission
Display "The commission is $", commission
```

This calculates the first salesperson's commission.

From Chapter 5 of *Starting Out with Programming Logic and Design,* Third Edition. Tony Gaddis.
Copyright © 2013 by Pearson Education, Inc. Published by Pearson Addison-Wesley. All rights reserved.

```
// Get the amount of sales.
Display "Enter the amount of sales."
Input sales

// Calculate the commission.
Set commission = sales * COMMISSION_RATE

// Display the commission
Display "The commission is $", commission
```

This calculates the second salesperson's commission.

And this code goes on and on . . .

As you can see, this is one long sequence structure containing a lot of duplicated code. There are several disadvantages to this approach, including the following:

- The duplicated code makes the program large.
- Writing a long sequence of statements can be time consuming.
- If part of the duplicated code has to be corrected or changed, then the correction or change has to be done many times.

Instead of writing the same sequence of statements over and over, a better way to repeatedly perform an operation is to write the code for the operation once, and then place that code in a structure that makes the computer repeat it as many times as necessary. This can be done with a *repetition structure*, which is more commonly known as a *loop*.

Condition-Controlled and Count-Controlled Loops

In this chapter, we will look at two broad categories of loops: condition-controlled and count-controlled. A *condition-controlled loop* uses a true/false condition to control the number of times that it repeats. A *count-controlled loop* repeats a specific number of times. We will also discuss the specific ways that most programming languages allow you to construct these types of loops.

 Checkpoint

1 What is a repetition structure?

2 What is a condition-controlled loop?

3 What is a count-controlled loop?

 ## Condition-Controlled Loops: `While`, `Do-While`, **and** `Do-Until`

CONCEPT: Both the `While` and `Do-While` loops cause a statement or set of statements to repeat as long as a condition is true. The `Do-Until` loop causes a statement or set of statements to repeat until a condition is true.

The While Loop

The While loop gets its name from the way it works: *While a condition is true, do some task*. The loop has two parts: (1) a condition that is tested for a true or false value, and (2) a statement or set of statements that is repeated as long as the condition is true. Figure 1 shows the logic of a While loop.

Figure 1 The logic of a While loop

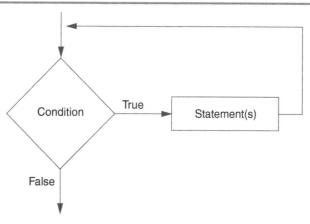

VideoNote

The While Loop

The diamond symbol represents the condition that is tested. Notice what happens if the condition is true: one or more statements are executed and the program's execution flows back to the point just above the diamond symbol. The condition is tested again, and if it is true, the process repeats. If the condition is false, the program exits the loop. In a flowchart, you will always recognize a loop when you see a flow line going back to a previous part of the flowchart.

Writing a While Loop in Pseudocode

In pseudocode, we will use the While statement to write a While loop. Here is the general format of the While statement:

```
While condition
    statement
    statement
    etc.
End While
```

These statements are the body of the loop. They are repeated while the condition is true.

In the general format, the *condition* is a Boolean expression, and the statements that appear on the lines between the While and the End While clauses are called the *body of the loop*. When the loop executes, the *condition* is tested. If it is true, the statements that appear in the body of the loop are executed, and then the loop starts over. If the *condition* is false, the program exits the loop.

As shown in the general format, you should use the following conventions when you write a While statement:

- Make sure the While clause and the End While clause are aligned.
- Indent the statements in the body of the loop.

By indenting the statements in the body of the loop you visually set them apart from the surrounding code. This makes your program easier to read and debug. Also, this is similar to the style that most programmers follow when writing loops in actual code.

Program 1 shows how we might use a While loop to write the commission calculating program that was described at the beginning of this chapter.

Program 1

```
 1  // Variable declarations
 2  Declare Real sales, commission
 3  Declare String keepGoing = "y"
 4
 5  // Constant for the commission rate
 6  Constant Real COMMISSION_RATE = 0.10
 7
 8  While keepGoing == "y"
 9      // Get the amount of sales.
10      Display "Enter the amount of sales."
11      Input sales
12
13      // Calculate the commission.
14      Set commission = sales * COMMISSION_RATE
15
16      // Display the commission
17      Display "The commission is $", commission
18
19      Display "Do you want to calculate another"
20      Display "commission? (Enter y for yes.)"
21      Input keepGoing
22  End While
```

Program Output (with Input Shown in Bold)

```
Enter the amount of sales.
10000.00 [Enter]
The commission is $1000
Do you want to calculate another
commission? (Enter y for yes.)
y [Enter]
Enter the amount of sales.
5000.00 [Enter]
The commission is $500
Do you want to calculate another
commission? (Enter y for yes.)
y [Enter]
Enter the amount of sales.
12000.00 [Enter]
The commission is $1200
Do you want to calculate another
commission? (Enter y for yes.)
n [Enter]
```

In line 2, we declare the `sales` variable, which will hold the amount of sales, and the `commission` variable, which will hold the amount of commission. Then, in line 3 we declare a `String` variable named `keepGoing`. Notice that the variable is initialized with the value "y." This initialization value is important, and in a moment you will see why. In line 6 we declare a constant, `COMMISSION_RATE`, which is initialized with the value 0.10. This is the commission rate that we will use in our calculation.

Line 8 is the beginning of a `While` loop, which starts like this:

```
While keepGoing == "y"
```

Notice the condition that is being tested: `keepGoing == "y"`. The loop tests this condition, and if it is true, the statements in the body of the loop (lines 9 through 21) are executed. Then, the loop starts over at line 8. It tests the expression `keepGoing == "y"` and if it is true, the statements in the body of the loop are executed again. This cycle repeats until the expression `keepGoing == "y"` is tested in line 8 and found to be false. When that happens, the program exits the loop. This is illustrated in Figure 2.

In order for this loop to stop executing, something has to happen inside the loop to make the expression `keepGoing == "y"` false. The statements in lines 19 through 21 take care of this. Lines 19 and 20 display a message asking "Do you want to calculate another commission? (Enter y for yes)." Then, the `Input` statement in line 21 reads the user's input and stores it in the `keepGoing` variable. If the user enters y (and it must be a lowercase y), then the expression `keepGoing == "y"` will be true when the loop starts over. This will cause the statements in the body of the loop to execute again. But, if the user enters anything other than lowercase y, the expression will be false when the loop starts over, and the program will exit the loop.

Figure 2 The `While` loop

```
                          This condition is tested.
                                   |
                          ┌────────┴────────┐
                  While  keepGoing == "y"

                          // Get the amount of sales.
                          Display "Enter the amount of sales."
                          Input sales

If the condition is true,
these statements are       // Calculate the commission.
executed, and then the     Set commission = sales * COMMISSION_RATE
loop starts over.

                          // Display the commission
If the condition is false,  Display "The commission is $", commission
these statements are
skipped and the            Display "Do you want to calculate another"
program exits the loop.    Display "commission? (Enter y for yes.)"
                          Input keepGoing

                  End While
```

Now that you have examined the pseudocode, look at the program output in the sample run. First, the program prompted the user to enter the amount of sales. The user entered 10000.00, and then the program displayed the commission for that amount, which is $1000.00. Then, the user is prompted "Do you want to calculate another commission? (Enter y for yes.)" The user entered y, and the loop started the steps over. In the sample run, the user went through this process three times. Each execution of the body of a loop is known as an *iteration*. In the sample run, the loop iterated three times.

Figure 3 shows a flowchart for Program 1. By looking at this flowchart you can see that we have a repetition structure (the while loop) with a sequence structure (the body of the loop) nested inside it. The fundamental structure of the while loop is still present, however. A condition is tested, and if it is true one or more statements are executed and the flow of execution returns to the point just above the conditional test.

Figure 3 Flowchart for Program 1

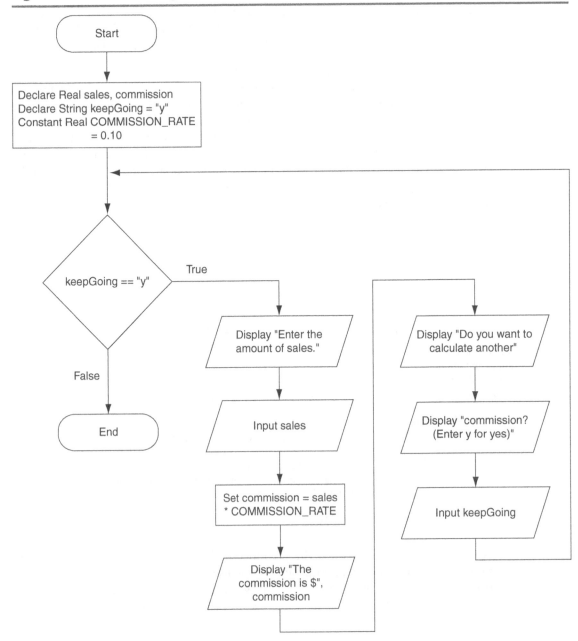

The `While` Loop Is a Pretest Loop

The `While` loop is known as a *pretest* loop, which means it tests its condition *before* performing an iteration. Because the test is done at the beginning of the loop, you usually have to perform some steps prior to the loop to make sure that the loop executes at least once. For example, the loop in Program 1 starts like this:

```
While keepGoing == "y"
```

The loop will perform an iteration only if the expression `keepGoing == "y"` is true. To make sure the expression is true the first time that the loop executes, we declared and initialized the `keepGoing` variable in line 3 as follows:

```
Declare String keepGoing = "y"
```

If `keepGoing` had been initialized with any other value (or not initialized at all), the loop would never execute. This is an important characteristic of the `While` loop: it will never execute if its condition is false to start with. In some programs, this is exactly what you want. The following *In the Spotlight* section gives an example.

In the Spotlight:
Designing a `While` Loop

A project currently underway at Chemical Labs, Inc. requires that a substance be continually heated in a vat. A technician must check the substance's temperature every 15 minutes. If the substance's temperature does not exceed 102.5, then the technician does nothing. However, if the temperature is greater than 102.5, the technician must turn down the vat's thermostat, wait five minutes, and check the temperature again. The technician repeats these steps until the temperature does not exceed 102.5. The director of engineering has asked you to design a program that guides the technician through this process.

Here is the algorithm:

1. Get the substance's temperature.
2. Repeat the following steps as long as the temperature is greater than 102.5:
   a. Tell the technician to turn down the thermostat, wait five minutes, and check the temperature again.
   b. Get the substance's temperature.
3. After the loop finishes, tell the technician that the temperature is acceptable and to check it again in 15 minutes.

After reviewing this algorithm, you realize that steps 2(a) and 2(b) should not be performed if the test condition (temperature is greater than 102.5) is false to begin with. The `While` loop will work well in this situation, because it will not execute even once if its condition is false. Program 2 shows the pseudocode for the program, and Figure 4 shows a flowchart.

Program 2

```
 1 // Variable to hold the temperature
 2 Declare Real temperature
 3
 4 // Constant for the maximum temperature
 5 Constant Real MAX_TEMP = 102.5
 6
 7 // Get the substance's temperature.
 8 Display "Enter the substance's temperature."
 9 Input temperature
10
11 // If necessary, adjust the thermostat.
12 While temperature > MAX_TEMP
13     Display "The temperature is too high."
14     Display "Turn the thermostat down and wait"
15     Display "five minutes. Take the temperature"
16     Display "again and enter it here."
17     Input temperature
18 End While
19
20 // Remind the user to check the temperature
21 // again in 15 minutes.
22 Display "The temperature is acceptable."
23 Display "Check it again in 15 minutes."
```

Program Output (with Input Shown in Bold)

```
Enter the substance's temperature.
104.7 [Enter]
The temperature is too high.
Turn the thermostat down and wait
five minutes. Take the temperature
again and enter it here.
103.2 [Enter]
The temperature is too high.
Turn the thermostat down and wait
five minutes. Take the temperature
again and enter it here.
102.1 [Enter]
The temperature is acceptable.
Check it again in 15 minutes.
```

Program Output (with Input Shown in Bold)

```
Enter the substance's temperature.
102.1 [Enter]
The temperature is acceptable.
Check it again in 15 minutes.
```

Figure 4 Flowchart for Program 2

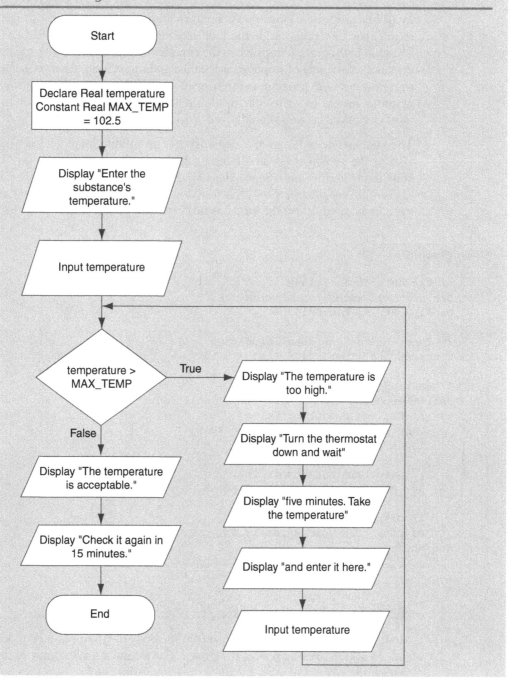

Infinite Loops

In all but rare cases, loops must contain within themselves a way to terminate. This means that something inside the loop must eventually make the test condition false. The loop in Program 1 stops when the expression keepGoing == "y" is false. If a loop does not have a way of stopping, it is called an infinite loop. An *infinite loop* continues to repeat until the program is interrupted. Infinite loops usually occur when the programmer forgets to write code inside the loop that makes the test condition false. In most circumstances you should avoid writing infinite loops.

The pseudocode in Program 3 demonstrates an infinite loop. This is a modified version of the commission calculating program. In this version, we have removed the code that modifies the keepGoing variable in the body of the loop. Each time the expression keepGoing == "y" is tested in line 9, keepGoing will contain the string "y". As a consequence, the loop has no way of stopping.

Program 3

```
 1 // Variable declarations
 2 Declare Real sales, commission
 3 Declare String keepGoing = "y"
 4
 5 // Constant for the commission rate
 6 Constant Real COMMISSION_RATE = 0.10
 7
 8 // Warning! Infinite loop!
 9 While keepGoing == "y"
10     // Get the amount of sales.
11     Display "Enter the amount of sales."
12     Input sales
13
14     // Calculate the commission.
15     Set commission = sales * COMMISSION_RATE
16
17     // Display the commission
18     Display "The commission is $", commission
19 End While
```

Modularizing the Code in the Body of a Loop

Modules can be called from statements in the body of a loop. In fact, modularizing the code in a loop often improves the design. For example, in Program 1, the statements that get the amount of sales, calculate the commission, and display the commission can easily be placed in a module. That module can then be called in the loop. Program 4 shows how this might be done. This program has a main module, which executes when the program runs, and a showCommission module, which handles all of the steps related to calculating and displaying a commission. Figure 5 shows a flowchart for the main module, and Figure 6 shows a flowchart for the showCommission module.

Program 4

```
 1 Module main()
 2      // Local variable
 3      Declare String keepGoing = "y"
 4
 5      // Calculate as many commissions
 6      // as needed.
 7      While keepGoing == "y"
 8         // Display a salesperson's commission.
 9         Call showCommission()
10
11         // Do it again?
12         Display "Do you want to calculate another"
13         Display "commission? (Enter y for yes.)"
14         Input keepGoing
15      End While
16 End Module
17
18 // The showCommission module gets the
19 // amount of sales and displays the
20 // commission.
21 Module show Commission()
22      // Local variables
23      Declare Real sales, commission
24
25      // Constant for the commission rate
26      Constant Real COMMISSION_RATE = 0.10
27
28      // Get the amount of sales.
29      Display "Enter the amount of sales."
30      Input sales
31
32      // Calculate the commission.
33      Set commission = sales * COMMISSION_RATE
34
35      // Display the commission
36      Display "The commission is  $", commission
37 End Module
```

The output of this program is the same as that of Program 1

Figure 5 The `main` module of Program 4

Figure 6 The `showCommission` module

```
┌──────────┐
│  Start   │
└──────────┘
     │
     ▼
┌─────────────────────┐
│ Declare String keepGoing │
│       = "y"          │
└─────────────────────┘
     │
     ▼
  ◇ keepGoing == "y" ◇ ──True──▶ ┌──────────────┐
     │                            │ showCommission() │
   False                          └──────────────┘
     │                                   │
     ▼                                   ▼
┌──────────┐                    ╱ Display "Do you want to ╱
│   End    │                    ╱ calculate another"      ╱
└──────────┘                             │
                                         ▼
                                ╱ Display "commission? ╱
                                ╱ (Enter y for yes)"   ╱
                                         │
                                         ▼
                                ╱ Input keepGoing ╱
```

```
┌────────────────┐
│ showCommission( ) │
└────────────────┘
     │
     ▼
┌─────────────────────┐
│ Declare Real sales, │
│    commission       │
│  Constant Real      │
│ COMMISSION_RATE = 0.10 │
└─────────────────────┘
     │
     ▼
╱ Display "Enter the ╱
╱ amount of sales."  ╱
     │
     ▼
╱ Input sales ╱
     │
     ▼
┌─────────────────────┐
│ Set commission = sales │
│  * COMMISSION_RATE  │
└─────────────────────┘
     │
     ▼
╱ Display "The      ╱
╱ commission is $", ╱
╱ commission        ╱
     │
     ▼
┌──────────┐
│  Return  │
└──────────┘
```

VideoNote

The Do-While Loop

The `Do-While` Loop

You have learned that the `While` loop is a pretest loop, which means it tests its condition before performing an iteration. The `Do-While` loop is a *posttest* loop. This means it performs an iteration before testing its condition. As a result, the `Do-While` loop always performs at least one iteration, even if its condition is false to begin with. The logic of a `Do-While` loop is shown in Figure 7.

Figure 7 The logic of a Do-While loop

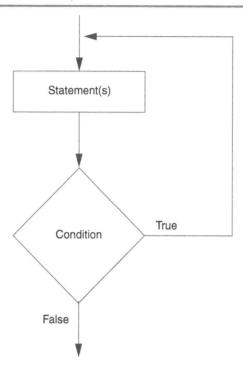

In the flowchart, one or more statements are executed, and then a condition is tested. If the condition is true, the program's execution flows back to the point just above the first statement in the body of the loop, and this process repeats. If the condition is false, the program exits the loop.

Writing a Do-While Loop in Pseudocode

In pseudocode, we will use the Do-While statement to write a Do-While loop. Here is the general format of the Do-While statement:

```
Do
    statement
    statement
    etc.
While condition
```

These statements are the body of the loop. They are always performed once, and then repeated while the condition is true.

In the general format, the statements that appear in the lines between the Do and the While clauses are the body of the loop. The *condition* that appears after the While clause is a Boolean expression. When the loop executes, the statements in the body of the loop are executed, and then the *condition* is tested. If the *condition* is true, the loop starts over and the statements in the body are executed again. If the condition is false, however, the program exits the loop.

As shown in the general format, you should use the following conventions when you write a Do-While statement:

- Make sure the Do clause and the While clause are aligned.
- Indent the statements in the body of the loop.

As shown in Program 5, the commission calculating program can be easily modified to use a Do-While loop instead of a While loop. Notice that in this version of the program, in line 3, we do not initialize the keepGoing variable with the string "y". It isn't necessary because the Do-While loop, in lines 7 through 15, will always execute at least once. This means that the Input statement in line 14 will read a value into the keepGoing variable before the condition is ever tested in line 15.

Figure 8 shows a flowchart for the main module.

Program 5

```
1  Module main()
2      // Local variable
3      Declare String keepGoing
4
5      // Calculate commissions as many
6      // times as needed.
7      Do
8          // Display a salesperson's commission.
9          Call showCommission()
10
11         // Do it again?
12         Display "Do you want to calculate another"
13         Display "commission? (Enter y for yes.)"
14         Input keepGoing
15     While keepGoing == "y"
16 End Module
17
18 // The showCommission module gets the
19 // amount of sales and displays the
20 // commission.
21 Module showCommission()
22     // Local variables
23     Declare Real sales, commission
24
25     // Constant for the commission rate
26     Constant Real COMMISSION_RATE = 0.10
27
28     // Get the amount of sales.
29     Display "Enter the amount of sales."
30     Input sales
31
32     // Calculate the commission.
33     Set commission = sales * COMMISSION_RATE
34
35     // Display the commission
36     Display "The commission is $", commission
37 End Module
```

The output of this program is the same as that of Program 1

Figure 8 Flowchart for the main module in Program 5

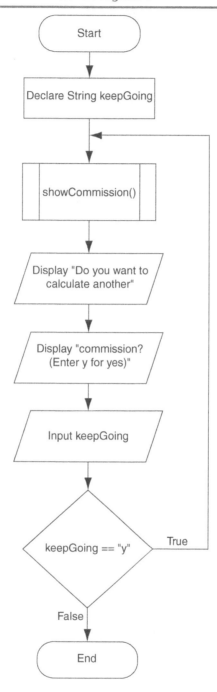

Although the Do-While loop is convenient to use in some circumstances, it is never required. Any loop that can be written as a Do-While loop can also be written as a While loop. As previously mentioned, some circumstances require that you initialize data prior to executing a While loop, to ensure that it executes at least once.

In the Spotlight:

Designing a Do-While Loop

Samantha owns an import business and she calculates the retail prices of her products with the following formula:

$$Retail\ Price = Wholesale\ Cost \times 2.5$$

She has asked you to design a program to do this calculation for each item that she receives in a shipment. You learn that each shipment contains various numbers of items, so you decide to use a loop that calculates the price for one item, and then asks her whether she has another item. The loop will iterate as long as she indicates that she has another item. Program 6 shows the pseudocode for the program, and Figure 9 shows the flowchart.

Program 6

```
 1 Module main()
 2     // Local variable
 3     Declare String doAnother
 4
 5     Do
 6         // Calculate and display a retail price.
 7         Call showRetail()
 8
 9         // Do this again?
10         Display "Do you have another item? (Enter y for yes.)"
11         Input doAnother
12     While doAnother == "y" OR doAnother == "Y"
13 End Module
14
15 // The showRetail module gets an item's wholesale cost
16 // from the user and displays its retail price.
17 Module showRetail()
18     // Local variables
19     Declare Real wholesale, retail
20
21     // Constant for the markup percentage
22     Constant Real MARKUP = 2.50
23
24     // Get the wholesale cost.
25     Display "Enter an item's wholesale cost."
26     Input wholesale
27
28     // Calculate the retail price.
29     Set retail = wholesale * MARKUP
30
31     // Display the retail price.
32     Display "The retail price is $", retail
33 End Module
```

Program Output (with Input Shown in Bold)

```
Enter an item's wholesale cost.
10.00 [Enter]
The retail price is $25
Do you have another item? (Enter y for yes.)
y [Enter]
Enter an item's wholesale cost.
15.00 [Enter]
The retail price is $37.50
Do you have another item? (Enter y for yes.)
y [Enter]
Enter an item's wholesale cost.
12.50 [Enter]
The retail price is $31.25
Do you have another item? (Enter y for yes.)
n [Enter]
```

Figure 9 Flowchart for Program 6

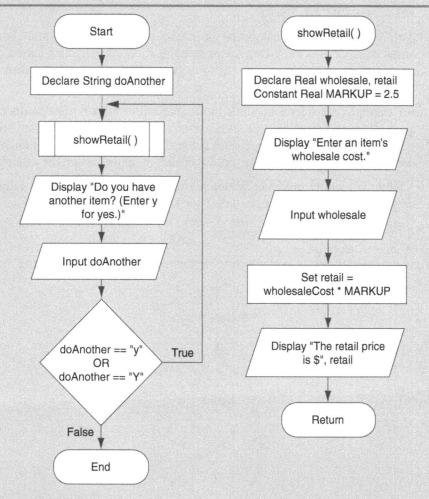

This program has two modules: `main`, which executes when the program runs, and `showRetail`, which calculates and displays an item's retail price. In the `main` module, a `Do-While` loop appears in lines 5 through 12. In line 7, the loop calls the `showRetail` module. Then, in line 10 the user is prompted "Do you have another item? (Enter y for yes.)" In line 11, the user's input is stored in the `doAnother` variable. In line 12, the following statement is the end of the `Do-While` loop:

```
While doAnother == "y" OR doAnother == "Y"
```

Notice that we are using the logical OR operator to test a compound Boolean expression. The expression on the left side of the OR operator will be true if `doAnother` is equal to lowercase `"y"`. The expression on the right side of the OR operator will be true if `doAnother` is equal to uppercase `"Y"`. If either of these subexpressions is true, the loop will iterate. This is a simple way to make a case insensitive comparison, which means that it does not matter whether the user enters uppercase or lowercase letters.

The `Do-Until` Loop

Both the `While` and the `Do-While` loops iterate as long as a condition is true. Sometimes, however, it is more convenient to write a loop that iterates *until* a condition is true—that is, a loop that iterates as long as a condition is false, and then stops when the condition becomes true.

For example, consider a machine in an automobile factory that paints cars as they move down the assembly line. When there are no more cars to paint, the machine stops. If you were programming such a machine, you would want to design a loop that causes the machine to paint cars until there are no more cars on the assembly line.

A loop that iterates until a condition is true is known as a `Do-Until` loop. Figure 10 shows the general logic of a `Do-Until` loop.

Figure 10 The logic of a `Do-Until` loop

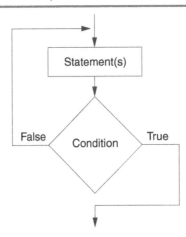

Notice that the Do-Until loop is a posttest loop. First, one or more statements are executed, and then a condition is tested. If the condition is false, the program's execution flows back to the point just above the first statement in the body of the loop, and this process repeats. If the condition is true, the program exits the loop.

Writing a Do-Until Loop in Pseudocode

In pseudocode, we will use the Do-Until statement to write a Do-Until loop. Here is the general format of the Do-Until statement:

```
Do
    statement
    statement        These statements are the body of the loop. They are always
    etc.             performed once, and then repeated until the condition is true.
Until condition
```

In the general format, the statements that appear in the lines between the Do and the Until clauses are the body of the loop. The *condition* that appears after the While clause is a Boolean expression. When the loop executes, the statements in the body of the loop are executed, and then the *condition* is tested. If the *condition* is true, the program exits the loop. If the *condition* is false, the loop starts over and the statements in the body are executed again.

As shown in the general format, you should use the following conventions when you write a Do–Until statement:

- Make sure the Do clause and the Until clause are aligned.
- Indent the statements in the body of the loop.

The pseudocode in Program 7 shows an example of the Do-Until loop. The loop in lines 6 through 16 repeatedly asks the user to enter a password until the string "prospero" is entered. Figure 11 shows a flowchart for the program.

Program 7

```
 1 // Declare a variable to hold the password.
 2 Declare String password
 3
 4 // Repeatedly ask the user to enter a password
 5 // until the correct one is entered.
 6 Do
 7    // Prompt the user to enter the password.
 8    Display "Enter the password."
 9    Input password
10
11    // Display an error message if the wrong
12    // password was entered.
13    If password != "prospero" Then
14       Display "Sorry, try again."
15    End If
16 Until password == "prospero"
17
18 // Indicate that the password is confirmed.
19 Display "Password confirmed."
```

Program Output (with Input Shown in Bold)

```
Enter the password.
ariel [Enter]
Sorry, try again.
Enter the password.
caliban [Enter]
Sorry, try again.
Enter the password.
prospero [Enter]
Password confirmed.
```

Figure 11 Flowchart for Program 7

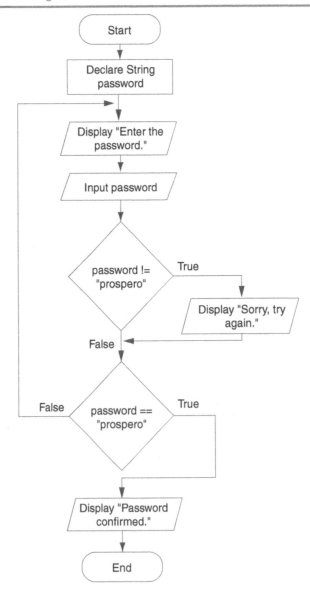

NOTE: Not all programming languages provide a Do-Until loop because you can write a Do-While loop that is logically equivalent to any Do-Until loop.

Deciding Which Loop to Use

In this section, we have introduced three different types of condition-controlled loop: the While loop, the Do-While loop, and the Do-Until loop. When you write a program that requires a condition-controlled loop, you will have to decide which loop to use.

You want to use the While loop to repeat a task as long as a condition is true. The While loop is ideal in situations where the condition might be false to start with, and in such cases you do not want the loop to iterate at all. The pseudocode that you saw in Program 2 is a good example.

The Do-While loop is also a candidate in situations where a task must be repeated as long as a condition is true. It is the best choice, however, when you always want the task to be performed at least once, regardless of whether the condition is true or false to start with.

The Do-Until loop also performs a task at least once. It is the best choice, however, when you want to perform a task *until* a condition is true. The Do-Until loop will repeat as long as its condition is false. When the condition is true, the Do-Until loop stops.

Checkpoint

4 What is a loop iteration?

5 What is the difference between a pretest loop and a posttest loop?

6 Does the While loop test its condition before or after it performs an iteration?

7 Does the Do-While loop test its condition before or after it performs an iteration?

8 What is an infinite loop?

9 What is the difference between a Do-While loop and a Do-Until loop?

3 Count-Controlled Loops and the For Statement

CONCEPT: A count-controlled loop iterates a specific number of times. Although you can write the logic of a condition-controlled loop so it iterates a specific number of times, most languages provide a loop known as the **For** loop, which is specifically designed as a count-controlled loop.

As mentioned at the beginning of this chapter, a count-controlled loop iterates a specific number of times. Count-controlled loops are commonly used in programs. For example, suppose a business is open six days per week, and you are going to write a program that calculates the total sales for a week. You will need a loop that iterates exactly six times. Each time the loop iterates, it will prompt the user to enter the sales for one day.

The way that a count-controlled loop works is simple: the loop keeps a count of the number of times that it iterates, and when the count reaches a specified amount, the loop stops. A count-controlled loop uses a variable known as a *counter variable*, or simply *counter*, to store the number of iterations that it has performed. Using the counter variable, the loop typically performs the following three actions: *initialization, test,* and *increment:*

1. **Initialization:** Before the loop begins, the counter variable is initialized to a starting value. The starting value that is used will depend on the situation.
2. **Test:** The loop tests the counter variable by comparing it to a maximum value. If the counter variable is less than or equal to the maximum value, the loop iterates. If the counter is greater than the maximum value, the program exits the loop.
3. **Increment:** To *increment* a variable means to increase its value. During each iteration, the loop increments the counter variable by adding 1 to it.

Figure 12 shows the general logic of a count-controlled loop. The initialization, test, and increment operations are indicated with the ①, ②, and ③ callouts.

Figure 12 Logic of a count-controlled loop

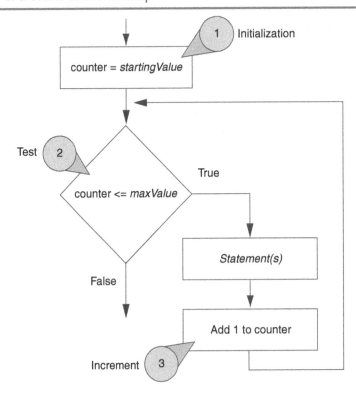

In the flowchart, assume that `counter` is an `Integer` variable. The first step is to set `counter` to the appropriate starting value. Then, determine whether `counter` is less than or equal to the maximum value. If this is true, the body of the loop executes. Otherwise, the program exits the loop. Notice that in the body of the loop one or more statements are executed, and then 1 is added to `counter`.

For example, look at the flowchart in Figure 13. First, an `Integer` variable named `counter` is declared and initialized with the starting value 1. Then, the expression `counter <= 5` is tested. If this expression is true the message "Hello world" is displayed and 1 is added to `counter`. Otherwise, the program exits the loop. If you follow the logic of this program you will see that the loop will iterate five times.

Figure 13 A count-controlled loop

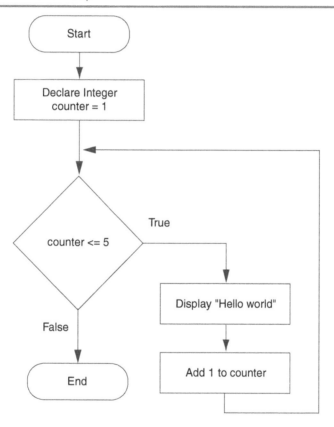

VideoNote

The For Statement

The `For` Statement

Count-controlled loops are so common in programming that most languages provide a statement just for them. This is usually called the `For` statement. The `For` statement is specifically designed to initialize, test, and increment a counter variable. Here is the general format that we will use to write the `For` statement in pseudocode:

For *counterVariable* = *startingValue* To *maxValue*
    statement
    statement   These statements are the body of the loop.
    statement
    etc.
End For

In the general format, *counterVariable* is the name of a variable that is used as a counter, *startingValue* is the value that the counter will be initially set to, and *maxValue* is the maximum value that the counter can contain. When the loop executes, the following actions are performed:

1. The *counterVariable* is set to the *startingValue*.
2. The *counterVariable* is compared to the *maxValue*. If the *counterVariable* is greater than *maxValue*, the loop stops. Otherwise:
   a. The statements that appear in the body of the loop are executed.
   b. The *counterVariable* is incremented.
   c. The loop starts over again at Step 2.

An actual For loop is easy to understand, so let's look at one. The pseudocode in Program 8 uses a For loop to display "Hello world" five times. The flowchart in Figure 14 shows the logic of the program.

Program 8

```
1 Declare Integer counter
2 Constant Integer MAX_VALUE = 5
3
4 For counter = 1 To MAX_VALUE
5     Display "Hello world"
6 End For
```

Program Output

```
Hello world
Hello world
Hello world
Hello world
Hello world
```

Line 1 declares an Integer variable that will be used as the counter variable. You do not have to name the variable counter (you are free to name it anything you wish), but in many cases that is an appropriate name. Line 2 declares a constant named MAX_VALUE that will be used as the counter's maximum value. The For loop begins in line 4 with the statement For counter = 1 To MAX_VALUE. This specifies that the counter variable will start with the value 1 and will end with the value 5. At the end of each loop iteration, the counter variable will be incremented by 1, so this loop will iterate five times. Each time it iterates, it displays "Hello world."

Notice that the loop does not contain a statement to increment the counter variable. This happens automatically in a For loop, at the end of each iteration. For that reason, you should be careful not to place a statement that modifies the counter variable inside the body of a For loop. Doing so will usually disrupt the way the For loop works.

Figure 14 Flowchart for Program 8

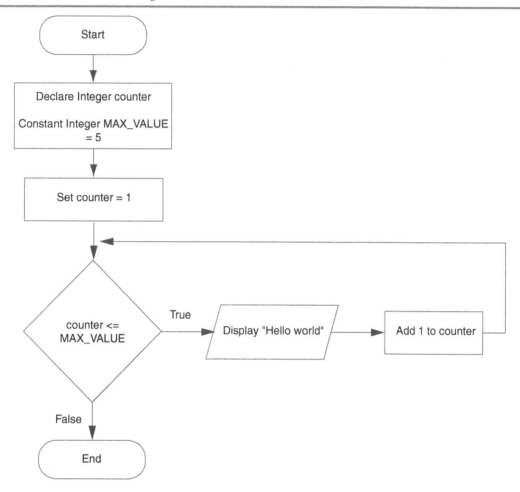

TIP: Program 8 has a constant, MAX_VALUE, that represents the counter variable's maximum value. The first line of the loop could have been written as follows, to achieve the same result:

```
For counter = 1 To 5
```

Although creating the named constant is not necessary for this simple program, creating named constants to represent important values is a good habit. Recall that named constants make a program easier to read and easier to maintain.

Using the Counter Variable in the Body of the Loop

In a count-controlled loop, the primary purpose of the counter variable is to store the number of times that the loop has iterated. In some situations, it is also helpful to use the counter variable in a calculation or other task within the body of the loop. For example, suppose you need to write a program that displays the numbers 1 through 10 and their squares, in a table similar to the following:

Number	Square
1	1
2	4
3	9
4	16
5	25
6	36
7	49
8	64
9	81
10	100

This can be accomplished by writing a count-controlled loop that iterates 10 times. During the first iteration, the counter variable will be set to 1, during the second iteration it will be set to 2, and so forth. Because the counter variable will take on the values 1 through 10 during the loop's execution, you can use it in the calculation inside the loop.

The flowchart in Figure 15 shows the logic of such a program. Notice that in the body of the loop, the counter variable is used in the following calculation:

```
Set square = counter^2
```

This assigns the result of counter^2 to the square variable. After performing this calculation, the contents of the counter variable and the square variable are displayed. Then, 1 is added to counter and the loop starts over again.

Program 9 shows the pseudocode for the program. Notice that the word Tab is used in the Display statements in lines 8 and 18. This is simply a way of indicating in pseudocode that we are indenting the screen output. For example, look at the following statement, which appears in line 18:

```
Display counter, Tab, square
```

This statement displays the contents of the counter variable, indents (or "tabs over"), and then displays the contents of the square variable. As a result, the numbers that are displayed will be aligned in two columns. Most programming languages provide a way to indent, or tab, screen output.

Figure 15 Displaying the numbers 1 through 10 and their squares

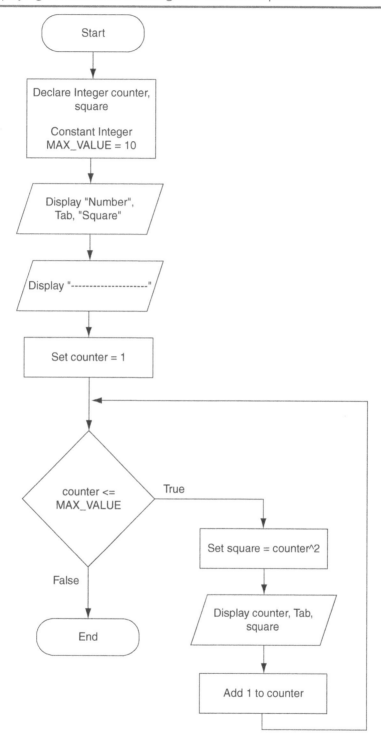

Program 9

```
1 // Variables
2 Declare Integer counter, square
3
4 // Constant for the maximum value
5 Constant Integer MAX_VALUE = 10
6
7 // Display table headings.
8 Display "Number", Tab, "Square"
9 Display "----------------------"
10
11 // Display the numbers 1 through 10 and
12 // their squares.
13 For counter = 1 To MAX_VALUE
14    // Calculate number squared.
15    Set square = counter^2
16
17    // Display number and number squared.
18    Display counter, Tab, square
19 End For
```

Program Output

```
Number              Square
----------------------
      1                1
      2                4
      3                9
      4               16
      5               25
      6               36
      7               49
      8               64
      9               81
     10              100
```

Incrementing by Values Other Than 1

The amount by which the counter variable is incremented in a For loop is known as the *step amount*. By default, the step amount is 1. Most languages provide a way to change the step amount. This gives you the ability to increment the counter variable by any value you wish.

In pseudocode, we will use the Step clause to specify a step value in a For loop. For example, look at the following pseudocode:

```
For counter = 0 To 100 Step 10
    Display counter
End For
```

In this loop, the starting value of the counter variable is 0, and its ending value is 100. The Step clause specifies a step value of 10, which means that 10 is added to the counter variable at the end of each iteration. During the first iteration, counter is 0, during the second iteration, counter is 10, during the third iteration, counter is 20, and so forth.

The pseudocode in Program 10 gives another demonstration. The program displays all of the odd numbers from 1 through 11.

Program 10

```
 1 // Declare a counter variable
 2 Declare Integer counter
 3
 4 // Constant for the maximum value
 5 Constant Integer MAX_VALUE = 11
 6
 7 // Display the odd numbers from 1 through 11.
 8 For counter = 1 To MAX_VALUE Step 2
 9    Display counter
10 End For
```

Program Output

```
1
3
5
7
9
11
```

In the Spotlight:

Designing a Count-Controlled Loop with the For Statement

Your friend Amanda just inherited a European sports car from her uncle. Amanda lives in the United States, and she is afraid she will get a speeding ticket because the car's speedometer works in kilometers per hour. She has asked you to write a program that displays a table of speeds in kilometers per hour with their values converted to miles per hour. The formula for converting kilometers per hour to miles per hour is:

$$MPH = KPH \times 0.6214$$

In the formula, *MPH* is the speed in miles per hour and *KPH* is the speed in kilometers per hour.

The table that your program displays should show speeds from 60 kilometers per hour through 130 kilometers per hour, in increments of 10, along with their values converted to miles per hour. The table should look something like this:

KPH	MPH
60	37.284
70	43.498
80	49.712
etc. . . .	
130	80.782

After thinking about this table of values, you decide that you will write a For loop that uses a counter variable to hold the kilometer-per-hour speeds. The counter's starting value will be 60, its ending value will be 130, and a step value of 10 will be used. Inside the loop you will use the counter variable to calculate a speed in miles-per-hour. Program 11 shows the pseudocode for the program, and Figure 16 shows a flowchart.

Program 11

```
 1 // Declare variables to hold speeds in MPH and KPH.
 2 Declare Real mph
 3 Declare Integer kph
 4
 5 // Display the table headings.
 6 Display "KPH", Tab, "MPH"
 7 Display "----------------------"
 8
 9 // Display the speeds.
10 For kph = 60 To 130 Step 10
11     // Calculate the miles-per-hour.
12     Set mph = kph * 0.6214
13
14     // Display KPH and MPH.
15     Display kph, Tab, mph
16 End For
```

Program Output

```
KPH            MPH
----------------------
60             37.284
70             43.498
80             49.712
90             55.926
100            62.14
110            68.354
120            74.568
130            80.782
```

Notice that a variable named kph is used as the counter. Until now we have used the name counter for our counter variables. In this program, however, kph is a better name for the counter because it will hold speeds in kilometers-per-hour.

Figure 16 Flowchart for Program 11

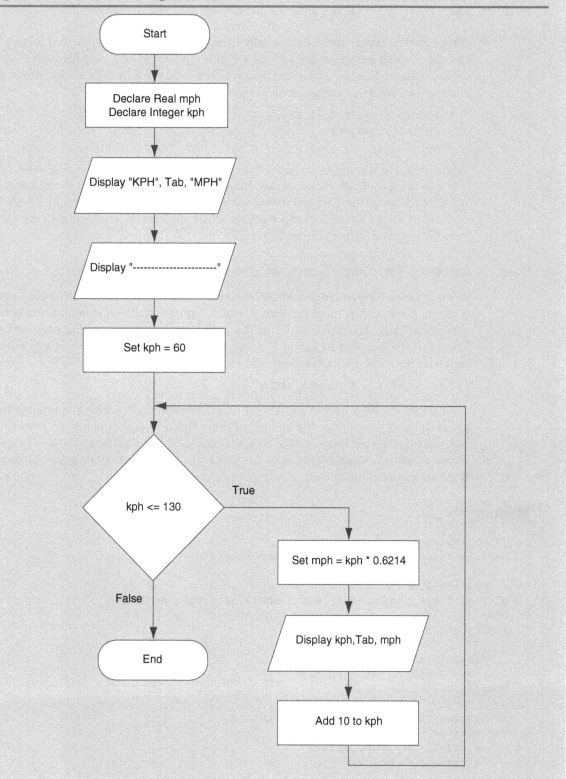

Counting Backward by Decrementing the Counter Variable

Although the counter variable is usually incremented in a count-controlled loop, you can alternatively decrement the counter variable. To *decrement* a variable means to decrease its value. In a For statement, you specify a negative step value to decrement the counter variable. For example, look at the following loop:

```
For counter = 10 To 1 Step -1
    Display counter
End For
```

In this loop, the starting value of the counter variable is 10, and its ending value is 1. The step value is –1, which means that 1 is subtracted from counter at the end of each iteration. During the first iteration, counter is 10; during the second iteration, counter is 9; and so forth. If this were an actual program, it would display the numbers 10, 9, 8, and so forth, down to 1.

Letting the User Control the Number of Iterations

In many cases, the programmer knows the exact number of iterations that a loop must perform. For example, recall Program 9, which displays a table showing the numbers 1 through 10 and their squares. When the pseudocode was written, the programmer knew that the loop had to iterate 10 times. A constant named MAX_VALUE was initialized with the value 10, and the loop was written as follows:

```
For counter = 1 To MAX_VALUE
```

As a result, the loop iterates exactly 10 times. Sometimes, however, the programmer needs to let the user decide the number of times that a loop should iterate. For example, what if you want Program 9 to be a bit more versatile by allowing the user to specify the maximum value displayed by the loop? The pseudocode in Program 12 shows how you can accomplish this.

Program 12

```
 1 // Variables
 2 Declare Integer counter, square, upperLimit
 3
 4 // Get the upper limit.
 5 Display "This program displays numbers, starting at 1,"
 6 Display "and their squares. How high should I go?"
 7 Input upperLimit
 8
 9 // Display table headings.
10 Display "Number", Tab, "Square"
11 Display "------------------------"
12
13 // Display the numbers and their squares.
14 For counter = 1 To upperLimit
15     // Calculate number squared.
16     Set square = counter^2
17
18     // Display number and number squared.
19     Display counter, Tab, square
20 End For
```

Program Output

```
This program displays numbers, starting at 1,
and their squares. How high should I go?
5 [Enter]
Number          Square
-------------------
    1               1
    2               4
    3               9
    4              16
    5              25
```

Lines 5 and 6 ask the user how high the numbers in the table should go, and the statement in line 7 stores the user's input in the upperLimit variable. Then, the For loop uses the upperLimit variable as the counter's ending value:

```
For counter = 1 To upperLimit
```

As a result, the counter variable starts with 1, and ends with the value in upperLimit. In addition to specifying the counter's ending value, you can also specify its starting value. The pseudocode in Program 13 shows an example. In this program, the user specifies both the starting value and the ending value of the numbers displayed in the table. Notice that in line 20 the For loop uses variables to specify both the starting and ending values of the counter variable.

Program 13

```
 1 // Variables
 2 Declare Integer counter, square,
 3      lowerLimit, upperLimit
 4
 5 // Get the lower limit.
 6 Display "This program displays numbers and"
 7 Display "their squares. What number should"
 8 Display "I start with?"
 9 Input lowerLimit
10
11 // Get the upper limit.
12 Display "What number should I end with?"
13 Input upperLimit
14
15 // Display table headings.
16 Display "Number", Tab, "Square"
17 Display "----------------------"
18
19 // Display the numbers and their squares.
20 For counter = lowerLimit To upperLimit
21     // Calculate number squared.
22     Set square = counter^2
23
24     // Display number and number squared.
25     Display counter, Tab, square
26 End For
```

Program Output

```
This program displays numbers and
their squares. What number should
I start with?
3 [Enter]
What number should I end with?
7 [Enter]
Number          Square
-------------------
    3              9
    4             16
    5             25
    6             36
    7             49
```

Designing a Count-Controlled `While` Loop

In most situations, it is best to use the `For` statement to write a count-controlled loop. Most languages, however, make it possible to use any looping mechanism to create a count-controlled loop. For example, you can create a count-controlled `While` loop, a count-controlled `Do-While` loop, or a count-controlled `Do-Until` loop. Regardless of the type of mechanism that you use, all count-controlled loops perform an initialization, test, and increment operation on a counter variable.

In pseudocode, you can use the following general format to write a count-controlled `While` loop:

① `Declare Integer counter = ` *startingValue* ◄————— Initialize a counter variable to the starting value.

② `While counter <= ` *maxValue* ◄————— Compare the counter to the maximum value.

    statement
    statement
    statement

③   `Set counter = counter + 1` ◄————— Add 1 to the counter variable during each iteration.

`End While`

The ①, ②, and ③ callouts show where the initialization, test, and increment actions are performed.

- ① shows the declaration of an `Integer` variable that will be used as the counter. The variable is initialized with the appropriate starting value.
- ② shows where the `While` loop tests the expression `counter <= ` *maxValue*. In this general format, *maxValue* is the maximum value that the counter variable can be set to.
- ③ shows where 1 is added to the `counter` variable. In a `While` loop, the counter variable will not automatically be incremented. You have to explicitly write a statement that performs this action. It's important that you understand how this statement works, so let's take a closer look at it:

    `Set counter = counter + 1`

This is how the statement would be executed by the computer: First, the computer would get the value of the expression on the right side of the = operator, which is counter + 1. Then, that value would be assigned to the counter variable. The effect of the statement is that 1 is added to the counter variable.

 WARNING! If you forget to increment the counter variable in a count-controlled While loop, the loop will iterate an infinite number of times.

The pseudocode in Program 14 shows an example of a count-controlled While loop. This program follows the same logic that you previously saw in Figure 13, and displays "Hello world" five times. Figure 17 points out where the counter variable's initialization, test, and increment occur in the pseudocode.

Program 14

```
 1 // Declare and initialize a counter variable.
 2 Declare Integer counter = 1
 3
 4 // Constant for the maximum value
 5 Constant Integer MAX_VALUE = 5
 6
 7 While counter <= MAX_VALUE
 8    Display "Hello world"
 9    Set counter = counter + 1
10 End While
```

Program Output

```
Hello world
Hello world
Hello world
Hello world
Hello world
```

Figure 17 The initialization, test, and increment of the counter variable

```
                        // Declare and initialize a counter variable.
Initialization    1  ─► Declare Integer counter = 1

                        // Constant for the maximum value
                        Constant Integer MAX_VALUE = 5

                        While counter <= MAX_VALUE  ◄──  2  Test
                            Display "Hello world"
Increment         3  ─►    Set counter = counter + 1
                        End While
```

The pseudocode in Program 15 shows another example. This program produces the same output that was produced by Program 9: the numbers 1 through 10 and their squares. The flowchart that you previously saw in Figure 15 shows the logic of this program.

Program 15

```
 1 // Variables
 2 Declare Integer counter = 1
 3 Declare Integer square
 4
 5 // Constant for the maximum value
 6 Constant Integer MAX_VALUE = 10
 7
 8 // Display table headings.
 9 Display "Number", Tab, "Square"
10 Display "----------------------"
11
12 // Display the numbers 1 through 10 and
13 // their squares.
14 While counter <= MAX_VALUE
15     // Calculate the square of a number.
16     Set square = counter^2
17
18     // Display the number and its square.
19     Display counter, Tab, square
20
21     // Increment counter.
22     Set counter = counter + 1
23 End While
```

Program Output

```
Number          Square
----------------------
    1               1
    2               4
    3               9
    4              16
    5              25
    6              36
    7              49
    8              64
    9              81
   10             100
```

Incrementing by Values Other Than 1

In Programs 14 and 15 the counter variable is incremented by 1 during each loop iteration, with a statement such as this:

```
Set counter = counter + 1
```

This statement can be easily modified to increment the counter variable by values other than 1. For example, you could add 2 to the counter variable with the following statement:

```
Set counter = counter + 2
```

The pseudocode in Program 16 demonstrates how you can use this statement in a count-controlled `While` loop. The program displays all of the odd numbers from 1 through 11.

Program 16

```
 1 // Declare a counter variable
 2 Declare Integer counter = 1
 3
 4 // Constant for the maximum value
 5 Constant Integer MAX_VALUE = 11
 6
 7 // Display the odd numbers from 1
 8 // through 11.
 9 While counter <= MAX_VALUE
10    Display counter
11    Set counter = counter + 2
12 End While
```

Program Output

```
1
3
5
7
9
11
```

Counting Backward by Decrementing

Previously you saw how a negative step value can be used to decrement the counter variable in a `For` statement. In a count-controlled `While` loop, you decrement the counter variable with a statement such as the following:

```
Set counter = counter − 1
```

This statement subtracts 1 from the `counter` variable. If the `counter` variable is set to the value 5 before this statement executes, it will be set to 4 after the statement executes. The pseudocode in Program 17 demonstrates how you can use this statement in a `While` loop. The program counts backward from 10 down to 1.

Program 17

```
 1 // Declare a counter variable
 2 Declare Integer counter = 10
 3
 4 // Constant for the minimum value
 5 Constant Integer MIN_VALUE = 1
 6
 7 // Display a count-down.
 8 Display "And the countdown begins..."
```

```
 9 While counter >= MIN_VALUE
10    Display counter
11    Set counter = counter - 1
12 End While
13 Display "Blast off!"
```

Program Output

```
And the countdown begins...
10
9
8
7
6
5
4
3
2
1
Blast off!
```

Let's take a closer look at this program. Notice that line 11 subtracts 1 from the counter variable. Because we are counting backward, we have to reverse many parts of the logic. For example, in line 2 the counter variable must be initialized with the value 10 instead of 1. This is because 10 is the counter's starting value in this program. Also, in line 5 we create a constant to represent the counter's minimum value (which is 1) instead of the maximum value. Because we are counting down, we want the loop to stop when it reaches 1. Finally, notice that we are using the >= relational operator in line 9. In this program we want the loop to iterate as long as the counter is greater than or equal to 1. When the counter becomes less than 1, the loop should stop.

Checkpoint

10 What is a counter variable?

11 What three actions do count-controlled loops typically perform using the counter variable?

12 When you increment a variable, what are you doing? When you decrement a variable, what are you doing?

13 Look at the following pseudocode. If it were a real program, what would it display?

```
Declare Integer number = 5
Set number = number + 1
Display number
```

14 Look at the following pseudocode. If it were a real program, what would it display?

```
Declare Integer counter
For counter = 1 To 5
    Display counter
End For
```

15 Look at the following pseudocode. If it were a real program, what would it display?

```
Declare Integer counter
For counter = 0 To 500 Step 100
   Display counter
End For
```

16 Look at the following pseudocode. If it were a real program, what would it display?

```
Declare Integer counter = 1
Constant Integer MAX = 8
While counter <= MAX
   Display counter
   Set counter = counter + 1
End While
```

17 Look at the following pseudocode. If it were a real program, what would it display?

```
Declare Integer counter = 1
Constant Integer MAX = 7
While counter <= MAX
   Display counter
   Set counter = counter + 2
End While
```

18 Look at the following pseudocode. If it were a real program, what would it display?

```
Declare Integer counter
Constant Integer MIN = 1
For counter = 5 To MIN Step -1
   Display counter
End For
```

Calculating a Running Total

CONCEPT: A running total is a sum of numbers that accumulates with each iteration of a loop. The variable used to keep the running total is called an accumulator.

Many programming tasks require you to calculate the total of a series of numbers. For example, suppose you are writing a program that calculates a business's total sales for a week. The program would read the sales for each day as input and calculate the total of those numbers.

Programs that calculate the total of a series of numbers typically use two elements:

- A loop that reads each number in the series.
- A variable that accumulates the total of the numbers as they are read.

The variable that is used to accumulate the total of the numbers is called an *accumulator*. It is often said that the loop keeps a *running total* because it accumulates the total as it reads each number in the series. Figure 18 shows the general logic of a loop that calculates a running total.

Figure 18 General logic for calculating a running total

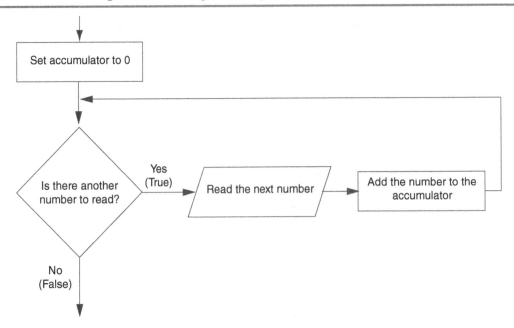

When the loop finishes, the accumulator will contain the total of the numbers that were read by the loop. Notice that the first step in the flowchart is to set the accumulator variable to 0. This is a critical step. Each time the loop reads a number, it adds it to the accumulator. If the accumulator starts with any value other than 0, it will not contain the correct total when the loop finishes.

Let's look at the design of a program that calculates a running total. The pseudocode shown in Program 18 allows the user to enter five numbers, and it displays the total of the numbers entered.

Program 18

```
 1 // Declare a variable to hold each number
 2 // entered by the user.
 3 Declare Integer number
 4
 5 // Declare an accumulator variable,
 6 // initialized with 0.
 7 Declare Integer total = 0
 8
 9 // Declare a counter variable for the loop.
10 Declare Integer counter
```

```
11
12 // Explain what we are doing.
13 Display "This program calculates the"
14 Display "total of five numbers."
15
16 // Get five numbers and accumulate them.
17 For counter = 1 To 5
18    Display "Enter a number."
19    Input number
20    Set total = total + number
21 End For
22
23 // Display the total of the numbers.
24 Display "The total is ", total
```

Program Output (with Input Shown in Bold)

```
This program calculates the
total of five numbers.
Enter a number.
2 [Enter]
Enter a number.
4 [Enter]
Enter a number.
6 [Enter]
Enter a number.
8 [Enter]
Enter a number.
10 [Enter]
The total is 30
```

First, let's look at the variable declarations. The number variable, declared in line 3, will be used to hold a number entered by the user. The total variable, declared in line 7, is the accumulator. Notice that it is initialized with the value 0. The counter variable, declared in line 10, will be used as a counter by the loop.

The For loop, in lines 17 through 21, does the work of getting the numbers from the user and calculating their total. Line 18 prompts the user to enter a number, and line 19 gets the user's input and stores it in the number variable. Then, the following statement in line 20 adds number to total:

```
Set total = total + number
```

After this statement executes, the value in the number variable will be added to the value in the total variable. When the loop finishes, the total variable will hold the sum of all the numbers that were added to it. This value is displayed in line 24. Figure 19 shows a flowchart for the Program 18.

Figure 19 Flowchart for Program 18

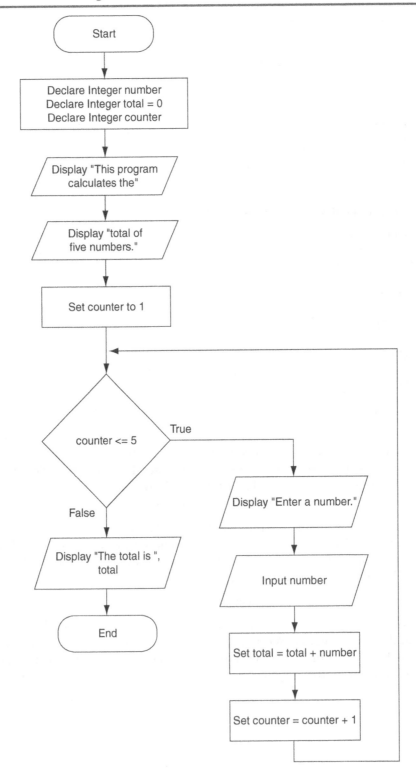

 **Checkpoint**

19 A program that calculates the total of a series of numbers typically has what two elements?

20 What is an accumulator?

21 Should an accumulator be initialized to any specific value? Why or why not?

22 Look at the following pseudocode. If it were a real program, what would it display?

```
Declare Integer number1 = 10, number2 = 5
Set number1 = number1 + number2
Display number1
Display number2
```

23 Look at the following pseudocode. If it were a real program, what would it display?

```
Declare Integer counter, total = 0
For counter = 1 To 5
    Set total = total + counter
End For
Display total
```

 ## 5 Sentinels

CONCEPT: A sentinel is a special value that marks the end of a list of values.

Consider the following scenario: You are designing a program that will use a loop to process a long list of values. At the time you are designing the program, you do not know the number of values that will be in the list. In fact, the number of values in the list could be different each time the program is executed. What is the best way to design such a loop? Here are some techniques that you have seen already in this chapter, along with the disadvantages of using them when processing a long list of values:

- Simply ask the user, at the end of each loop iteration, whether there is another value to process. If the list of values is long, however, asking this question at the end of each loop iteration might make the program cumbersome for the user.
- Ask the user at the beginning of the program how many items the list contains. This might also inconvenience the user, however. If the list is very long, and the user does not know the number of items in the list, it will require the user to count them.

When processing a long list of values with a loop, perhaps a better technique is to use a sentinel. A *sentinel* is a special value that marks the end of a list of items. When a program reads the sentinel value, it knows it has reached the end of the list, so the loop terminates. For example, suppose a doctor wants a program to calculate the average weight of all her patients. The program might work like this: A loop prompts the user to enter either a patient's weight, or 0 if there are no more weights. When the program reads 0 as a weight, it interprets this as a signal that there are no more weights. The loop ends and the program displays the average weight.

A sentinel value must be unique enough that it will not be mistaken as a regular value in the list. In the example cited above, the doctor (or her medical assistant) enters 0 to signal the end of the list of weights. Because no patient's weight will be 0, this is a good value to use as a sentinel.

In the Spotlight:
Using a Sentinel

The county tax office calculates the annual taxes on property using the following formula:

$$\textit{Property Tax} = \textit{Property Value} \times 0.0065$$

Every day, a clerk in the tax office gets a list of properties and has to calculate the tax for each property on the list. You have been asked to design a program that the clerk can use to perform these calculations.

In your interview with the tax clerk, you learn that each property is assigned a lot number, and all lot numbers are 1 or greater. You decide to write a loop that uses the number 0 as a sentinel value. During each loop iteration, the program will ask the clerk to enter either a property's lot number, or 0 to end. Program 19 shows the pseudocode for the program, and Figure 20 shows a flowchart.

Program 19

```
 1 Module main()
 2    // Local variable for the lot number
 3    Declare Integer lotNumber
 4
 5    // Get the first lot number.
 6    Display "Enter the property's lot number"
 7    Display "(or enter 0 to end)."
 8    Input lotNumber
 9
10    // Continue processing as long as the user
11    // does not enter lot number 0.
12    While lotNumber != 0
13       // Show the tax for the property.
14       Call showTax()
15
```

```
16        // Get the next lot number.
17        Display "Enter the lot number for the"
18        Display "next property (or 0 to end)."
19        Input lotNumber
20     End While
21 End Module
22
23 // The showTax module gets a property's
24 // value and displays its tax.
25 Module showTax()
26     // Local variables
27     Declare Real propertyValue, tax
28
29     // Constant for the tax factor.
30     Constant Real TAX_FACTOR = 0.0065
31
32     // Get the property's value.
33     Display "Enter the property's value."
34     Input propertyValue
35
36     // Calculate the property's tax.
37     Set tax = propertyValue * TAX_FACTOR
38
39     // Display the tax.
40     Display "The property's tax is $", tax
41 End Module
```

Program Output (with Input Shown in Bold)

```
Enter the property's lot number
(or enter 0 to end).
417 [Enter]
Enter the property's value.
100000 [Enter]
The property's tax is $650
Enter the lot number for the
next property (or 0 to end).
692 [Enter]
Enter the property's value.
60000 [Enter]
The property's tax is $390
Enter the lot number for the
next property (or 0 to end).
0 [Enter]
```

Figure 20 Flowchart for Program 19

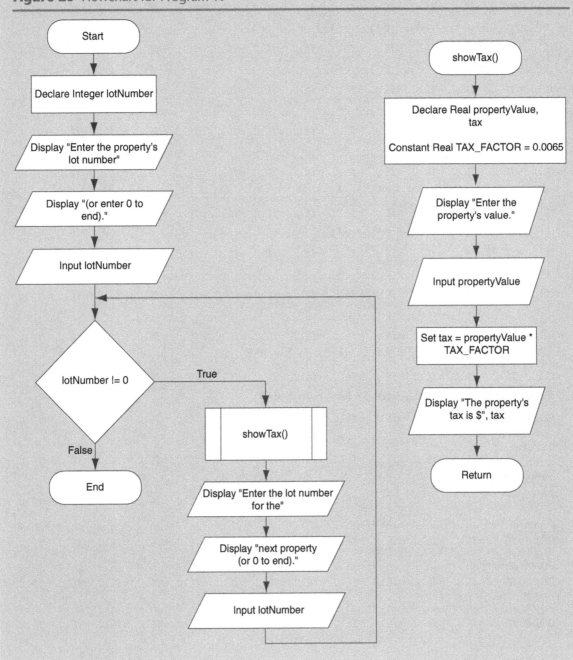

Checkpoint

24 Why should you take care to choose a unique value as a sentinel?

25 What is a sentinel?

6 Nested Loops

CONCEPT: A loop that is inside another loop is called a nested loop.

A nested loop is a loop that is inside another loop. A clock is a good example of something that works like a nested loop. The second hand, minute hand, and hour hand all spin around the face of the clock. The hour hand, however, only makes 1 revolution for every 12 of the minute hand's revolutions. And it takes 60 revolutions of the second hand for the minute hand to make 1 revolution. This means that for every complete revolution of the hour hand, the second hand has revolved 720 times. Here is pseudocode with a loop that partially simulates a digital clock. It displays the seconds from 0 to 59:

```
Declare Integer seconds
For seconds = 0 To 59
    Display seconds
End For
```

We can add a `minutes` variable and nest the loop above inside another loop that cycles through 60 minutes:

```
Declare Integer minutes, seconds
For minutes = 0 To 59
    For seconds = 0 To 59
        Display minutes, ":", seconds
    End For
End For
```

To make the simulated clock complete, another variable and loop can be added to count the hours:

```
Declare Integer hours, minutes, seconds
For hours = 0 To 23
    For minutes = 0 To 59
        For seconds = 0 To 59
            Display hours, ":", minutes, ":", seconds
        End For
    End For
End For
```

If this were a real program, its output would be:

```
0:0:0
0:0:1
0:0:2
```

(The program will count through each second of 24 hours.)

```
23:59:59
```

The innermost loop will iterate 60 times for each iteration of the middle loop. The middle loop will iterate 60 times for each iteration of the outermost loop. When the outermost loop has iterated 24 times, the middle loop will have iterated 1,440 times and the innermost loop will have iterated 86,400 times! Figure 21 shows a flowchart for the complete clock simulation program previously shown.

Figure 21 Flowchart for a clock simulator

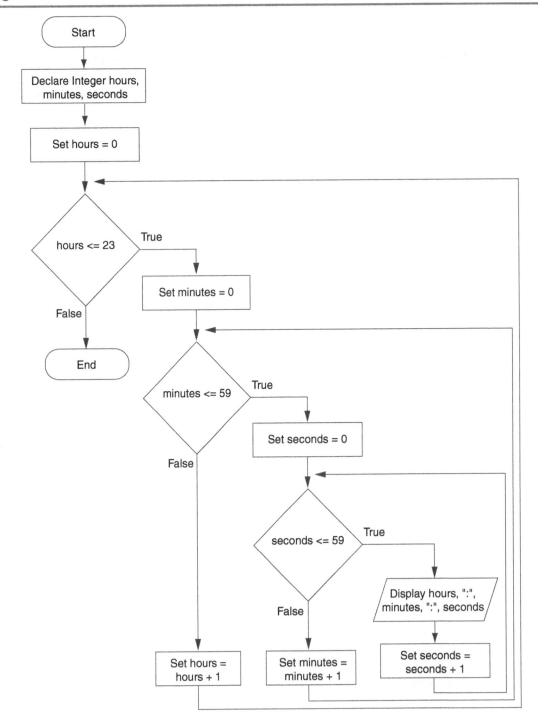

The simulated clock example brings up a few points about nested loops:

- An inner loop goes through all of its iterations for every single iteration of an outer loop.
- Inner loops complete their iterations faster than outer loops.
- To get the total number of iterations of a nested loop, multiply the number of iterations of all the loops.

Program 20 shows another example in pseudocode. It is a program that a teacher might use to get the average of each student's test scores. The statement in line 13 gets the number of students, and the statement in line 17 gets the number of test scores per student. The For loop that begins in line 20 iterates once for each student. The nested inner loop, in lines 27 through 31, iterates once for each test score.

Program 20

```
 1  // This program averages test scores. It asks the user for the
 2  // number of students and the number of test scores per student.
 3  Declare Integer numStudents
 4  Declare Integer numTestScores
 5  Declare Integer total
 6  Declare Integer student
 7  Declare Integer testNum
 8  Declare Real score
 9  Declare Real average
10
11  // Get the number of students.
12  Display "How many students do you have?"
13  Input numStudents
14
15  // Get the number of test scores per student.
16  Display "How many test scores per student?"
17  Input numTestScores
18
19  // Determine each student's average test score.
20  For student = 1 To numStudents
21      // Initialize an accumulator for test scores.
22      Set total = 0
23
24      // Get a student's test scores.
25      Display "Student number ", student
26      Display "------------------"
27      For testNum = 1 To numTestScores
28          Display "Enter test number ", testNum, ":"
29          Input score
30          Set total = total + score
31      End For
32
33      // Calculate the average test score for this student.
34      Set average = total / numTestScores
35
36      // Display the average.
37      Display "The average for student ", student, " is ", average
38      Display
39  End For
```

Program Output (with Input Shown in Bold)

```
How many students do you have?
3 [Enter]
How many test scores per student?
3 [Enter]
Student number 1
-----------------
Enter test number 1:
100 [Enter]
Enter test number 2:
95 [Enter]
Enter test number 3:
90 [Enter]
The average for student number 1 is 95.0

Student number 2
-----------------
Enter test number 1:
80 [Enter]
Enter test number 2:
81 [Enter]
Enter test number 3:
82 [Enter]
The average for student number 2 is 81.0

Student number 3
-----------------
Enter test number 1:
75 [Enter]
Enter test number 2:
85 [Enter]
Enter test number 3:
80 [Enter]
The average for student number 3 is 80.0
```

Review Questions

Multiple Choice

1. A _____-controlled loop uses a true/false condition to control the number of times that it repeats.

   a. Boolean
   b. condition
   c. decision
   d. count

2. A _____-controlled loop repeats a specific number of times.

    a. Boolean
    b. condition
    c. decision
    d. count

3. Each repetition of a loop is known as a(n) _____.

    a. cycle
    b. revolution
    c. orbit
    d. iteration

4. The `While` loop is a _____ type of loop.

    a. pretest
    b. posttest
    c. prequalified
    d. post iterative

5. The `Do-While` loop is a _____ type of loop.

    a. pretest
    b. posttest
    c. prequalified
    d. post iterative

6. The `For` loop is a _____ type of loop.

    a. pretest
    b. posttest
    c. prequalified
    d. post iterative

7. A(n) _____ loop has no way of ending and repeats until the program is interrupted.

    a. indeterminate
    b. interminable
    c. infinite
    d. timeless

8. A _____ loop always executes at least once.

    a. pretest
    b. posttest
    c. condition-controlled
    d. count-controlled

9. A(n) _____ variable keeps a running total.

    a. sentinel
    b. sum
    c. total
    d. accumulator

10. A(n) _____ is a special value that signals when there are no more items from a list of items to be processed. This value cannot be mistaken as an item from the list.
    a. sentinel
    b. flag
    c. signal
    d. accumulator

True or False

1. A condition-controlled loop always repeats a specific number of times.

2. The While loop is a pretest loop.

3. The Do-While loop is a pretest loop.

4. You should not write code that modifies the contents of the counter variable in the body of a For loop.

5. You cannot display the contents of the counter variable in the body of a loop.

6. It is not possible to increment a counter variable by any value other than 1.

7. The following statement decrements the variable x: Set x = x - 1.

8. It is not necessary to initialize accumulator variables.

9. In a nested loop, the inner loop goes through all of its iterations for every single iteration of the outer loop.

10. To calculate the total number of iterations of a nested loop, add the number of iterations of all the loops.

Short Answer

1. Why should you indent the statements in the body of a loop?

2. Describe the difference between pretest loops and posttest loops.

3. What is a condition-controlled loop?

4. What is a count-controlled loop?

5. What three actions do count-controlled loops typically perform using the counter variable?

6. What is an infinite loop? Write the code for an infinite loop.

7. A For loop looks like what other loop in a flowchart?

8. Why is it critical that accumulator variables are properly initialized?

9. What is the advantage of using a sentinel?

10. Why must the value chosen for use as a sentinel be carefully selected?

Algorithm Workbench

1. Design a `While` loop that lets the user enter a number. The number should be multiplied by 10, and the result stored in a variable named `product`. The loop should iterate as long as `product` contains a value less than 100.

2. Design a `Do-While` loop that asks the user to enter two numbers. The numbers should be added and the sum displayed. The loop should ask the user whether he or she wishes to perform the operation again. If so, the loop should repeat; otherwise it should terminate.

3. Design a `For` loop that displays the following set of numbers:

   0, 10, 20, 30, 40, 50 . . . 1000

4. Design a loop that asks the user to enter a number. The loop should iterate 10 times and keep a running total of the numbers entered.

5. Design a `For` loop that calculates the total of the following series of numbers:

$$\frac{1}{30} + \frac{2}{29} + \frac{3}{28} + \ldots \frac{30}{1}$$

6. Design a nested loop that displays 10 rows of # characters. There should be 15 # characters in each row.

7. Convert the `While` loop in the following code to a `Do-While` loop:

```
Declare Integer x = 1
While x > 0
    Display "Enter a number."
    Input x
End While
```

8. Convert the `Do-While` loop in the following code to a `While` loop:

```
Declare String sure
Do
    Display "Are you sure you want to quit?"
    Input sure
While sure != "Y" AND sure != "y"
```

9. Convert the following `While` loop to a `For` loop:

```
Declare Integer count = 0
While count < 50
    Display "The count is ", count
    Set count = count + 1
End While
```

10. Convert the following `For` loop to a `While` loop:

```
Declare Integer count
For count = 1 To 50
    Display count
End For
```

Debugging Exercises

1. Find the error in the following pseudocode.

```
Declare Boolean finished = False
Declare Integer value, cube

While NOT finished
    Display "Enter a value to be cubed."
    Input value;
    Set cube = value^3
    Display value, " cubed is ", cube
End While
```

2. The programmer intended the following pseudocode to display the numbers 1 through 60, and then display the message "Time's up!" It will not function as intended, however. Find the error.

```
Declare Integer counter = 1
Const Integer TIME_LIMIT = 60

While counter < TIME_LIMIT
    Display counter
    Set counter = counter + 1
End While
Display "Time's up!"
```

3. The programmer intended the following pseudocode to get five sets of two numbers each, calculate the sum of each set, and calculate the sum of all the numbers entered. It will not function as intended, however. Find the error.

```
// This program calculates the sum of five sets of two numbers.
Declare Integer number, sum, total
Declare Integer sets, numbers

Constant Integer MAX_SETS = 5
Constant Integer MAX_NUMBERS = 2

Set sum = 0;
Set total = 0;

For sets = 1 To MAX_NUMBERS
    For numbers = 1 To MAX_SETS
        Display "Enter number ", numbers, " of set ", sets, "."
        Input number;
        Set sum = sum + number
    End For
    Display "The sum of set ", sets, " is ", sum "."
    Set total = total + sum
    Set sum = 0
End For
Display "The total of all the sets is ", total, "."
```

Programming Exercises

VideoNote
The Bug Collector Problem

1. Bug Collector

    A bug collector collects bugs every day for seven days. Design a program that keeps a running total of the number of bugs collected during the seven days. The loop should ask for the number of bugs collected for each day, and when the loop is finished, the program should display the total number of bugs collected.

2. **Calories Burned**

   Running on a particular treadmill you burn 3.9 calories per minute. Design a program that uses a loop to display the number of calories burned after 10, 15, 20, 25, and 30 minutes.

3. **Budget Analysis**

   Design a program that asks the user to enter the amount that he or she has budgeted for a month. A loop should then prompt the user to enter each of his or her expenses for the month, and keep a running total. When the loop finishes, the program should display the amount that the user is over or under budget.

4. **Sum of Numbers**

   Design a program with a loop that asks the user to enter a series of positive numbers. The user should enter a negative number to signal the end of the series. After all the positive numbers have been entered, the program should display their sum.

5. **Tuition Increase**

   At one college, the tuition for a full-time student is $6,000 per semester. It has been announced that the tuition will increase by 2 percent each year for the next five years. Design a program with a loop that displays the projected semester tuition amount for the next five years.

6. **Distance Traveled**

   The distance a vehicle travels can be calculated as follows:

   $$Distance = Speed \times Time$$

   For example, if a train travels 40 miles per hour for three hours, the distance traveled is 120 miles. Design a program that asks the user for the speed of a vehicle (in miles per hour) and how many hours it has traveled. It should then use a loop to display the distance the vehicle has traveled for each hour of that time period. Here is an example of the output:

   ```
   What is the speed of the vehicle in mph? 40 [Enter]
   How many hours has it traveled? 3 [Enter]
   Hour          Distance Traveled
   ─────────────────────────────────
     1                40
     2                80
     3                120
   ```

7. **Average Rainfall**

   Design a program that uses nested loops to collect data and calculate the average rainfall over a period of years. The program should first ask for the number of years. The outer loop will iterate once for each year. The inner loop will iterate twelve times, once for each month. Each iteration of the inner loop will ask the user for the inches of rainfall for that month. After all iterations, the program should display the number of months, the total inches of rainfall, and the average rainfall per month for the entire period.

8. **Celsius to Fahrenheit Table**

   Design a program that displays a table of the Celsius temperatures 0 through 20 and their Fahrenheit equivalents. The formula for converting a temperature from Celsius to Fahrenheit is

   $$F = \frac{9}{5}C + 32$$

   where F is the Fahrenheit temperature and C is the Celsius temperature. Your program must use a loop to display the table.

9. **Pennies for Pay**

   Design a program that calculates the amount of money a person would earn over a period of time if his or her salary is one penny the first day, two pennies the second day, and continues to double each day. The program should ask the user for the number of days. Display a table showing what the salary was for each day, and then show the total pay at the end of the period. The output should be displayed in a dollar amount, not the number of pennies.

10. **Largest and Smallest**

    Design a program with a loop that lets the user enter a series of numbers. The user should enter –99 to signal the end of the series. After all the numbers have been entered, the program should display the largest and smallest numbers entered.

11. **First and Last**

    Design a program that asks the user for a series of names (in no particular order). After the final person's name has been entered, the program should display the name that is first alphabetically and the name that is last alphabetically. For example, if the user enters the names Kristin, Joel, Adam, Beth, Zeb, and Chris, the program would display Adam and Zeb.

12. **Calculating the Factorial of a Number**

    In mathematics, the notation $n!$ represents the factorial of the nonnegative integer n. The factorial of n is the product of all the nonnegative integers from 1 up through n. For example:

    $$7! = 1 \times 2 \times 3 \times 4 \times 5 \times 6 \times 7 = 5{,}040$$

    and

    $$4! = 1 \times 2 \times 3 \times 4 = 24$$

    Design a program that asks the user to enter a nonnegative integer and then displays the factorial of that number.

Answers to Checkpoint Questions

1 A structure that causes a section of code to repeat.

2 A loop that uses a true/false condition to control the number of times that it repeats.

3 A loop that repeats a specific number of times.

4 An execution of the statements in the body of the loop.

5 A pretest loop tests its condition before it performs an iteration. A posttest loop tests its condition after it performs an iteration.

6 Before

7 After

8 A loop that has no way of stopping, and repeats until the program is interrupted.

9 A Do-While loop iterates while a condition is true. When the condition is false, the Do-While loop stops. A Do-Until loop iterates until a condition is true. When the condition is true, the Do-Until loop stops.

10 A variable that is used to store the number of iterations that it has performed.

11 Initialization, test, and increment.

12 Incrementing a variable means increasing its value. Decrementing a variable means decreasing its value.

13 6

14 1
   2
   3
   4
   5

15 0
   100
   200
   300
   400
   500

16 1
   2
   3
   4
   5
   6
   7
   8

17 1
   3
   5

      7

18 5
    4
    3
    2
    1

19 1. A loop that reads each number in the series.
    2. A variable that accumulates the total of the numbers as they are read.

20 A variable that is used to accumulate the total of a series of numbers.

21 Yes, it should be initialized with the value 0. This is because values are added to the accumulator by a loop. If the accumulator does not start at the value 0, it will not contain the correct total of the numbers that were added to it when the loop ends.

22 15

23 5

24 15

25 A sentinel is a special value that marks the end of a list of values.

26 A sentinel value must be unique enough that it will not be mistaken as a regular value in the list.

ASCII/Unicode Characters

The following table lists the ASCII (American Standard Code for Information Interchange) character set, which is the same as the first 127 Unicode character codes. This group of character codes is known as the *Latin Subset of Unicode*. The code columns show character codes and the character columns show the corresponding characters. For example, the code 65 represents the letter A. Note that the first 31 codes and code 127 represent control characters that are not printable.

Code	Character	Code	Character	Code	Character	Code	Character	Code	Character
0	NUL	26	SUB	52	4	78	N	104	h
1	SOH	27	Escape	53	5	79	O	105	i
2	STX	28	FS	54	6	80	P	106	j
3	ETX	29	GS	55	7	81	Q	107	k
4	EOT	30	RS	56	8	82	R	108	l
5	ENQ	31	US	57	9	83	S	109	m
6	ACK	32	(Space)	58	:	84	T	110	n
7	BEL	33	!	59	;	85	U	111	o
8	Backspace	34	"	60	<	86	V	112	p
9	HTab	35	#	61	=	87	W	113	q
10	Line Feed	36	$	62	>	88	X	114	r
11	VTab	37	%	63	?	89	Y	115	s
12	Form Feed	38	&	64	@	90	Z	116	t
13	CR	39	'	65	A	91	[	117	u
14	SO	40	(	66	B	92	\	118	v
15	SI	41	)	67	C	93	]	119	w
16	DLE	42	*	68	D	94	^	120	x
17	DC1	43	+	69	E	95	_	121	y
18	DC2	44	,	70	F	96	`	122	z
19	DC3	45	–	71	G	97	a	123	{
20	DC4	46	.	72	H	98	b	124	|
21	NAK	47	/	73	I	99	c	125	}
22	SYN	48	0	74	J	100	d	126	~
23	ETB	49	1	75	K	101	e	127	DEL
24	CAN	50	2	76	L	102	f		
25	EM	51	3	77	M	103	g		

From Appendix A of *Starting Out with Programming Logic and Design,* Third Edition. Tony Gaddis. Copyright © 2013 by Pearson Education, Inc. Published by Pearson Addison-Wesley. All rights reserved.

Flowchart Symbols

This page shows the flowchart symbols that are used in this text.

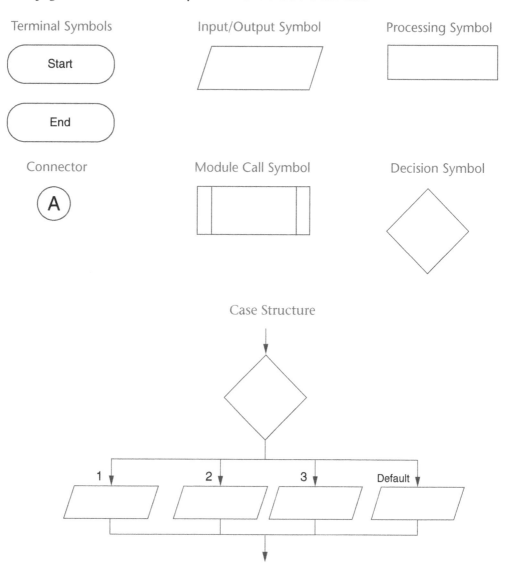

Pseudocode Reference

This appendix serves as a quick reference for the pseudocode that is used in this text. This reference concisely covers the text's statements and operators. (It does not cover the library functions, however.)

Data Types	Description
Integer	Used for variables that will store whole numbers
Real	Used for variables that will store numbers with a fractional part
String	Used for variables that will store strings
Character	Used for variables that will store a single character

Variables

To declare a variable, you use the `Declare` statement. Here is the general format:

```
Declare DataType VariableName
```

In the general format, *DataType* is the variable's data type and *VariableName* is the variable's name. Here are some examples:

```
Declare Integer distance
Declare Real grossPay
Declare String name
Declare Character letter
```

You can optionally initialize a variable with a starting value when you declare it. Here is an example:

```
Declare Real price = 49.95
```

Named Constants

You create a named constant by using the `Constant` statement instead of the `Declare` statement. Here is the general format:

```
Constant DataType Name = Value
```

In the general format, *DataType* is the constant's data type, *Name* is the constant's name, and *Value* is the contstant's value. Here is an example:

```
Constant Real INTEREST_RATE = 0.072
```

Arrays

Here is the general format of an array declaration:

```
Declare DataType ArrayName[Size]
```

In the general format, `DataType` is the array's data type, `ArrayName` is the array's name, and `Size` is the number of elements in the array. Here is an example:

```
Declare Integer units[10]
```

This statement declares an array of `Integer` values. The array's name is `units`, and it has 10 elements.

Two-Dimensional Arrays

Here is the general format of a two-dimensional array declaration:

```
Declare DataType ArrayName[Rows][Cols]
```

In the general format, `DataType` is the array's data type, `ArrayName` is the array's name, `Rows` is the number of rows in the array, and `Cols` is the number of columns. Here is an example:

```
Declare Integer values[10][20]
```

This statement declares an array of `Integer` values. The array's name is `values`, and it has 10 rows and 20 columns.

Displaying Output

To display output you use the `Display` statement. The `Display` statement displays a line of output on the screen. Here is the general format to use when you are displaying one item of data:

```
Display Item
```

To display multiple items, you separate the items with commas, as shown in the following general format:

```
Display Item, Item, Item ...
```

Here are some examples:

```
Display "Hello world"
Display grossPay
Display "My name is ", name
```

You can use the word `Tab` to indent screen output to the next tab position. Here is an example:

```
Display amount1, Tab, amount2, Tab, amount3
```

Reading Input

You use the `Input` statement to read keyboard input. Here is the general format:

```
Input VariableName
```

In the general format, `VariableName` is the name of the variable that will receive the input. Here is an example:

```
Input hours
```

Comments

In this text, we begin a comment with two forward slashes. Everything appearing on the line after the slashes is a comment. Here is an example:

```
// Get the number of hours worked.
```

Math Operators

Symbol	Operator	Description
+	Addition	Adds two numbers
–	Subtraction	Subtracts one number from another
*	Multiplication	Multiplies one number by another
/	Division	Divides one number by another and gives the quotient
MOD	Modulus	Divides one number by another and gives the remainder
^	Exponent	Raises a number to a power

Relational Operators

Operator	Meaning
>	Greater than
<	Less than
>=	Greater than or equal to
<=	Less than or equal to
==	Equal to
!=	Not equal to

Logical Operators

Operator	Meaning
AND	The AND operator connects two Boolean expressions into one compound expression. Both subexpressions must be true for the compound expression to be true.
OR	The OR operator connects two Boolean expressions into one compound expression. One or both subexpressions must be true for the compound expression to be true. It is only necessary for one of the subexpressions to be true, and it does not matter which.
NOT	The NOT operator is a unary operator, meaning it works with only one operand. The operand must be a Boolean expression. The NOT operator reverses the truth of its operand. If it is applied to an expression that is true, the operator returns false. If it is applied to an expression that is false, the operator returns true.

The If-Then Statement

General format:

```
If condition Then
    statement
    statement          } These statements are conditionally
    etc.               } executed.
End If
```

In the general format, the *condition* is a Boolean expression. If the expression is true, the statements appearing between the If clause and the End If clause are executed. Otherwise, the statements are skipped. Here is an example:

```
If sales > 50000 Then
    Set bonus = 500.0
    Set commissionRate = 0.12
    Display "You've met your sales quota!"
End If
```

The If-Then-Else Statement

General format:

```
If condition Then
    statement
    statement          } These statements are executed if the
    etc.               } condition is true.
Else
    statement
    statement          } These statements are executed if the
    etc.               } condition is false.
End If
```

In the general format, the *condition* is a Boolean expression. If the expression is true, the statements appearing between the If clause and the Else clause are executed. Otherwise, the statements between the Else clause and the End If clause are executed. Here is an example:

```
If temperature < 40 Then
    Display "A little cold, isn't it?"
Else
    Display "Nice weather we're having."
End If
```

The Select Case Statement

General format:

```
Select testExpression  ← This is a variable or an expression.
    Case value_1:
        statement
        statement      } These statements are executed if the
        etc.           } testExpression is equal to value_1.
```

```
Case value_2:
    statement
    statement
    etc.
```
> These statements are executed if the *testExpression* is equal to *value_2*.

Insert as many Case *sections as necessary*

```
Case value_N:
    statement
    statement
    etc.
```
> These statements are executed if the *testExpression* is equal to *value_N*.

```
Default:
    statement
    statement
    etc.
```
> These statements are executed if the *testExpression* is not equal to any of the values listed after the Case statements.

```
End Select  ◄─────────
```
This is the end of the structure.

The first line of the structure starts with the word Select, followed by a *testExpression*. Inside the structure there is one or more blocks of statements that begin with a Case statement. Notice that the word Case is followed by a value.

When the Select Case statement executes, it compares the value of the *testExpression* with the values that follow each of the Case statements (from top to bottom). When it finds a Case value that matches the *testExpression's* value, the program branches to the Case statement. The statements that immediately follow the Case statement are executed, and then the program jumps out of the structure. If the *testExpression* does not match any of the Case values, the program branches to the Default statement and executes the statements that immediately follow it. Here is an example:

```
Select month
   Case 1:
      Display "January"
   Case 2:
      Display "February"
   Case 3:
      Display "March"
   Default:
      Display "Error: Invalid month"
End Select
```

The While Loop

General format:

```
While condition
    statement
    statement
    etc.
End While
```
> These statements are the body of the loop. They are repeated while the condition is true.

In the general format, the *condition* is a Boolean expression, and the statements that appear on the lines between the While and the End While clauses are the body of the loop. When the loop executes, the *condition* is tested. If it is true, the statements that appear in the body of the loop are executed, and then the loop starts over. If the *condition* is false, the program exits the loop. The following pseudocode shows an example:

```
Set count = 0
While count < 10
    Display count
    Set count = count + 1
End While
```

The Do-While Loop

General format:

```
Do
    statement
    statement
    etc.
While condition
```

These statements are the body of the loop. They are always performed once, and then repeated while the condition is true.

In the general format, the statements that appear in the lines between the Do and the While clauses are the body of the loop. The *condition* that appears after the While clause is a Boolean expression. When the loop executes, the statements in the body of the loop are executed, and then the *condition* is tested. If the *condition* is true, the loop starts over and the statements in the body are executed again. If the condition is false, however, the program exits the loop. Here is an example:

```
Set count = 10
Do
    Display count
    Set count = count - 1
While count > 0
```

The Do-Until Loop

General format:

```
Do
    statement
    statement
    etc.
Until condition
```

These statements are the body of the loop. They are always performed once, and then repeated until the condition is true.

In the general format, the statements that appear in the lines between the Do and the Until clauses are the body of the loop. The *condition* that appears after the While clause is a Boolean expression. When the loop executes, the statements in the body of the loop are executed, and then the *condition* is tested. If the *condition* is true, the program exits the loop. If the *condition* is false, the loop starts over and the statements in the body are executed again. Here is an example:

```
Set count = 10
Do
    Display count
    Set count = count - 1
Until count == 0
```

The For Loop

General format:

```
For counterVariable = startingValue To maxValue
    statement
    statement          These statements are the body of the loop.
    statement
    etc.
End For
```

In the general format, *counterVariable* is the name of a variable that is used as a counter, *startingValue* is the value that the counter will be initially set to, and *maxValue* is the maximum value that the counter can contain. When the loop executes, the following actions are performed:

1. The *counterVariable* is set to the *startingValue*.
2. The *counterVariable* is compared to the *maxValue*. If the *counterVariable* is greater than *maxValue*, the loop stops. Otherwise:
   a. The statements that appear in the body of the loop are executed.
   b. The *counterVariable* is incremented.
   c. The loop starts over again at step 2.

Here is an example:

```
For counter = 1 To 10
    Display "Hello world"
End For
```

The For Each Loop

General format:

```
For Each var In array
    statement
    statement
    statement
    etc.
End For
```

In the general format, *var* is the name of a variable and *array* is the name of an array. The loop will iterate once for every element in the *array*. Each time the loop iterates, it copies an array element to the *var* variable. For example, the first time the loop iterates, *var* will contain the value of *array*[0], the second time the loop iterates *var* will contain the value of *array*[1], and so forth. This continues until the loop has stepped through all of the elements in the array. The following pseudocode shows an example:

```
Constant Integer SIZE = 5
Declare Integer numbers[SIZE] = 5, 10, 15, 20, 25
Declare Integer num
For Each num In numbers
    Display num
End For
```

Defining a Module

To create a module you write its definition, which has two parts: a header and a body. The header indicates the starting point of the module, and the body is a list of statements that belong to the module. Here is the general format used in this book to write a module definition in pseudocode:

```
Module name()
    statement
    statement        } These statements are the body of the module.
    etc.
End Module
```

Calling a Module

To call a module you use the `Call` statement. Here is the general format:

```
Call ModuleName()
```

In the general format, *ModuleName* is the name of the module being called. In the following example, a module named `showMessage` is being called:

```
Call showMessage()
```

Parameter Variables

If you want a module or function to receive arguments when it is called, you must equip the module or function with one or more parameter variables. Parameter variables are declared inside the parentheses of the module definition. Here is an example of a pseudocode module that has an `Integer` parameter variable:

```
Module doubleNumber(Integer value)
   Declare Integer result
   Set result = value * 2
   Display result
End Module
```

When this module is called, an `Integer` argument will be passed to it by value. To pass an argument by reference, the word `Ref` is used in the parameter variable declaration, and shown here:

```
Module setToZero(Integer Ref value)
   value = 0
End Module
```

Defining a Function

A function definition is similar to a module definition. Here is the general format:

```
Function DataType FunctionName(ParameterList)
    statement
    statement
    etc.
    Return value        ← A function must have a Return statement. This causes a
                          value to be sent back to the part of the program that called
End Function            the function.
```

The first line is the function header. It begins with the word `Function`, followed by these items:

- *DataType* is the data type of the value that the function returns.
- *FunctionName* is the name of the function.
- An optional parameter list appears inside a set of parentheses. If the function does not accept arguments, then an empty set of parentheses will appear.

Beginning at the line after the function header, one or more statements will appear. These statements are the function's body, and are performed any time the function is executed. One of the statements in the body must be a `Return` statement, which takes the following form:

```
Return value
```

The *value* that follows the word `Return` is the value that the function will send back to the part of the program that called the function. Here is an example:

```
Function Integer sum(Integer num1, Integer num2)
   Declare Integer result
   Set result = num1 + num2
   Return result
End Function
```

Opening an Output File and Writing Data To It

In our pseudocode, we first declare an `OutputFile` variable, and then we use the `Open` statement to open the file. Here is an example:

```
Declare OutputFile customerFile
Open customerFile "customers.dat"
```

We then use the `Write` statement to write data to the file. Here is an example:

```
Write customerFile "Charles Pace"
```

When finished writing to the file, we use the `Close` statement to close the file. Here is an example:

```
Close customerFile
```

Opening an Input File and Reading Data from It

In our pseudocode, we first declare an `InputFile` variable, and then we use the `Open` statement to open the file. Here is an example:

```
Declare InputFile inventoryFile
Open inventoryFile "inventory.dat"
```

We then use the `Read` statement to read data from the file. Here is an example:

```
Read inventoryFile itemName
```

This statement reads an item from the file and stores it in the `itemName` variable. When finished reading the file, we use the `Close` statement to close the file. Here is an example:

```
Close inventoryFile
```

Detecting the End of an Input File

In our pseudocode we use the `eof` function to determine whether we have reached the end of an input file. Here is the function's general format:

```
eof(internalFileName)
```

The `eof` function accepts a file's internal name as an argument, and returns true if the end of the file has been reached, or false if the end of the file has not been reached. The following pseudocode shows an example:

```
// Declare an input file
Declare InputFile salesFile

// A variable to hold a sales amount
// that is read from the file
Declare Real sales

// Open the sales.dat file.
Open salesFile "sales.dat"

// Read all of the items in the file
// and display them.
While NOT eof(salesFile)
   Read salesFile sales
   Display currencyFormat(sales)
End While

// Close the file.
Close salesFile
```

Deleting a File

To delete a file we use the `Delete` statement. Here is the general format:

```
Delete Filename
```

In the general format, `Filename` is the name of the file on the system's disk. Here is an example:

```
Delete "customers.dat"
```

Renaming a File

To rename a file we use the `Rename` statement. Here is the general format:

```
Rename ExistingName, NewName
```

In the general format, `ExistingName` is the file's existing name (on the system's disk), and `NewName` is the file's new name. Here is an example:

```
Rename "temp.dat", "customers.dat"
```

Defining a Class

General format:

```
Class ClassName
```

   Field declarations and method definitions go here...

```
End Class
```

The first line starts with the word `Class`, followed by the name of the class. Next you write the declarations for the class's fields and the definitions of the class's methods. The words `End Class` appear at the end of the class definition. Here is a `CellPhone` example:

```
Class CellPhone
   // Field declarations
   Private String manufacturer
   Private String modelNumber
   Private Real retailPrice

   // Method definitions
   Public Module setManufacturer(String manufact)
      Set manufacturer = manufact
   End Module

   Public Module setModelNumber(String modNum)
      Set modelNumber = modNum
   End Module

   Public Module setRetailPrice(Real retail)
      Set retailPrice = retail
   End Module

   Public Function String getManufacturer()
      Return manufacturer
   End Function

   Public Function String getModelNumber()
      Return modelNumber
   End Function

   Public Function Real getRetailPrice()
      Return retailPrice
   End Function
End Class
```

Creating an Instance of a Class

To create an instance of a class (in other words, an object), you declare a variable to reference the object, and then you use the `New` operator to create the instance. Here is an example that creates an instance of the `CellPhone` class previously shown:

```
Declare CellPhone myPhone
Set myPhone = New CellPhone()
```

The first statement declares a variable named `myPhone`. The second statement creates an instance of the `CellPhone` class and assigns its memory address to the `myPhone` variable.